Conflict, Nationhood and Corporeality
in Modern Literature

Also by Petra Rau:

ENGLISH MODERNISM, NATIONAL IDENTITY AND THE GERMANS, 1890–1950

Conflict, Nationhood and Corporeality in Modern Literature

Bodies-at-War

Edited by

Petra Rau
University of Portsmouth

First published 2010 by
PALGRAVE MACMILLAN

Palgrave Macmillan in the UK is an imprint of Macmillan Publishers Limited,
registered in England, company number 785998, of Houndmills, Basingstoke,
Hampshire RG21 6XS.

Palgrave Macmillan in the US is a division of St Martin's Press LLC,
175 Fifth Avenue, New York, NY 10010.

Palgrave Macmillan is the global academic imprint of the above companies
and has companies and representatives throughout the world.

Palgrave® and Macmillan® are registered trademarks in the United States,
the United Kingdom, Europe and other countries.

ISBN 978–0–230–23152–8   hardback

This book is printed on paper suitable for recycling and made from fully
managed and sustained forest sources. Logging, pulping and manufacturing
processes are expected to conform to the environmental regulations of the
country of origin.

A catalogue record for this book is available from the British Library.

A catalog record for this book is available from the Library of Congress.

10   9   8   7   6   5   4   3   2   1
19   18   17   16   15   14   13   12   11   10

Printed and bound in Great Britain by
CPI Antony Rowe, Chippenham and Eastbourne

Contents

List of Illustrations		vii
Acknowledgements		viii
Notes on Contributors		ix

Introduction: Between Absence and Ubiquity – on the
Meanings of the Body-at-War   1
Petra Rau

1   'Isn't This Worth Fighting For?' The First World War and the
(Ab)Uses of the Pastoral Tradition   26
Christine Berberich

2   Violence and the Pacifist Body in Vernon Lee's *The Ballet of
the Nations*   46
Patricia Pulham

3   Incommensurate Histories: the Remaindered Irish
Bodies of the Great War   64
Eugene McNulty

4   'Soft-skinned Vehicle': Reading the Second World War
in Tom Paulin's *The Invasion Handbook*   83
Mark Rawlinson

5   'A stiff is still a stiff in this country': the Problem
of Murder in Wartime   104
Gill Plain

6   Masculinity, Masquerade and the Second World War:
Betty Miller's *On the Side of the Angels*   124
Victoria Stewart

7   'One step closer to the dreamers of the nightmare':
the Fascinating Fascist Corpus in Contemporary
British Fiction   143
Petra Rau

8   'Resentments': the Politics and Pathologies of War Writing   164
Marina MacKay

9   'The dangerous edge of things': Geopolitical Bodies and
    Cold War Fiction   185
    Richard Robinson

Index   205

List of Illustrations

1.1 *Your Country's Call* (1915), Imperial War Museum, London 32

1.2 Herbert Cole, in Ernest Rhys (ed.), *The Old Country*
(London: J.M. Dent, 1917) 34

1.3 Herbert Cole, in Ernest Rhys (ed.), *The Old Country*
(London: J.M. Dent, 1917) 35

1.4 Herbert Cole, in Ernest Rhys (ed.), *The Old Country*
(London: J.M. Dent, 1917) 35

1.5 Herbert Cole, in Ernest Rhys (ed.), *The Old Country*
(London: J.M. Dent, 1917) 36

Acknowledgements

This edited collection had its beginning in a symposium on war writing and the body held at the University of Portsmouth in 2007. While not everybody who contributed to this stimulating event is represented here, I would like to express my gratitude to all participants for setting in motion and sustaining the lively dialogue that has made this project possible.

The Centre of European and International Social Research and the Centre for Studies in Literature at the University of Portsmouth have both opened their coffers to support the symposium and this collection, and I am very grateful for their generosity. Finally, I would like to thank the contributors for their patience with this most pedantic of editors.

Gloucestershire, 2010
Petra Rau

Notes on Contributors

Christine Berberich is Senior Lecturer in Nineteenth and Twentieth-Century English and European Literature at the University of Portsmouth. She has published on Englishness, George Orwell, Anthony Powell, Evelyn Waugh, Kazuo Ishiguro, Julian Barnes and W.G. Sebald. Her book *The Image of the English Gentleman in Twentieth-Century Literature: Englishness and Nostalgia* was published in 2008.

Marina MacKay teaches at Washington University in St Louis. She is the author of *Modernism and World War II* (2007), editor of *The Cambridge Companion to the Literature of World War II* (2009) and co-editor with Lyndsey Stonebridge of *British Fiction After Modernism* (Palgrave, 2007). Her most recent articles have appeared in *PMLA, ELH* and *Modern Fiction Studies*.

Eugene McNulty is a lecturer in the English Department of St Patrick's College, Dublin. His main interests centre on Irish literature and theatre history, and the intersection between postcolonial and Irish studies. He has a particular interest in the cultural history of the north of Ireland, and is the author of *The Ulster Literary Theatre and the Northern Revival* (2008). His chapter for this collection emerges out of a wider and ongoing interest in the legacy of the Great War period in Irish literature and cultural politics.

Gill Plain is Professor of English Literature and Popular Culture at the University of St Andrews. She has research interests in war and representation, gender, national identity and crime fiction. Her publications include *Women's Fiction of the Second World War* (1996), *Twentieth-Century Crime Fiction: Gender, Sexuality and the Body* (2001) and *John Mills and British Cinema: Masculinity, Identity and Nation* (2006). She is currently working on a literary history of the 1940s.

Patricia Pulham is Senior Lecturer in English Literature at the University of Portsmouth. She is co-editor with Catherine Maxwell of the first annotated edition of selected short stories by Vernon Lee, *Hauntings and Other Fantastic Tales* (2006), and of *Vernon Lee: Decadence, Ethics, Aesthetics*, the first collection of critical essays on Lee's work (Palgrave Macmillan, 2006). Her monograph *Art and the Transitional Object in Vernon Lee's Supernatural Tales* was published in 2008. With Rosario

Arias, she has co-edited a collection of essays: *Haunting and Spectrality in Neo-Victorian Fiction: Possessing the Past* (Palgrave Macmillan, 2009).

Richard Robinson is Lecturer in English at Swansea University. He specializes in twentieth-century fiction, and has published articles on James Joyce, Italo Svevo and Kazuo Ishiguro. His monograph *Narratives of the European Border: a History of Nowhere* (Language, Discourse, Society series) was published by Palgrave Macmillan in 2007. He is currently working on the fiction of John McGahern.

Petra Rau is Senior Lecturer in English Literature at the University of Portsmouth. She has published on modernism, travel writing, war literature and Freudian aesthetics. Her book *English Modernism, National Identity and the Germans, 1890–1950* was published in 2009. She is currently working on a monograph about the Second World War in contemporary fiction.

Mark Rawlinson is Senior Lecturer in the School of English and Academic Director of the College of Arts, Humanities and Law at the University of Leicester. He is the author of *British Writing of the Second World War* (2000) and *Pat Barker* (2009), editor of the Norton Critical Edition of *A Clockwork Orange* (2010), and co-editor, with Adam Piette, of *The Edinburgh Companion to Twentieth-Century British and American War Literature* (forthcoming). He has written numerous essays about the cultural representations of war from the Napoleonic period onwards, and is currently working on the Second World War in fiction after 1945 and on camouflage.

Victoria Stewart is Senior Lecturer in the Department of English, University of Leicester. She is the author of *Women's Autobiography: War and Trauma* (Palgrave 2003) and *Narratives of Memory: British Writing of the 1940s* (Palgrave 2006). Currently she is working on a monograph on secrecy in fiction of the Second World War.

Introduction: Between Absence and Ubiquity – on the Meanings of the Body-at-War

Petra Rau

War is about killing people. This is not necessarily the aim of war (other than in genocide), but it is its chief mode of operation. Governments authorizing war now go to great lengths to deny this simple fact by reiterating that advances in training, equipment and the technology of mechanized warfare have minimized casualties on either side, or they focus on the purposes of war rather than its cost – the defence of territory and borders, national honour or cohesion, the liberation of a people, or the containment of an ideology or religion perceived to be hostile to one's own 'way of life'. However, the creative response to war more often than not takes the perspective of the soldier, focusing on the physical conditions of war and their impact on the body. The disjunction between official ways of obscuring the physical destruction of human life and artists' and writers' insistence on representing the vicissitudes of the body-at-war is striking. This collection of essays is, in many ways, a critical response to this discrepancy of corporeal representations in our modern war culture. In this introduction I want to briefly retrace and contextualize this politically expedient vanishing act and juxtapose it with the ubiquity of corporeal suffering in visual and literary renditions of war.

'The body' has become a focus of renewed academic interest in the last thirty years. Through the rediscovery of Freud's theories and in the wake of Michel Foucault's influential studies *The History of Sexuality* (1976) and *Discipline and Punish* (1977), much work in the Humanities has focused on recognizing the body as a historically shifting cultural construction that signifies within a multiplicity of overlapping and intersecting discourses: medicine, law, religion, art and literature, even engineering.[1] In his 1991 essay 'History of the Body' the medical historian Roy Porter declared his impatience with the lack of interplay

1

between the study of vital statistics and methods of decoding corporeal representations in the pursuit of such an enterprise. Porter was dissatisfied with the lack of a cultural history of the body, criticizing both the work of literary scholars like Elaine Scarry's *The Body in Pain* (1985) for ignoring empirical evidence and medical practitioners' narrow interpretation of the body as a biological given.[2] Indeed, the conceptual gap between the body as an empirical, biological reality and the way it is made to 'mean' in culture has narrowed most noticeably when historians and literary scholars have brought the two into dialogue, most successfully in relation to the body-at-war.[3] John Keegan's *The Face of Battle* (1977) examined the physical conditions of men at war from Agincourt to Waterloo and the Somme. In *A History of Warfare* (1993) the structuring principle of his study remains the materiality of war (stone, flesh, iron, fire) and its effects on the 'warrior', even if his contention of the soldier as a tribal caste apart and as the origin of civilization may be controversial. Joanna Bourke's *Dismembering the Male: Men's Bodies, Britain and the Great War* (1996) and *An Intimate History of Killing* (1999) paid close attention to the physical and psychological experiences of soldiers and how governments respond to them. Keegan and Bourke represent the different approaches to legitimate mass killing: that of the military historian and historiographer on the one hand, and that of the cultural historian on the other. The former is interested in the evolution of warfare as a technique or political strategy, the latter focuses on the experience of the individual soldier as a result of such developments. Whether 'evolution' is the right word for technological progress in the service of mass destruction is disputed by the contributors to George Kassimeris's edited collection *The Barbarisation of Warfare* (2006) who analyse the reasons for the degradation of military ethics and its consequences for its victims and the political landscape of Western democracies.

The concern that informs this collection of essays is the representation of the body-at-war (the body in uniform, the wounded and suffering body, the corpse) as well as its various appropriations by the nation and its signifying systems (a canon of national literature which suggests hegemonic readings of war; commemoration and cultural memory of war). Scarry's *The Body in Pain* remains one of the most influential studies even if her main thesis, that pain elides verbal representation, is surely contestable. However, her formulation that 'war is injuring' and that its perpetuation would not be possible without disowning this reality still holds, as we shall see.[4] While Scarry suggested that it is not merely governments authorizing war that are responsible for this disavowal, her analysis of how injury disappears from view through strategies of omission, redescription and metaphorization has been tremendously influential for cultural historians such as Bourke and for political journalists, for instance in Stephen Poole's *Unspeak* (2006). That war and its official versions make language itself a casualty became a reason for modernists to be highly distrustful of a medium they saw abused by the liberal politicians who had endorsed the slaughter of the First World War, as Vincent Sherry has argued.[5] Examining the war writing of Helen Zenna Smith (Evadne Price), Enid Bagnold, Mary Borden and Vera Brittain, Jane Marcus traces one of the origins of the fragmentation often held to be the prime formal and stylistic innovation of modernist writing to the writing practice of women nurses and ambulance drivers.[6] Marcus also credits such women's war writing with an ability to foreground the corporeality with which middle-class literature representing civilian life and values continued to struggle.[7]

Bourgeois culture has constructed the (respectable) body as inconspicuous and invisible. The normative body 'means' precisely because it has gone from social awareness. Bodies in war, however, are neither respectable nor inconspicuous, not least because war is a rupture of cultural norms on so many levels. The body-at-war, then, becomes precisely the site in which such ruptures first become manifest. As a result, modern war writing remains obsessed with the physical ordeal and the indignities war imposes on the body: from the discomfort of lice-ridden bodies in Smith's *Not so Quiet* (1930) to the bloated corpses in Ernst Jünger's *Storm of Steel* (1920) or the grotesque dismemberments in Henri Barbusse's *Under Fire* (1916); from the debilitating humidity and filth in J.G. Ballard's Japanese internment camp in *Empire of the Sun* (1984) to the dull ache that plagues the freezing GI in Richard Bausch's *Peace* (2009). Yet there is also room for pleasure and physical delight: much joy is gained from the local wine in *Peace* and the local women in Erich Maria Remarque's *All Quiet on the Western Front* (1929). While the sex in Puzo's *The Dark Arena* (1955) is rough, it undoubtedly affords both participants distraction from the hunger and dereliction around them. Sexual opportunities along a wide spectrum of preferences and modes are not just a staple of contemporary re-imaginings of war – as in Joseph Kanon's *The Good German* (2002), Adam Thorpe's *The Rules of Perspective* (2005), Louis de Bernière's *Captain Corelli's Mandolin* (1994), Sarah Waters's *The Night Watch* (2005) or Thomas Keneally's *The Office of Innocence* (2002) – but also informed the consciousness of wartime writers such as Graham Greene, Elizabeth Bowen, Patrick Hamilton or Henry Green. Santanu Das has also argued recently that sentient experiences under wartime conditions between 1914 and 1918 were not uniformly awful, but affected soldiers' and nurses' subjectivities in manifold ways that shaped the way they wrote about the war in letters, poems and memoirs.[8] In her Kleinian analysis of First World War narratives, Trudi Tate argued that the relationship between the historical events of war and their creative rendition may be rather complex: 'moments of terror and suffering are remembered (or imagined) as producing oddly eroticised forms of pleasure': history and fantasy meet through the sight of the suffering human body.[9]

For Sara Cole, corporeal experiences are the common denominator for the participants in war and therefore undermine the binary oppositions war sets up: civilian and combatant, enemy and friend, man and woman, injured and healthy.[10] Perhaps this is the most compelling reason for officially obscuring corporeality from images and words in modern war culture. Yet in our visual age, it is images – TV reportage and war photography – that purport to represent reality and that shape our relationship to war. Their distribution or withholding condition our desire for different sorts of information about violent conflict. In *Regarding the Pain of Others* (2003), the late Susan Sontag argued, 'the understanding of war among people who have not experienced war is now chiefly a product of the impact of these images'.[11] It is not merely those ignorant and innocent of war whose idea of war is moulded thus. For Paul Fussell censorship of word and image also affects the manner in which writerly sensibilities relate the combat experience. The wider the gap between official (mis)representation and the soldier's own experience, the more incommunicable the combatants' experience of physical danger and destruction to the 'home front', the harder it is to write against a collective national consciousness of war from which he or she may feel entirely alienated.[12] There is, then, political significance in writing about the body-at-war. Not only do the literary analyses in this collection aim to reinstate the body to the centre of attention (irrespective of ideological or methodological positions); they also respond to ways of reading war and war writing that have appropriated the body for political expediency or have obscured its meanings.

Modern war and the vanishing body: embodiment, nation, technology

Let me illustrate my case with a very recent example of a vanishing body. On 5 October 2009, British Guardsman Jamie Janes from the 1st Battalion The Grenadier Guards was killed in an explosion while on foot patrol in Helmand province, Afghanistan. Subsequently he, or rather his death, became the subject of a minor scandal between various stakeholders in the war in Afghanistan (the government, the military, the families of service personnel and the press). On the death of all service personnel killed in action while on operational duties, the British Prime Minister now writes to the bereaved families (the letters are drafted by military officials but handwritten by the Prime Minister). In the case of Guardsman Janes, his letter of condolence was ill-received by Janes's mother, who dismissed it angrily as 'a hastily-scrawled insult' in an interview with the *Sun* newspaper: not only was Gordon Brown's hand barely legible, the letter also appeared to contain other mistakes such as the misspelling of the Guardsman's surname.[13] The *Sun* printed a copy of the PM's letter amongst a flurry of headlines that included this gaffe alongside other offending signs of casual disrespect, such as Brown's failure to bow his head at the Cenotaph on Remembrance Day. When the premier subsequently apologized for his poor handwriting in a telephone conversation, reassuring Mrs Janes that the mistakes had been unintentional, a transcript of the recorded call was posted on the *Sun*'s website, not least because it gave a wider audience to Mrs Janes's criticism of the government's alleged failure to better equip British troops.[14]

Unsurprisingly, in this proxy row over major issues, Guardsman Janes and his maimed body disappeared from view almost as soon as he had become an occasion for official appreciation, maternal grief and anger, political manoeuvring, and journalistic grandstanding in notoriously ephemeral forms of writing (letters, news items). He was written about badly, disrespectfully and hyperbolically. However, the stakeholders in this debate were in fact united in their attempts to give meaning to a military death because our culture's conflicted attitude to war demands that we justify licensed killing and dying: the more controversial the conflict, the greater the need to validate its corpses. The newsworthiness of the PM's etiquette blunders, commented the BBC's Nick Robinson, did not lie in his alleged unpatriotic lack of commitment to the mission in Afghanistan and, by implication, to the service men and women on duty in British campaigns in past and present wars. Rather, the story was a symptom of a widespread doubt about 'whether "our boys" are fighting and dying in vain'.[15] In the course of the recent wars in Afghanistan and Iraq we see a widening gulf between public criticism of the government's military policy and public empathy for the troops (an empathy that must necessarily put aside any doubts over a career choice in which individual agency is professionally suspended). Charity organizations have inhabited this disjunction to mobilize greater support for ex-service personnel, renaming veterans 'heroes'.[16] In this strategy, the connotations with ageing men and with the temporal remoteness of the two world wars are replaced by an epithet that revives a concept of patriotism, honour and duty which those global conflicts dismissed as hopelessly outdated. Indeed, according to the website of the Royal British Legion:

> Heroes is one of those words that is bandied about too readily these days, devaluing and diminishing the actions of real heroes.
>
> The brave young men and women in our Armed Forces, especially those who are serving on the front lines in Afghanistan and Iraq, wake up every morning knowing that it could be their last. These are the people who are our true heroes.[17]

'Real' and 'true' heroes are those who do their duty in the face of mortal danger in the front lines of combat in remote areas. Part of the work of interest groups such as the British Legion consists in keeping in the public eye the troops' effort when it has long disappeared from headlines and television screens; in acknowledging their service as an act of patriotic bravery even if the conflicts in question are controversial; and in drawing attention to the inadequate financial provision and psychological care provided by the state for its corps post-service. Turning veterans and currently serving personnel into 'heroes' is a strategy to remind the public that the military is not synonymous with the government and that the former should not be held responsible for the latter's policies or failures. While both institutions represent a nation's citizens, they are separate corporate bodies operating in different spheres – the government at the centre of power, the military literally at the geopolitical borders to which this power extends.

It is perhaps more important to emphasize the consistency with which veterans throughout the twentieth century have remained marginalized socially and economically[18] despite annual rituals of commemoration and sentiment. Acts of remembrance such as the laying of wreaths at the Cenotaph allow us to forget war and conflict the rest of the time. In such rituals, however, the soldier's service is elevated to a national sacrifice, and the act of mourning and remembrance converted into a state function that requires strictly choreographed roles and gestures for the head of state and the head of government. Honouring a representative dead body invokes the continuation of the nation (in some way, he or she died 'for us'). This elevation of the soldier stands in stark contrast to the spectacular waste of human life that war produces.

It retrospectively validates this state-ordained wastage as 'somehow' necessary for the life of the nation: while many contemporary citizens in Britain and Germany are aware of the colossal loss of life in the First World War, few would actually be able to recall why this war was fought or what its war aims were.

These acts of remembrance, then, confirm rather than belie the absence of the soldier's suffering in the national consciousness for which the retrospective promotion to 'hero' is also meant to compensate. At best, soldiers' services remain at the margins of our awareness. In *Blood Sacrifice and the Nation* Carolyn Marvin and David Ingle argue that soldiers become sacrificial designates that ensure national cohesion by forming a class that allows societies to expel internal violence to a border of conflict with an external enemy.[19] In doing so, societies resort to a totemic practice that is both primitive and religious, while the predominantly secular self-perception of many Western nations helps to deny their capacity for ritual as well as the religious elements in the construction of national identity: 'At the behest of the group, the life-blood of community members must be shed. Group solidarity, or sentiment, flows from the value of this sacrifice.'[20] Marvin and Ingle's theory of sacrificial bodies and national symbols is the result of their trenchant analysis of how embodiment functions in the context of US history:

> The flag symbolizes the sacrificed body of the *citizen*. This label has meaning only in relation to the group that defines it, the *nation*. Blood sacrifice links the citizen to the nation. It is a ritual in the most profound sense, for it creates the nation from the flesh of its citizens. The flag is the sign and agent of the nation formed in blood sacrifice.[21]

This logic may sound more atavistic than it is, or rather, our scepticism towards such radical formulations may be grounded in a civilized delusion that wishes to see war as the last resort of political strategy rather than to acknowledge it as an essential element of nation-building and nationalism. We can see such potent embodiment at work in political iconographies outside the US, across a broad ideological spectrum, and on various levels of official acknowledgement. For instance, it is manifest in Eugène Delacroix's *Liberty Leading the People* (1830). It explicitly permeates the entire inventory of Nazi semiotics from SS initiation ceremonies to political anthems, from annual mass events to architectural sculpture.[22] Nor is the flag the only symbol of national embodiment. As I have suggested above, commemorative events may serve a similar purpose. British popular 'memory' of the Second World War – perhaps the most pervasive amongst the nations participating in that conflict – consolidates into a narrative of national unity entirely impervious to historiographical or literary revision precisely because it constitutes a cornerstone of post-war national identity and citizenship.[23]

For Marvin and Ingle, there is an inverse relationship between the invisibility of the sacrificial body at the border and cultural consciousness of it at the centre. It is entirely appropriate that military staff should be repatriated and buried in coffins draped with the national flag; but it is alarming when images of such rituals are disseminated, firstly because they highlight the cost of war that military rhetoric so studiously obfuscates and secondly because they allow for an identificatory link, via the flag, between the soldier's sacrifice and the civilian's responsibility: both are citizens of the same nation.[24] It is increasingly important for this sacrifice to be honourable and honoured whenever it does become visible. Hence the personal letters by state representatives, the pageants, the commemorations, the retrospective medals and recognitions, or the epithet 'hero'.

Paradoxically, this reclaiming of heroism *also* works on the basis of diminished corporeality such as maimed bodies, absent bodies and proxy representations (grieving families, photographs of service personnel and memorials). The Royal British Legion, which organizes the annual poppy appeal, recently launched a poster campaign with the mottos 'for his sake' (displaying a soldier in combat fatigues with a full leg prosthesis next to him) and 'for their sake', showing a serviceman's female partner and child in a domestic setting with a photograph of the deceased in uniform.[25] If charities foreground survivors and their families to personalize operational statistics, official government bodies focus on individualizing 'fatalities': the Ministry of Defence website lists all British deaths in service individually with date, place and circumstances of death[26] with a webpage for each service person outlining their career and life. Great effort is being made to counteract any hint that upon death, the soldier becomes a lifeless statistic. In fact, it is mostly upon death that the soldier becomes publicly visible. The response to death in service is often precisely a lot of (formal) writing: condolence letters and online obituaries, casualty lists and a bureaucracy of 'vital records', newspaper reports, names on memorials.

The corpse's vanishing act stands in contrast to the body's elevation at the beginning of a service career: many recruitment ads for the armed forces stress the necessity of physical fitness, and slogans such as

'99.9% need not apply' turn the career choice and the tough selection process into a contest from which the soldier emerges as superior to the civilian in physique, resolve and mental strength. The subsequent submersion of the individual soldier in the units organizing a corporate body that in turn represents the military forces of a nation may contribute to making the soldier's body vanish in literal and figurative ways. That armed forces represent nations is a relatively recent phenomenon, part of the development of modern nation-states. Feudal obligation, membership of a warrior caste or mercenary belligerence used to be the reasons for going to battle. By the eighteenth century, however, soldiers had become professionals and servants of the state. In the case of France and Prussia, the history of these countries and the history of their armed forces cannot really be separated. The cost and maintenance of a standing army required a centralized bureaucratic framework which enabled the crown to gain unprecedented control over economic resources and activities.[27] According to Michael Howard, a number of factors contributed to the coalescence of armed forces and nation: the introduction of compulsory military service; the rise of educational standards; population growth that allowed for a large standing army of qualified and trained men; technological progress that through the railway network and the telegraph system allowed for efficient troop movement, supply and communication; and finally, the formation of nation-states in which the idea of the 'country' as a set of values, customs and essences (*la patrie*; *Vaterland*) became a war aim that informed operations and was embodied in the head of state.[28] As early as the Napoleonic era, but certainly by the late nineteenth century, war had begun to have a much more profound impact on the entire population since its representative armed forces required the mobilization of all available resources. War was no longer an affair of armies; it had become total and involved entire societies. With the help of war reporters, the telegraph and daguerreotype, it was also brought closer to home: news often meant news of or about war. And reading about war often meant reading about someone who had been watching the spectacle of war and was trying to make sense of it.

Verbal and visual forms of (mis)representing war in official communications and journalistic reportage range from (pre-)censorship to fabrication; from omission to manipulation. Conflicting readings of war or of the outcomes of battle are not infrequent. It was not always easy to assess quickly who had gained or lost more territory and manpower. In situ post-battle interpretation of the fighting by generals and commanders might score victory where the result was at best a stalemate with spectacular loss of life, such as at the battle of Eylau (1807). The justification of such corrections to reality is usually the well-worn notion of keeping up morale (the soldiers' as well as the citizens') and, if the conflict is ongoing, the strategic advantage over the enemy gained by restricting information. Since the Boer War, corpses could neither be shown nor written about unless they were 'foreign bodies' whose existence or discovery justified one's own operations. In the First World War, little could officially be said about the horrors inflicted by technological warfare on the bodies of men engaged in highly mechanized fighting on the Western Front, or about the ghastly conditions in the trenches. However, Allied propaganda made the most of so-called atrocities inflicted by the enemy on innocent foreign bodies, as in the case of 'the rape of Belgium', with its well-known trope of a feminized, sexualized national body that fell victim to a bestial force; or the story of the 'crucified Canadian soldier' nailed to a barn door.[29] There is a sense that any injury done to a soldier's body is also inflicted on the nation he represents, hence the reluctance to show images of one's fallen soldiers or of coffins shipped home. These unwelcome reminders of the cost of war seem to be the main reason why the body is written out of war before it might make an awkward reappearance as a corpse.

The nation-at-war in modern times replaces the individual with an allegorical body (imperious Britannia, the Statue of Liberty, Marianne), heads of state (the Kaiser, Churchill) with symbols (the flag, the eagle, the lion), or with synecdoches of national character: a landscape, a song, the model citizen. As Christine Berberich argues in her chapter, the embodiment of national values in such portable artefacts as poetry anthologies patriotically tether the soldier to the homeland. They transform that proverbial corner of a foreign field (where Britain mostly fights its wars) into 'England'. Hence the idealized countryside on British recruitment posters in the First and Second World Wars ('Isn't this worth fighting for? Enlist Now!', 'Your Britain – Fight for it Now'); hymns and popular songs incorporating national legend, poetry or values ('Jerusalem', 'The White Cliffs of Dover'); the propaganda posters instructing civilians about how to behave in wartime in order to forge national unity, that is to synchronize the effort by civilian and military forces. In the latter phenomenon we can see an authoritarian discourse in which by dint of maximizing modes of production and restricting consumption in a wartime economy, bodies are rigorously policed: 'Eat less bread!', 'Keep mum!', 'Come into the Factories', 'Post Early'. In a total war, every area of life becomes subject to regulation, from the contents of pots and pans to topics of conversation; from leisure time to sexual conduct. Just as the civilian body is regimented under conditions of total war, the military body has been increasingly mechanized: the soldier is an integral part of the *machinery* of war, a human operator of sophisticated high-cost equipment.

This process of mechanization begins not just with modern industrialized warfare and professional armies whose equipment is state-funded and part of a national budget. As Mark Seltzer has demonstrated in *Bodies and Machines*, late nineteenth-century culture was profoundly preoccupied with the boundaries between the animate and the inanimate, with the relationship between consuming bodies and machines that enabled production.[30] To think of the body as a machine became a predominant metaphor in the early twentieth century, to the extent that cultural, medico-pedagogical and socio-economic discourses used those terms almost interchangeably, as the titles of a range of publications demonstrate: Jacques Loeb's *The Mechanistic Conception of Life* (1912), Arnold Bennett's *The Human Machine* (1913), Arthur Keith's *The Engines of the Human Body* (1919), or Fritz Kahn's *Der Mensch als Industriepalast* (1930) [Man as an Industrial Palace].[31] Oswald Spengler's cultural analysis in *Man and Technics* (1932) saw mechanization as a symptom of the decline of the West: 'the Civilization itself has become a machine that does, or tries to do, everything in mechanical fashion'.[32]

Modern modes of mass-production and administration coralled masses of workers to fit into and around labour-, time- and cost-saving machines, if they did not altogether increasingly replace the human element in those processes. In his analysis of the manufacturing process for his Model T, Henry Ford observed that only 12 per cent of the almost 8000 operations required able-bodied men; the rest could be performed by partially able men:[33] modern manufacturing disabled and dispensed with men even before the First World War could dismember them. In a similar vein, armies were increasingly treated like a labour force, subjected to the same rules of efficiency, division of labour, and target achievements. D.H. Lawrence was one of the first writers to spot the cataclysmic link between modern industrial and military organization in an article for the *Manchester Guardian* shortly after the outbreak of the First World War. For him, militarism was a symptom of the modern technological age that deprived men of an organic corporeal existence. Observing military exercises in Bavaria in 1913, he commented that war would be 'an affair entirely of machines, with men attached to the machines as the subordinate part thereof, as the butt is the part of a rifle'.[34]

In official representations of battle or of armies on ancient reliefs and friezes, on murals and in panoramic painting, on propaganda posters and photography flesh is gradually replaced with iron as technology and weaponry advance; even the bodies of the monarch or commander are mere embodiments, symbolizing the state power that both mobilizes force and is sustained by military prowess whether we think of outsized pharaohs leading chariot fights, Trajan leading his men on his eponymous column in Rome, Meissonnier's *Napoleon III at the Battle of Solferino*, Churchill's bulk before an RAF formation and a tank squadron on 'Let us go forward together' or, famously, Jockel Fink's photograph of Margaret Thatcher riding a Challenger tank in Fallingbostel in 1986.

It has become a critical truism to see the highly mediated Gulf War of 1991 as a marker of modern war's vanishing bodies, not least because it presented a very different image of war from the earlier conflict in Vietnam where narrative and photography presented combat in marked contrast to the US administration's official version. If Vietnam brought war into the living room, the Gulf sanitized the domesticated battlefield of its corpses. Since missile damage became invisible on impact, it did not provoke moral assessments despite the ubiquity of this conflict on TV screens. As the central record of the Gulf War is dominated by the US military's own description to which the pre-censored reportage hardly offered a corrective, one could do worse than believe that this was a robot Blitz, a war of 'targets', in which 'installations', 'assets' and 'units' were 'attrited', 'neutralized' and 'pounded' by remote-controlled missiles with video cameras. As both Joanna Bourke and Richard Overy have argued, such language is symptomatic of a barbarization of warfare in which increasing levels of violence are enabled by a rhetoric that obfuscates the reality of war.[35] Such language obliterates bodies twice – once in the actual attack and again in the lack of acknowledgment of the human victims of conflict. The Gulf War's rhetoric carefully concealed the death toll, primarily that of over 100,000 Iraqi soldiers who were quietly incorporated in such disembodied language. Intellectuals were highly disturbed less by the war itself than by the way in which it was presented to the world as a war without bodies in which superior technology and state power controlled the visibility of human cost.[36]

Yet the history of the vanishing body at war reaches back much further, to the invention of weaponry that increased the distance between combatants from face-to-face fighting to hundreds of feet, even miles: catapults, crossbows, cannons, firearms and long-range artillery. Even such an awkward tool as the Dreyse needle gun (the first rifled breechloader, used in the Austro-Prussian War of 1866) or Krupp's steel breechloading cannon, deployed in the Franco-Prussian war of 1870, kept the enemy at a distance of between several hundred and 3000 yards. In the 1880s, high explosives increased the range of all weapons to hitherto inconceivable distances. By the late nineteenth century, soldiers did not need to see the enemy to fight him nor need they present a visible or physical target during attack.[37] The battle was now between manually-operated machines obliterating men and territory, rather than consisting in man-to-man combat. The result of such 'impersonalisation', as John Keegan calls it in *The Face of Battle*, is the soldier's sense of vanishing, subject to vast unlocalized forces, lost in demolished, depopulated landscapes in which any sense of time disappears, particularly in the major wars of the twentieth century: the overwhelming feeling of insignificance and littleness encouraged soldiers to think of their opponents as equally unimportant.[38] Despite continual addenda to the Geneva Conventions, modern warfare made the boundaries between perpetrators and victims, lawful and unlawful acts, more and more ambiguous.

Sophisticated weaponry and 'total war' did not only increase the destructiveness of war, it shifted its impact and its target towards civilians. The war of attrition on the Western Front affected predominantly military personnel, and it was the first war in which more soldiers died from battle injury than through disease. Already in the Second World War, over 60 per cent of the casualties were civilians while in today's conflicts the figure is closer to 90 per cent.[39] Yet death toll and body count are not synonymous but depend on national perspectives. By the standards of twentieth-century history, Allied casualty figures in the Gulf War, in Iraq and in Afghanistan are very low and might be interpreted as indicative of the superior force and strategies applied in these conflicts. Yet this reading depends on the lack of precise information about, and interest in recording, the death toll incurred by the designated enemy or the resident population. Such unilateral accountancy also neglects the range of physical suffering brought about by anti-civilian strategies such as rape, torture, forced expulsion, famine, impoverishment and disease, which may severely traumatize but do not necessarily always lead to death.[40]

If I have so far used the terms 'war' and 'conflict' interchangeably, this is a reflection of the instability of the meaning and purpose of war. As Hew Strachan argues in his essay 'The Idea of War', the ways in which war is defined have changed considerably, from Carl von Clausewitz's dictum 'an act of force to compel our enemy to do our will' (a political strategy) to the current 'war on terror', which leaves purpose and enemies indeterminate. Most literature on war was less philosophical than strategic: it did not wish to define or understand war, as Clausewitz tried to, but offered suggestions for superior strategy that would lead to victory.[41] Where are the boundaries, one might ask, between civil war, rebellion, revolution or insurgency? What is the difference between 'armed conflict', 'hostilities' and 'war'? Does genocide count as war, is it a separate category or a mere by-product? *Who* defines organized violence may or may not validate a conflict as war, as is borne out by the different names for the 'Sepoy Rebellion' of 1857: calling it the 'Indian Mutiny' emphasizes an unlawful and insurgent act by colonial military subjects from an imperialist perspective; calling it 'India's First War of Independence' integrates it into a history of national counter-imperialist measures that spans almost a hundred years and succeeds in gaining self-government. 'War' at this time designated a conflict between sovereign nation-states; avoiding this term nominally reduced the significance of the violence even if the conflict lasted for years or incurred enormous casualties. It also relegated the enemy to an irregular guerrilla force, a mere partisan faction; it denied suzerainty altogether or occluded the purpose and the nature of military intervention, hence terms like 'the Boxer Rebellion', 'the Tibet Expedition', 'the Troubles', 'the Malayan Emergency'.

Reading the body-at-war: war writing and corporeal signification

War writing is now as recognized a genre as the *Bildungsroman*, science fiction or autobiography, with a host of textbooks and anthologies to support its study. If the academy has become more attentive to literary responses to war this is not least because writers got there first – and because, deplorably, they have so many wars to represent, remember or re-imagine. In fact, one of the first works of Western literature, Homer's *The Iliad* (c. 750 BC) is the *urtext* of war writing, an epic poem that translates violence into myth. For Kate McLoughlin, writing about war fulfils a range of purposes: it retrospectively imposes verbal order on the chaos of battle; it keeps a record which may serve to imaginatively explain death on a large scale; it may be therapeutic as well as exhilarating or serve as a protection against war's brutalizing effects.[42] Fredric Jameson suggests that war novels and films 'are pretty much the same and have few enough surprises for us' whether they fall into stereotypical narrative variants and situations or defamiliarize known patterns.[43] Yet both agree that war literature is caught in and motivated by the paradox that such violence is an unimaginable collective reality which exceeds representation while it 'ceaselessly tempt[s] and exasperate[s] narrative ambitions, conventional and experimental alike'.[44] McLoughlin notes the recurring rhetorical figure of the adynaton as indicative of the writer's sense of ineptitude in the face of war. Such disclaimers ('it is impossible to convey', 'I cannot adequately express', 'there are no words to describe') call upon the reader's imagination to fill in, supplement, and aggravate through his or her apprehension what has been put on paper.

Taken more literally, such disclaimers suggest that combatants cannot understand war precisely because of the disorientating effects of warfare on the senses: the chaos of the mêlée and the deafening noise of artillery fire mark literary and military accounts of warfare from the Battle of Waterloo (Tolstoy, Stendhal), the Franco-Prussian War (Zola) through to the trenches of the Western Front (Barbusse, Jünger). Terrain and location are other challenges to comprehension. In Grimmelshausen's portrayal of the Thirty Years' War, *Simplicissimus* (1668), we see war represented as a mind-boggling culture of violence, as fighting cannot be contained on conventional battlefields but spreads across Central Europe through marauding, looting and torturing mercenaries: it is an assault on all humanity into which everyone is drawn. Traversing the vast snowy plains of the Russian steppe, which defeated Napoleon's armies, is vividly evoked in its effects on the soldiers of both sides in Lt Heinrich Vossler's contemporary diary *With Napoleon in Russia 1812* (1831) and in Jeanette Winterson's magical realist novel *The Passion* (1984). How a siege debilitates both sides is the subject of Theodor Plivier's *Stalingrad* (1954) and Vasily Grossmann's *Life and Fate* (completed 1960, published 1980). The works of Remarque and Jünger challenged the boundaries between the dead and the living: in their novels of the First World War labyrinthine subterranean passages, burrows and corpse-strewn mud fields gradually turn into unholy cemeteries. Elizabeth Bowen's 'Mysterious Kôr' and 'The Demon Lover' (both 1944), Gert Ledig's *Payback* (1956) and Sarah Waters's *The Night Watch* (2006) all describe surreal or uncanny cityscapes in which bombed-out citizens lose their homes, their lives or their minds. The dense forests on the Eastern Front harbour 'partisans', but such primeval accommodation also challenges their humanity (Levi, Michaelis). Life in the 'underground', in hiding or in ghettos requires survival skills that can construct new realities from which it is impossible to fully exit post-war, as is shown in Jurek Becker's *Jakob the Liar* (1990) or Louis Begley's *Wartime Lies* (1991). The large body of writing about the Shoah combines physical deprivation and mental trauma in particularly poignant ways. In Biyi Bandele's *Burma Boy* (2007) and Michael Herr's *Despatches* (1977), set in the jungles of Burma and Vietnam, combatants are not just assaulted by terrain-savvy enemies but also by hostile, alien environments. All these conditions produce intense sentient impressions as well as specific physical conditions, from the pain of injury to that of hunger and thirst; from frostbite to jungle rot; from maggot-infested ulcers to cannibalism. While they all give us a sense of war, and its senselessness, these narratives also suggest the artificiality of representation in a range of implicit or self-conscious ways. In his analysis of Tolstoy and Stendhal's novels of the Napoleonic wars, Jan Mieszkowski argues that these grand narratives of war already ironically present conflict as a spectacle that has to be imagined rather than observed, although the mind can grasp no better what defies the eye.[45]

Panoramic positions, from which the progress of battle can be viewed and assessed may be a retrospective construction if not a myth although both war painting and military historiography often assume such vantage points. As the narrator comments in W.G. Sebald's *The Rings of Saturn* (1995) on viewing Louis-Jules Dumoulin's massive Waterloo Panorama of 1912:

> This then, I thought as I looked around me, is the representation of history. It requires a falsification of perspective. We, the survivors, see everything from above, see everything at once, and still we do not know how it was. The desolate field extends all around where once fifty thousand soldiers and ten thousand horses met their end within a few hours. The night after the battle, the air must have been filled with death rattles and groans. Now there is nothing but the silent brown soil. Whatever became of the corpses and mortal remains? Are they buried under the memorial? Are we standing on a mountain of death? Is that our ultimate vantage point? Does one really have the much-vaunted historical overview from such a position? [...]
>
> No clear picture emerged. Neither then nor today. Only when I had shut my eyes, I well recall, did I see a cannon ball smash through a row of poplars at an angle, sending the green branches flying in tatters. And then I saw Fabrizio, Stendhal's young hero, wandering about the battlefield, pale but with his eyes aglow.[46]

Sebald's melancholic reflection alludes to Walter Scott's unseeing battlefield tourism, and, more importantly, to Walter Benjamin's notion of the 'Angel of History' who, with his back turned to the future, stands at the bottom of a pile of debris: for both Sebald and Benjamin, history clearly means a mountain of corpses. Yet Benjamin's angel is inspired by Paul Klee's painting *Angelus Novus*; Sebald's reflection, by Benjamin and Stendhal. The response to mountains of corpses – a history of war – is mediated through layers of textuality. It is only when the narrator closes his eyes that he sees, or rather, that he recalls visualizing, a famous scene from *The Charterhouse of Parma*. And while Fabrizio's eyes may well be aglow, he remains confused and uncomprehending. The obfuscating effect of war is the subject of this scene: precisely because we have turned war into something that can be looked upon or watched (on reliefs, tapestries, panoramas, memorials, cinema or TV screens), it cannot be understood. The visualization is misleading.

Can representing war assume the opposite strategy: a refusal to supply any (more) detail, to indulge in gore or evoke dulled images of conventional battle? Can it take refuge in synecdoches, symbols and abstractions? We find this strategy in combatants' narratives as well as in civilians'. I am thinking here of the pair of boots that is bequeathed to survivors in Remarque's *All Quiet on the Western Front* (and which develops into shorthand for 'yet another death') and of Jacob Flanders's boots in Woolf's elegiac *Jacob's Room* (1922) in which exploding shells, mud and rotting corpses are literally unknowable, unspeakable and therefore entirely absent. If both novels highlight the alienation between combatants and civilians due to the incommunicability of war experience, they also stress the banality of death. In the reverse tradition of Homer's *Iliad* they provide a life to commemorate *before* death in combat, although this undercuts any notion of heroism or noble warriorhood. Gert Ledig's *Payback* takes this commemorative strategy to absurd extremes, in the portrayal of a seventy-minute air attack on an unknown German city in the Second World War, during which new forms of dying are evenly distributed. Before we meet a character we hear their spectral voices reading their obituary paragraph; later in the chapter, they combust, melt into asphalt, are torn to shreds or buried alive, or asphyxiate in a firestorm. If war deprives humans of humanity, what is the point in the conventions of representing people? Patricia Pulham's Kristevaen reading of the pacifist Vernon Lee's versions of *The Ballet of the Nations* (and its later version *Satan the Waster*) emphasizes the tensions in the anti-representational politics of Lee's script and never-performed play. While Lee takes her inspiration from public Catholic rituals of suffering, she refuses to have that suffering performed on stage. The nations at war in her play about the First World War are embodied, but they are not visible. What we see in Lee's intentions (albeit not on stage) perhaps marks a collision between a traditional understanding of the suffering body mediated by images and religious or legal narratives on the one hand and one framed through propaganda and photography on the other. It also shifts any notion of the sacrificial body from the heroic soldier to the pacifist martyr, since Lee makes it clear that in the act of war governments abuse citizen's bodies. For her, there is nothing hallowed in mass slaughter. Lee's radical protest is less subtle than what Kate McLoughlin calls 'writerly tacitness' about war, in which that topic falls into 'lexical gaps, the spaces separating lines, the structural inter-stices of fragmented writing'.[47]

If Lee reclaims the body from the appropriation of the nations at war (at the cost of her own abuse), Tom Paulin engages in a similar project in *The Invasion Handbook*. In his chapter on Paulin's poems, Mark Rawlinson reads Paulin's work as a 'critique of the usurpation of the citizen's body by the state': body and voice emerge as 'alternatives to historical abstrac-tion' as we find them in national myths of war. Christine Berberich's interpretation of Siegfried Sassoon's *Memoirs of a Foxhunting Man* follows a similar policy of uncovering a writerly scepticism towards hegemonic versions of war. For her, the nostalgia that is habitually projected onto the bucolic idyll of a pre-war landscape that was strongly politicized dur-ing the First World War is a product of misreading Sassoon. Scrutinized more closely, the pastoral tropes of Sassoon's Edwardian England already harbour discord and offer a darker vision of a home that would be utterly defamiliarized by a war fought in a foreign field.

Lee and Paulin do not indulge in injured or maimed bodies. Appalled by the state's appropriation of the body they choose to focus on the mechanics of politics by showing how nations integrate it into national myths or propaganda or, in the case of Sassoon, how the state even recruits landscapes in its military service so that their evocation has to be rethought and rewritten. The consequences of the spectacular human waste of modern war, then, do not always lead to the repre-sentation of bodily casualties in various states of injury, mutilation or decay. Yet from its earliest examples, war writing does not shy from the brutality of conflict. There is certainly no writerly tacitness in Homer's *Iliad* in which heads roll, teeth fly from mouths, shoulders are speared, and corpses shamed. Here we see Hector's chariot-driver Cebriones killed by Patroclos in book XVI in which he

> smash[es] his forehead with the jagged stone.
> Both brows were hit at once, the frontal bone
> gave way, and both his eyes burst from their sockets
> dropping into the dust before his feet,
> as like a diver from the handsome car
> he plummeted, and life ebbed from his bones.[48]

There is an effort here at aestheticizing death (not killing) through the use of simile as if the rhetorical figure could restore dignity to such detailed disfiguration in dying. But perhaps most memorable in all this slaughter before the gates of Troy is the mutilation of Hector's body. Stabbed by each of the spectators to his death, he is subsequently stripped and strapped behind a chariot with which Achilles gallops around the city walls. Hector's mother tears her hair out and his wife Andromache faints at the sight of her husband's 'torn body', but Homer does not spare us the detail of how the corpse is prepared for such humiliation:

> Behind both feet he pierced
> the tendons, heel to ankle. Rawhide cords
> he drew through both and lashed them to his chariot,
> letting the man's head trail. Stepping aboard,
> bearing the great trophy of the arms,
> he shook the reins, and whipped the team ahead
> into a willing run. A dust-cloud rose
> above the furrowing body; the dark tresses
> flowed behind, and the head so princely once
> lay back in dust. Zeus gave him to his enemies
> to be defiled in his own fatherland.
> So his own head was blackened.[49]

In her wartime reading of this epic, Simone Weil noted that war is a force that transforms people into things (corpses, at the extreme end), or that it at least has a petrifactive effect on the mind. This transformation metaphorically turns sentient matter into stone, reducing it either to complete passivity (inert matter) or to a state in which it is carried away in a frenzy of momentum. She seems to suggest that whatever side one is on (the victim or perpetrator of violence) the effect of the transformation dehumanizes both: 'intolerable sufferings continue [...] because they have deprived the sufferer of the resources which might serve to extricate him'.[50] In such a reading Achilles's 'blind force' originates in his own 'intolerable suffering' over his lover Patroclos's death, which has unleashed a desire to wreak revenge on Hector, whose shame will, in turn, bring unbearable grief to his family. The process of wounding here is of course also a psychological one; 'trauma' is the Greek word for wound. Such a *perpetuum mobile* of violence sits uneasily with notions of torture, about which Marina MacKay writes in her chapter on Jean Améry. Nor does MacKay suggest that the psychoanalytic notion of trauma is an adequate approach to torture (or perhaps even the Shoah). Her interest in the response of Austrian Jewish survivors like Améry and Ruth Klüger to the assault on the Jewish body lies in their insistence on remembering the affront through resentment – a resentment that also reacts to their environment's ignorance of or anger at their marked body. The survivor insists on remaining stigmatized in the face of the future's oblivion.

To see the body of a friend or a loved one mutilated is a horrific experience, because it affects the way in which we remember them. Such injury literally defamiliarizes the already abject corpse. If post-mortem rituals such as washing, dressing and burial are predominantly for the bereaved, they serve to reassure them of the humanity of the deceased and of the humanity of the society to which the ritual returns the corpse. It is paramount for Priam to retrieve his son's body, as it must have been deeply troubling for the families of over 200,000 soldiers lost in the First World War to know that their sons' bodies were not even recovered, let alone buried. Burial makes death mean, but it depends on the readability of the corpse. Remembrance Day at the Cenotaph in London and similar war memorials is a necessary cultural ritual not least because many graves are overseas or because there is no grave. Therefore the Cenotaph does not represent the unknown warrior but the unknown grave, as Joanna Bourke states.[51] The monumental stone body of the Cenotaph stands for the corpse that, in death, has vanished or become unreadable: its literal meaning is 'empty tomb'.

If the absent corpse is at the heart of a ritual national commemoration (whose etiquette, as we have already seen, is strictly prescribed and involves other representative national bodies), it is perhaps apposite to think about the relationship between national memory, war writing and dead bodies. Eugene McNulty reads Sebastian Barry's novel *A Long Long Way* as dramatizing a 'schism in remembrance' occasioned by the Irish soldiers deployed in the Allied cause in Flanders and against their own countrymen in the Easter Rising. The division in the Irish body politic is played out in the commemorative practices and agendas of these conflicts. In such contexts, dead bodies are also bodies of evidence (even in their politically expedient vanishing acts) of imperialist appropriation or anti-imperialist self-fashioning. In my own discussion of Robert Harris's *Fatherland* and Ian McEwan's *Black Dogs*, I examine the ways in which these books position the fascist body in the material remnants of fascist ideology, most notably the camp. To what extent does our contemporary memorial culture appropriate the physical remnants of the Shoah and of Nazism to fashion an identity that insists on the radical otherness of victimhood and perpetration while remaining entranced by the spectacle of absolute power?

In war, and after war, bodies have to be readable as representing warring parties or ideologies. The uniform is a military marker of nationality and rank; it is a sign of who is and is not a combatant with the rights and duties attributed to such status. Two of the chapters in this collection focus on the meaning of uniforms and the erotic investments that adhere to them. Victoria Stewart argues that uniforms augment or decrease the value of bodies. Her essay on Betty Miller's novel *On the Side of the Angels* focuses on the complex relationship between gender and uniforms, while I am interested in the way in which contemporary writing fantasizes about the signifying power of the Nazi uniform way beyond its historical meaning and dramatizes ambiguous scenarios in which absolute power and democratic restraint uneasily coalesce. Yet it is not just the military body whose meaning poses problems: what happens to the civilian corpse in wartime, when killing has become lawful? Gill Plain examines literary corpses in popular fiction of the Second World War and the ways in which they, as well as murderers and detectives, come to signify in different ways. That individual bodies become representative of the national body, that corpses might embody the body politic and suffer its fate, is the subject of Richard Robinson's analysis of Ian McEwan's novel *The Innocent*, about the division of Germany. McEwan's corporeal trope of a gruesome dismemberment reminds Robinson of the surgical metaphors military historians use to describe war's effect on geopolitical territory.

That many of the chapters collected here are about British writing on the major conflicts of the twentieth century is perhaps no surprise. War remains a cornerstone of post-war British identity and the literary response to British wars takes this into account, not just by representing war in the first place (making it count, recording it) but by interpreting it – often against hegemonic readings of war. War writing is not always anti-war writing, but one would now be hard pressed, given the ubiquity of corpses, to find a writer who extols its so-called virtues. One would hope that those whose business it is to make war, endorse war and perpetuate war might take a closer look at its literary representations rather than at war memorials. It might tell them something about the certainty with which the body count will overwrite their 'legacy'.

Notes

1. To name just a few of the most influential studies: Julia Kristeva, *The Powers of Horror: an Essay on Abjection* (New York: Columbia University Press, 1982). Elaine Scarry, *The Body in Pain: the Making and Unmaking of the World* (Oxford: Oxford University Press, 1985). Thomas Walter Laqueur, *Making Sex: Body and*

Gender from the Greeks to Freud (Cambridge, MA: Harvard University Press, 1990). Mike Featherstone, Mike Hepworth and Bryan S. Turner (eds), *The Body: Social Process and Cultural Theory* (London: Sage, 1991). Elisabeth Bronfen, *Over Her Dead Body: Death, Femininity and the Aesthetic* (Manchester: Manchester University Press, 1992). Mark Seltzer, *Bodies and Machines* (London: Routledge, 1992). Judith Butler, *Bodies that Matter: on the Discursive Limits of Sex* (London: Routledge, 1993). Peter Brooks, *Body Work: Objects of Desire in Modern Narrative* (Cambridge, MA: Harvard University Press, 1993). Sander L. Gilman, *Health and Illness: Images of Difference* (London: Reaktion Books, 1995). Roy Porter and Lesley Hall, *The Facts of Life: the Creation of Sexual Knowledge in Britain, 1650–1950* (New Haven: Yale University Press, 1995). Tim Armstrong, *Modernism, Technology and the Body* (Cambridge: Cambridge University Press, 1998). Mitchell B. Merback, *The Thief, the Cross and the Wheel: Pain and the Spectacle of Punishment in Medieval and Renaissance Europe* (London: Reaktion, 1999). Dennis Patrick Slattery, *The Wounded Body: Remembering the Markings of Flesh* (New York: SUNY Press, 2000). Nigel Spivey, *Enduring Creation: Art, Pain and Fortitude* (London: Thames & Hudson, 2001). Robert Mills, *Suspended Animation: Pain, Pleasure and Punishment in Medieval Culture* (London: Reaktion, 2005).

2. Roy Porter, 'History of the Body', in Peter Burke (ed.), *New Perspectives on Historical Writing* (Cambridge: Polity Press, 1991), 206–33; 209–11.

3. For a start on this project see *Journal of War and Culture Studies* 1/2 (2008) which collects some of the contributions of the eighth annual conference of the Group for War and Culture Studies (2004), 'The Body at War: Somatic Cartographies of Western Warfare in the 19th and 20th Centuries'.

4. Scarry, *The Body in Pain*, 64.

5. Vincent Sherry, *The Great War and the Language of Modernism* (Oxford: Oxford University Press, 2003).

6. Laura Marcus, 'Corpus/Corps/Corpse: Writing the Body in/at War', in Helen Zenna Smith, *Not So Quiet: Stepdaughters of War* (New York: The Feminist Press, 1989), 241–300; 249.

7. Ibid., 267. Her prime example is of course Virginia Woolf's much cited statement on the topic of corporeal experience, in 'Professions for Women' (1931), that she has failed to tell the truth about her own body.

8. Santanu Das, *Touch and Intimacy in First World War Literature* (Cambridge: Cambridge University Press, 2005).

9. Trudi Tate, *Modernism, History and the First World War* (Manchester: Manchester University Press, 1998), 89; 95. In her analysis of writing about anxiety in late modernist writing and British psychoanalysis, Lyndsey Stonebridge offers a Kleinian reading for the later conflict. See *The Writing of Anxiety: Imagining Wartime in Mid-Century British Culture* (Basingstoke: Palgrave Macmillan, 2007).

10. Sara Cole, 'People in War', in Kate McLoughlin (ed.), *The Cambridge Companion to War Writing* (Cambridge: Cambridge University Press, 2009), 25–38; 26; 35–6.

11. Susan Sontag, *Regarding the Pain of Others* (London: Hamish Hamilton, 2003), 19.

12. Paul Fussell, *Wartime: Understanding and Behaviour in the Second World War* (Oxford: Oxford University Press, 1989), 268.

13. Tom Newton Dunn, 'PM Couldn't Even Get Our Name Right', *Sun*, 9 November 2009, http://www.thesun.co.uk/sol/homepage/news/campaigns/our_boys/2720283/Prime-Minister-Gordon-Brown-couldnt-even-get-our-name-right.html, accessed 22 December 2009.

14. See 'I Can't Believe I've Been Brought Down To The Level Of Having An Argument With The Prime Minister Of My Own Country', *Sun*, 10 November 2009, http://www.thesun.co.uk/sol/homepage/news/campaigns/our_boys/ 2722106/Mum-at-war-Jacqui-Janes-the-full-transcript. html, accessed 22 December 2009.
15. Nick Robinson, 'When Politics Matters', BBC Newslog, 9 November 2009, http://www.bbc.co.uk/blogs/nickrobinson/2009/11/when_politics_m.html, accessed 2 December 2009.
16. See the Help for Heroes campaign, http://www.helpforheroes.org.uk.
17. 'To our heroes', http://www.poppy.org.uk/remembrance/our-heroes-messageboard, accessed 3 December 2009.
18. In her seminal analysis of the socio-medical impact of war injuries on constructs of masculinity, Joanna Bourke noted a marked shift in attitudes towards maimed soldiers. While soldiers' mutilations were initially read as a badge of courage and patriotism, maimed veterans soon lost the status of wounded warriors and were treated like disabled children upon reintegration into the national economy. *Dismembering the Male: Men's Bodies and the Great War* (London: Reaktion, 1996), 56; 251.
19. Carolyn Marvin and David Ingle, *Blood Sacrifice and the Nation: Totem Rituals and the American Flag* (Cambridge: Cambridge University Press, 1999), 4; 72f.; 80.
20. Ibid., 4.
21. Ibid., 63.
22. See Jay W. Baird, *To Die For Germany: Heroes in the Nazi Pantheon* (Bloomington: Indiana University Press, 1990). Peter Reichel, *Der schöne Schein des dritten Reiches: Faszination und Gewalt des Faschismus*, 2nd edn (Frankfurt/Main: Fischer, 1993). J.A. Mangan (ed.), *Shaping the Superman: Fascist Body as Political Icon – Aryan Fascism* (London: Frank Cass, 1999); Daniel Wildmann, *Begehrte Körper: Konstruktion und Inszenierung des 'arischen' Mannerkörpers im 'Dritten Reich'* (Würzburg: Königshausen & Neumann, 1998).
23. See Angus Calder, *The Myth of the Blitz* (London: Pimlico, 1992) and Sonya O. Rose, *Which People's War? National Identity and Wartime Citizenship in Wartime Britain, 1939–45* (Oxford: Oxford University Press, 2004).
24. This identificatory link between the soldier's body and the citizen also operates via the uniform whenever the 'wrong' visibility is achieved, such as in the images about the prisoner abuses in Abu Ghraib. When Susan Sontag responded to these images with the trenchant analysis 'the photographs *are* us' in an essay in the *New York Times*, she implied that the US soldiers in these images had not only committed gross misconduct but that they had had reason to believe themselves to be beyond reproach. What Sontag highlights as a contemporary problem of political culture in the US is precisely the discrepancy between what the soldier does (commit obscene and brutal acts on naked foreign bodies) and what he/she should embody (American values). Her bold statement makes visible the process by which the centre (the US administration, US society) disassociates itself from its military representatives and 'sacrificial designates' at the border rather than acknowledging the cataclysmic shift in values that has produced a culture of abuse. Susan Sontag, 'Regarding the Torture of Others', in Paolo Dilonardo and Anne Jump (eds), *At the Same Time* (London: Hamish Hamilton, 2007), 128–45;

131; first published in the *New York Times*, Magazine, 23 May 2004, http://www.nytimes.com/2004/05/23/magazine/23PRISONS.html. See also Patrick Hagopian, 'The Abu Ghraib Photographs and the State of America: Defining Images', in Louise Purbrick, Jim Aulich and Graham Dawson (eds), *Contested Spaces: Sites, Representations and Histories of Conflict* (Basingstoke: Palgrave Macmillan 2007), 13–49.

25. See The Royal British Legion's poppy appeal, http://www.poppy.org.uk.

26. As at 9 May 2010, there have been 285 British fatalities in Afghanistan since the start of operations in October 2001, http://www.mod.uk/DefenceInternet/FactSheets/OperationsFactsheets/OperationsInAfghanistanBritishFatalities.htm. British casualty figures to 15 February 2010 stand at 333 seriously or very seriously wounded, with 1126 field hospital admissions through battle wounds and 2321 admissions through disease or non-battle injuries. As of July 2009 the British fatalities for the war in Iraq since its beginning in March 2003 are 179, http://www.mod.uk/DefenceInternet/FactSheets/OperationsFactsheets/OperationsInIraqBritishFatalities.htm. Casualty figures to 31 July 2009 stand at 222 seriously or very seriously wounded, with 315 field hospital admissions through battle wounds and 3283 admissions through disease or non-battle injuries, http://www.mod.uk/NR/rdonlyres/7E86BD05-D4FF-4677–97AA-CCFBDCFE4E34/0/optelic_31jul09.pdf.

27. Michael Howard, *War in European History*, updated edn (Oxford: Oxford University Press, 2009), 68–9.

28. Ibid., 97–110.

29. See Tate, *Modernism*, 41–62. Peter Buitenhuis, *The Great War of Words: British, American and Canadian Propaganda and Fiction, 1914–1933* (Vancouver: University of British Columbia Press, 1987). A rare exception to this othering of the body was a British propaganda poster showing British seamen forced to parade past jeering German civilians, who laughed at the humiliation that had been inflicted on their enemy by way of shaving one side of their heads and beards. It is part of the poster collection of the Imperial War Museum, London.

30. See Seltzer, *Bodies and Machines*.

31. See Petra Rau, *English Modernism, National Identity and the Germans, 1890–1950* (Aldershot: Ashgate, 2009), 141–4. See also Tim Armstrong, *Modernism*.

32. Oswald Spengler, *Man and Technics* (London: Allan & Unwin, 1963), 94.

33. Seltzer, *Bodies and Machines*, 157.

34. D.H. Lawrence, 'With the Guns', in *The Prussian Officer and Other Stories*, ed. Antony Atkins (Oxford: Oxford University Press, 1995), 246.

35. Joanna Bourke, 'Barbarisation vs. Civilisation in Time of War', in George Kassimeris (ed.), *The Barbarisation of Warfare* (London: Hurst, 2006), 19–39; 21–32. Richard Overy, 'The Second World War: a Barbarous Conflict?' in ibid., 39–58; 55.

36. See Allan Sekula, 'War without Bodies', *Artforum* 30/3 (1991): 107–10. Hugh Gusterson, 'Nuclear War, the Gulf War, and the Disappearing Body', *Journal of Urban and Cultural Studies* 2/1 (1991): 51. John Taylor, *Body Horror: Photojournalism, Catastrophe and War* (Manchester: Manchester University Press, 1998). Jean Baudrillard, *The Gulf War Did Not Take Place* (Sydney: Power, 1995).

37. Howard, *War in European History*, 102–3.

38. John Keegan, *The Face of Battle* (Harmondsworth: Penguin, 1983), 326–9.
39. Bourke, 'Barbarisation', 21.
40. See Hugo Slim, *Killing Civilians: Method, Madness and Morality in War* (London: Hurst, 2007).
41. Hew Strachan, 'The Idea of War', in *Cambridge Companion*, 7–15; 12.
42. Kate Mcloughlin, 'War and Words', in ibid., 15–25; 19–21.
43. Fredric Jameson, 'War and Representation', *PMLA* 124/5 (2009): 1532–47; 1533.
44. Ibid., 1547.
45. See Jan Mieszkowski, 'Watching War', *PMLA* 124/5 (2009): 1648–60.
46. W.G. Sebald, *The Rings of Saturn*, trans. Michael Hülse (London: Harvill, 1998), 125–6. Note that Sebald misspells the painter's name: it is not Dumontin but Dumoulin. For a 360 degree film of this panorama see Waterloo Panorama at http://www.youtube.com/watch?v=w1Tl8WGctzo, accessed 18 December 2009.
47. McLoughlin, 'War and Words', 17.
48. Homer, *The Iliad*, trans. Robert Fitzgerald, intro. G.S. Kirk (Oxford: Oxford University Press, 1998), 295.
49. Ibid., 392.
50. Simone Weil, 'The *Iliad*, or the Poem of Force' [1940], in Simone Weil, *An Anthology*, ed. Siân Miles (London: Penguin, 2005), 182–216; 202; 205.
51. Bourke, *Dismembering the Male*, 246–7.

1

'Isn't This Worth Fighting For?' The First World War and the (Ab)Uses of the Pastoral Tradition

Christine Berberich

The war, propaganda and the English countryside

For hundreds of years, the English countryside has been used as the most effective evocation of Englishness: in times of war and peace it has been conjured up, by the English and non-English alike, to express nostalgia and hope, a sense of belonging, a yearning for home; and as something that needs to be defended at all cost. However, the political dimension of this use of the countryside is still often ignored. This chapter examines how the English landscape was propagandistically held up to the soldiers of the Great War as 'what they were fighting for'; and how some select literature of the Great War subverts this notion. The chapter will be divided into three parts. The first part will set the theoretical framework that defines my use of terms such as 'pastoral'. Here I will briefly outline the historical and ideological development that saw the elevation of the countryside to a marker of Englishness as part of a conscious effort to mould an *imagined* body of the nation. The second part will assess three different wartime 'visions' of England as green and pleasant land, taking examples from propaganda (a recruitment poster), literature (an anthology for soldiers in the trenches) and music ('Jerusalem', the popular anthem based on William Blake's verse, 'And did those feet in ancient time', from his Preface to Milton). All three visions take recourse to stereotypical depictions of England. They focus on the rural and idyllic: rolling green fields, grazing sheep, picturesque little villages or homely thatched cottages. The final part will discuss some select representations of the English countryside in the writing of the Great War. Particular emphasis will be placed on Siegfried Sassoon's trilogy *Memoirs of George Sherston*, consisting of *Memoirs of a Foxhunting Man*, *Memoirs of an Infantry Officer* and *Sherston's Progress*. Sassoon started publishing his semi-autobiographical novels in 1928 (with volumes two and three published in 1930 and 1936 respectively), after a post-war gestation period of ten years which helped him to find the required distance to recreate the horrors he experienced in the trenches in prose form. The trilogy charts the life of George Sherston, from his protected, rural upbringing in pre-war Kent to his wartime experiences, which closely reflect Sassoon's own. Sassoon's work could be read as conjuring up a stereotypical, rural and potentially *mythical* Englishness that fits in seamlessly with the propaganda prevalent during the war. However, my contention is that, at closer reading, Sassoon's version of the English landscape undermines the traditional notion of the English pastoral. His *Memoirs of a Foxhunting Man* in particular both upholds and deconstructs the myth of the English countryside as being 'worth fighting for'. While the official war propaganda machinery made good use of the pastoral and the population's nostalgia for it, war writers such as Sassoon adapted the pastoral tradition to show that the Great War had destroyed the myth of the prelapsarian rural idyll of the English countryside once and for all.

The 'creation' of rural England

For centuries the countryside has held a special position in English collective consciousness. It has long since been equated with the country
as a whole. Whenever Englishness needs to be conjured up, be it for
political reasons, tourism or marketing, it is usually the image of the
green and pleasant land rather than that of industrial urban spaces that
is called upon. As such, the English landscape has become an ideological
tool. W.J.T. Mitchell has pointed out the relevance of landscape as both
'signifier' and 'signified'.[1] This pertinent distinction acknowledges that
the English countryside has come to represent a lot more than a merely
rural area used for agriculture; it has acquired its own signification as an
ideological space and, as such, has turned into a 'socially constructed
space [...] increasingly detached from geographically functional [...]
space'.[2] Rural reality and culturally constructed myth are thus at odds
in the English countryside. This is a crucial distinction, as it seems that
the ideological message of the English countryside has come to overwrite the notion of naturalness. Benedict Anderson's theory of nations
as 'imagined communities' is important here. Anderson believes that a
nation 'is an imagined political community' because it is built on an
abstract sense of comradeship consciously or unconsciously shared by
all its inhabitants.[3] In other words, in England, an 'imagined', idealized

countryside has not only been conjured up but has also been (ab)used for political means and has, effectively, become the dominant picture of English nationhood.

It is important to know about the historical and social development of landscape as an ideological tool in order to comprehend its impact on identity formation. Although 'landscape' had already played an important part in Renaissance self-fashioning – for example, in Sir Philip Sidney's *The Countess of Pembroke's Arcadia* – it was in particular the eighteenth century that saw important developments in the, quite literal, making of the English landscape. The onset of the industrial revolution changed the 'physical' appearance of England; it also altered its social make-up. While the nation's future and fortune depended on industrial and technological developments, those trends remained largely ignored by those in power. Martin J. Wiener has pointed out that late eighteenth and early nineteenth-century English upper-middle and upper-class society adopted 'a conception of Englishness that virtually excluded industrialism'.[4] While the middle classes gained increasing importance and influence, they still, largely, modelled themselves on the traditional landed gentry by aspiring to country estates and public-school education for their sons which would enable them to join the ranks of the upper classes. The newly affluent middle classes became important patrons of the arts and literature. But again they made sure that it was primarily their own views of the country that were upheld for future generations. The countryside played an important role here, as more and more emphasis was placed on the 'spiritual' quality of the English countryside as a place where the 'picturesque' could be experienced.[5] Images that were meant to commemorate England functioned on the 'exclusion' principle: unpleasant or displeasing aspects were ignored in favour of the 'sublime' and 'picturesque'. The focus was on the beauty of the land rather than the condition of the rural poor, or the scars that new industries left on the landscape.[6]

What started as a class-specific cultural practice to improve and show off private property to its best advantage soon had repercussions on the nation's conception of identity: the views and ideas of select social strata, namely the upper and upper-middle classes, came to dominate the nation's outlook as a whole. The countryside became the official representative of 'Englishness', as Wendy Joy Darby explains: 'The English countryside became the locus of timeless stability precisely as it was poised to undergo, or was indeed already undergoing, rapid change with the concomitant transformation of social relations.'[7]

It is important to see this link between the representation of national identity and ideology. In the case of England, then, we can say that the image of the countryside has actively been manipulated to represent the nation as a whole. John Short suggests:

> In England the two meanings of country, as countryside and nation, are collapsed into one another; the essence of England is popularly thought to be the green countryside – the enclosed fields, the secluded/excluded parklands of the country houses and the small villages. [...] *The countryside [...] is [...] the most important landscape in the national [...] ideology.*[8]

Ideological manipulation that started in the eighteenth century subsequently gained meaning for the nation as a whole, with repercussions to the present day. The countryside has been elevated to the status of 'cultural object', which can be manipulated and used to support various political discourses.

During the Great War it was particularly this traditional, rural England that was conjured up to raise the appropriate fighting spirit. Modris Eksteins makes it clear that for the Germans, the First World War 'was a war to *change* the world; for the British, this was a war to *preserve* a world'.[9] He also points out:

> [T]he German [war] adventure was a revolutionary threat [for this traditional England], a threat to security, prosperity, and integrity. It was a threat to the Wessex landscapes of Hardy's novels, to the Shropshire lad of A.E. Housman's imagination, and to Mr. Badger of Kenneth Grahame's *The Wind in the Willows*, who had built his house on the remains of an ancient civilization.[10]

Eksteins's use of literary landscapes, rather than real ones, emphasizes the status of landscape as something that is 'imagined' rather than 'real'. By linking the war effort to the landscapes described – but ultimately invented – by celebrated authors, he reinforces the fact that the soldiers were sent out to fight for a fiction: for something that only existed as the figment of somebody else's imagination.

It is here that we need to consider the notion of 'pastoralism' and question what the term implies. Most people will, correctly, link pastoralism to literature about a pleasant, often idealized landscape. However, the term is more complex than that. Brian Loughrey suggests that 'pastoralism'

is a 'contested term' as it now suggests so many different things.[11] Terry
Gifford differentiates three different meanings of pastoral:

> First, the pastoral is a historical form with a long tradition which
> began in poetry, developed into drama and more recently could be
> recognized in novels. [Secondly] there is a broader use of 'pastoral'
> to refer to an area of content. In this sense pastoral refers to any
> literature that describes the country with an implicit or explicit
> contrast to the urban. [Finally] that simple celebration of nature
> comes under scrutiny in the third use of 'pastoral'. [...] This is a
> sceptical use of the term – 'pastoral' as pejorative, implying that the
> pastoral vision is too simplified and thus an idealization of the reality
> of life in the country.[12]

While some critics have argued that the pastoral as a literary genre
lost impact with the end of the Romantic era,[13] others have suggested
that, in the twentieth century, the so-called Georgian poets (a group
gathering under the auspices of Edward Marsh, who also published
their work) 'established in English culture a discourse of escape into
rural reassurance' that effectively resurrected the pastoral mode.[14] Poets
such as Rupert Brooke, Edmund Blunden, Lascelles Abercrombie and
Edward Thomas adhered to this countryside ideal, and the Georgian
group, particularly the writers based around the village of Dymock
on the Gloucestershire/Herefordshire border, reached almost mythical
status in their lifetime. Their love and adulation of the English countryside stood in stark contrast to the modernist – and predominantly
urban – movement of the time, celebrating old, slow-moving rural
traditions and rituals rather than advocating the advent of new speed-
inducing machinery and technology. Countless anecdotes about the
Dymock set have become part of a modern pastoral myth, such as the
story of the poet Edward Thomas who, when asked why he was plan-
ning to enlist, simply bent down, picked up some soil and said 'Literally,
for this.'[15] Thomas, if one is to believe the story, thus showed himself
inextricably bound to the land he saw threatened by the war.[16] Similarly,
Edmund Blunden described himself in his memoirs *Undertones of War*
(1928) as 'a harmless young shepherd in a soldier's coat'.[17] This also
anchors Blunden in the pastoral tradition, and alludes to Gifford's
first meaning of the term 'pastoral', as well as to Leo Marx's rule: 'no
shepherd, no pastoral'.[18]

   However, Annabel Patterson has convincingly argued that the use
of the pastoral changes constantly, and that the pastoral can be used

as a political tool, namely to express a critique of, or retreat from, contemporary society.[19] I would like to suggest that Siegfried Sassoon, in particular in *Memoirs of a Foxhunting Man*, uses the pastoral in all of the senses of the word: first of all, in the long rural section that precedes his descriptions of the war, Sassoon employs the pastoral following the long literary tradition, potentially offering his readers a false sense of security before the (literal) onslaught of the war action. Secondly, his novel clearly foregrounds the rural and rural pursuits – which links back to Gifford's second explanation of the term. Finally, and most importantly, Sassoon uses the pastoral in a pejorative sense. His subtle allusions to the destruction of war, hidden among evocative descriptions of a verdant, idyllic landscape, suggest that Sassoon was aware that he depicted an 'idealization of life in the country'. His *Memoirs of a Foxhunting Man* can thus be seen as a political tool that expresses a critique of Sassoon's contemporary society that, all too willingly, wanted to forget about the horrors of the war by harking back to the idea of a prelapsarian rural idyll.

The green and pleasant land as war aim

The First World War was a full-blown propaganda war. In all participating countries, the civilian population was assaulted by a daily barrage of propaganda, from atrocity stories about German soldiers bayoneting Belgian babies to posters or uplifting music – all in the service of upholding morale and sustaining recruitment (Britain did not have conscription until 1916).[20] In Britain, images of the countryside were used to forge and perpetuate a sense of national identity and 'place' to unite the populace in support for the war. In this section, I would like to discuss a number of 'visions' of Englishness that were pressed into war duty: one visual, two literary, one of them with a link to music. Different media inevitably represent things differently; yet these three different 'visions' share a focus on the English landscape and succeed in sentimentalizing the link between country and countryside.

The first 'vision' of Englishness comes in the form of the war-time propaganda poster depicted in Figure 1.1.

In brilliant colours the poster depicts rolling green hills, a few sheep dotted here and there, a small village with picturesque thatched cottages. One of the cottages even comes with its own dovecote, complete with fluttering white doves, symbolizing peace. The sky is a bright blue, with some prettily contrasting fluffy white clouds. In short, it depicts what could be seen as a quintessential and stereotypical rural English idyll, one that is, today, often given the deprecatory adjective 'chocolate-box'.

Figure 1.1   Your Country's Call (1915), Imperial War Museum, London

The depicted idyll is not even disrupted by the presence of a 'Tommy' in the foreground, sporting his field uniform and a gun. He looks clean and relaxed, with a smile on his face, as he points at the model village, giving voice to 'your country's call', asking 'Isn't this worth fighting for?' The moral message and political agenda of the poster are explicit: the idyllic village stands for England as a whole; the innocent inhabitants of this rural arcadia, the happy sheep and carefree doves have to be protected from the onslaught of the enemy. And if England's young men do not understand this message, or choose to ignore its call to 'ENLIST NOW', then they are clearly no patriots.

However, the message of this poster, but also its design, with its seemingly clear-cut and simple call to arms, is more problematic than this. In particular, it is the figure of the soldier that deserves further attention: he is not an English but a Scottish soldier wearing a kilt. The fact that a Scottish soldier is transposed onto an English landscape, and here in particular a southern English landscape, immediately adds a considerable political dimension to this poster: southern England is chosen to represent Britain as a whole and is thus given a clear prominence over the other countries and regions encompassed by the term 'United Kingdom'. In this regard, the poster does not only have the immediate effect of calling young men to arms but also a wider-reaching political agenda in that it advertises *English* supremacy, epitomized by her unique landscape that soldiers flock from near and far to defend.

Ernest Rhys's book *The Old Country* is the second 'vision' of Englishness I would like to discuss. It was published in 1917 specifically for soldiers fighting in the trenches. In Rhys's words, it was intended as a 'kit-book or hut-book' whose 'practical use [lay] in its pocketable size and its effect as a golden remembrancer'.[21] The subtitle of the anthology clarifies its purpose: *A Book of Love and Praise of England*. Again, not Britain but England is highlighted, thus representing a geopolitical body celebrating and upholding *English* values for the *British* soldiers in the trenches. This subtitle is further problematized by the inclusion of 'Hen Wlad Fy Nhadam' (the patriotic Welsh anthem 'Land of My Fathers'), excerpts from Scottish greats like Burns and Scott, as well as contributions with telling titles such as 'A Gift of India' or 'Sunrise on the Veld: Outside Johannesburg'. While Rhys's anthology thus clearly includes the other countries of the United Kingdom and the Empire, its title explicitly excludes them. This point is further emphasized by A.G. Gardiner's contribution 'In Praise of England' which starts with the memorable words 'And when I say England, forgive me for once, O stern and wild Caledonian, if I mean Scotland too.'[22] Gardiner explains that the more appropriate terminology 'Great Britain' or 'United Kingdom' would merely conjure up 'solemn things' such as 'the British Constitution and Magna Carta' and justifies his substitution of England for all of Britain with his wish to '[think] of the springing grass and the budding trees, the lambs that I know are gambolling in the chequered shade and the lark that is shouting the news of spring in the vault of the sky' that, apparently, only 'England' can conjure up.[23] This imagery immediately recalls that of the recruitment poster above and again shows how a specifically English countryside[24] comes to represent the nation as a whole.

The Old Country contains an eclectic collection of poetry and prose ranging from William Hazlitt's 'Merry England' to Hilaire Belloc's 'A Song of the South Country'. While there are some excerpts that celebrate London, the English seafaring tradition, or 'patriotism' in general, the majority of the poetry and prose excerpts focus on the countryside, its flora and fauna: 'Lollingdon Downs', 'The Old Country House', 'Stonehenge', 'English Weather', 'In Praise of England', 'Two Rural Rides', 'Under the Greenwood Tree', 'England of my Heart' or 'A Country Cricket Match' are but a few examples. Significantly, Rhys's anthology is beautifully produced and illustrated by Herbert Cole with images of English villages, flowers and trees (see Figures 1.2–1.4).

The familiar connotations of the thatched cottage, the hay wain with rural workers (reminiscent of Constable's *The Hay Wain*) or the sweeping view of fields and trees immediately emphasize the patriotic message of the poems and prose pieces in the anthology. In fact, by merely looking at the illustrations, the patriotism of the target readership (the soldiers in the trenches) would be aroused. This collection shows that, at a time when pastoralism was effectively in crisis – after all, in Flanders and along the Somme the warring parties each did their utmost to blow another countryside to pieces – writers and publishers took recourse

Figure 1.2   Herbert Cole, in Ernest Rhys, *The Old Country* (1917, p. vii)

Figure 1.3　Herbert Cole, in Ernest Rhys, *The Old Country* (1917, p. 131)

Figure 1.4　Herbert Cole, in Ernest Rhys, *The Old Country* (1917, p. 149)

to established literary genres such as the pastoral to create a parallel, peaceful and ultimately illusionary world to further the troops' fighting spirit.

By sentimentalizing a national trope in such a suggestive manner, Rhys not only reinforced the aim of the war – 'Isn't this Worth Fighting For? Enlist Now!' – but, simultaneously, gave shape to a potentially shell-shocked sense of national identity in the soldiers who were suffering in the trenches. His collection, rather predictably, concludes with Rupert Brooke's already celebrated poem 'The Soldier' – 'If I should die' – and ends on the line 'In hearts at peace, under an English heaven'.[25] In his

Figure 1.5   Herbert Cole, in Ernest Rhys, *The Old Country* (1917, p. 161)

introduction to the collection, Sir Arthur Yapp appealed to each and
every individual soldier's imagination – an imagination that would
immediately fly towards his 'village home, which is all the world to
him'.[26] This again conjures up the image of the village in the propaganda
poster above, an image further reinforced by one of the anthology's
illustrations which evokes nostalgia for a peaceful pastoralism embodied
by the homely looking thatched cottage by the stream (Figure 1.5).

   Importantly, Yapp wanted to rouse the men's patriotism, and through
that, their fighting spirit: the sight of a ravaged village in France should,
for them, evoke images of the (potentially threatened) peaceful idyll left
behind in England – and consequently spur them on to further battle
action.

   Blake's verse, 'And did those feet in ancient time' (popularly referred
to as 'Jerusalem') is the last 'vision' of Englishness in this section.
Although originally published in 1804, the poem still has relevance
in conjunction with the other two visions that appear to have a more
immediate concern with the war effort. 'Jerusalem' aptly juxtaposes an
old, traditional England of 'mountains green' and 'pleasant pastures'
with the monstrosity of modernity's 'dark Satanic Mills' that need to
be combated at all cost, and with the help of a 'Bow of burning gold',
'Arrows of desire', a 'Spear' and a 'Chariot of Fire' calls to re-establish
the Arcadian idyll of 'Jerusalem' in 'England's green and pleasant
land'.[27] For Blake, modernity threatened to destroy pastoral idylls. More
than a hundred years later, the Great War takes 'modernity' one step

further: the modern age in the form of an enemy power trying to invade the peacefulness of traditional England.[28]

However, 'Jerusalem' is pertinent for yet another reason: it was in 1916, at the height of the Great War, that Hubert Parry wrote the musical score for Blake's poem that has since taken the standing of an unofficial English national anthem. While Parry's tune, from 1918 onwards, has been adopted by such stalwart institutions as the Women's Institute, its composition in 1916 is important as it was immediately recognizable as a rousing, patriotic tune to ring throughout the land and, probably, the trenches – and yet another reminder to the nation about what exactly it was they were fighting for: to defeat the enemy threatening England's 'green and pleasant land'.

Blake's poem is the first contribution in Rhys's *The Old Country*, both in the shape of the original poem and the musical score. As the opening and closing poems of the collection, Blake's 'Jerusalem' and Brooke's 'The Soldier' thus set an apt framework for the fighting man at the front: the first reminds them of what they are fighting for, the last reassures them that it is, in fact, worth dying for.

The three 'visions' of rural England as the 'green and pleasant land' – the propaganda poster, the anthology, the hymn based on the poem – all drummed up support for the war effort. They aimed to appeal to the soldiers' patriotism but effectively they did much more than that: they can be seen to *construct* a sense of national identity that serves a political purpose. The rural imagery in all three visions is in the service of political ideology: rural England is shown to be synonymous not only with England as a whole, but with all of Britain. The pastoral idyll is thus (ab)used for political expediency.

Literary landscapes of the Great War: subverting expectations?

Paul Fussell has written that 'if the opposite of war is peace, the opposite of experiencing moments of war is proposing moments of pastoral', and that 'recourse to the pastoral is an English mode of both fully gauging the calamities of the Great War and imaginatively protecting oneself against them'.[29] Fussell thus seems to suggest that the pastoral trope used by British writers of the Great War generation is inextricably linked to the horrors experienced in the trenches: writers consciously take recourse to pastoral images to block out the memories of warfare and destruction. This could suggest an escapist motivation, a conscious shutting out of shocking experiences that is very different from the unconscious closing of the mind due to severe wartime trauma. In that sense, Sassoon's work, particularly *Memoirs of a Foxhunting Man*, could be read as a work upholding and cherishing the uncritical notion of England as green and pleasant land. Many critics consider Sassoon's semi-autobiographical novel a mere celebration of nostalgia and old-fashioned values, determined to find solace in escapism rather than facing the horrors of trench warfare in Flanders. Christopher Lane, for example, has condemned Sassoon for 'virtually suspend[ing] the influence of the modern by reverting to scenes of pastoral tranquillity'.[30] Indeed, of the 313 pages of *Memoirs of a Foxhunting Man*, the first 243 describe the pre-war rural idyll of Butley in Kent, and the protagonist's carefree upbringing as a country gentleman interested only in genteel country pursuits such as hunting, cricket and point-to-pointing.

Sassoon's earlier career as a Georgian poet, part of a large and successful group celebrating the beauty of the countryside and advocating a return to nature, has served as a convenient reason for labelling him a pastoral writer. Indeed, his earlier lyrical poetry fits in seamlessly with the work of the Georgians and was included in some of the volumes of Georgian poetry published by Edward Marsh.[31] Even a later poem such as 'Nimrod in September' evocatively conjures up a misty early autumn morning in the countryside. Sassoon's love of the countryside is certainly reflected in *Memoirs of a Foxhunting Man* which is replete with lengthy and detailed depictions of aspects of the land that surrounds his fictional character Sherston. The following quotation exemplifies Sassoon's attention to detail: 'I can hear the creak of the saddle and the clop and clink of hoofs as we cross the bridge over the brook by Dundell Farm; there is a light burning in the farmhouse window, and the evening star glitters above a broken drift of half-luminous cloud.'[32] Sassoon's landscape descriptions succeed in making the reader feel part of the landscape, assuming familiarity with the scenery he describes, evoking a homely feeling of belonging. It is this that makes the contrast with the war chapters towards the end of the first volume so drastic, and that adds impact to the reading of Sassoon's pastoralism as pejorative – this safe world no longer exists. The *Memoirs* do, potentially, go even further than that as they come to show that this 'safe world' has never existed in the first place.

While Sassoon might initially have enlisted out of the same idealism that motivated Edward Thomas, a pure and unadulterated love of the land, 'circumstances', as Bergonzi points out, soon 'made [him] a realist; unlike other soldier poets he could not be content with using scenes of rural English life as a compensation and balance for the brutality of life at the Front'.[33] Much of his poetry is characterized by a brutal juxtaposition of rural scenes with vitriolic recollections of war, and he continues in the same vein in *Memoirs of a Foxhunting Man*. Crucially, what at first glance looks like pastoral reminiscences can be read as radical social criticism as the book condemns the futile, pre-war existence of its protagonist. Sassoon's novel thus has a binary vision: on the one hand, the pastoral idyll of pre-war Kent and genteel country pursuits; on the other, the trenches of the First World War. But the binary vision can also be applied to the seemingly nostalgic celebration of rural Englishness that precedes the war chapters.

The ambiguity of Sassoon's trilogy, but in particular *Memoirs of a Foxhunting Man*, may well reflect his own ambivalent attitude towards the land he simultaneously loves, mourns and debunks as mythical. Throughout even the most evocative landscape descriptions, Sassoon drops hints about the death and devastation that were to come. And these hints do not only lie in the subject matter itself (hunting), as Paul Fussell has argued: 'the book has begun with fox-hunting; it ends with Boche-hunting'.[34] Sassoon places his pointers towards things to come within his landscape depictions and in the midst of hunting action. In *Memoirs of a Foxhunting Man*, for example, there are several remarks about the barbed wire that farmers put up to demarcate their land and discourage riders and hunters. Sherston, in his persona of huntsman, resents the wire and denounces a landowner using it as a 'double-distilled blighter who's wired up all his fences' (134). As the war draws closer, the mention of 'wire' multiplies and the threat it poses to rider and horses increases – 'And then there was the wire, which was deplorably prevalent' (226) – culminating in Sherston's fall over some concealed wire shortly after joining the army training corps, which results in a broken arm (252). The barbed wire stands for the threat it poses to the soldiers at the front; Sherston's fall suitably symbolizes the increasing dangers he now has to face. Barbed wire, formerly a mere irritant to the eager huntsman, becomes a threat to life and limb at the front.

In many cases, however, Sassoon's hints at the devastation and turmoil of warfare are subtly concealed in the text and require careful close reading. At the beginning of *Memoirs of a Foxhunting Man*, Sassoon provides an evocative description of Sherston's childhood environment:

Looking back across the years I listen to the summer afternoon cooing of my aunt's white pigeons, and the soft clatter of their wings as they flutter upward from the lawn at the approach of one of the well-nourished cats. I remember, too, the smell of strawberry jam

being made; and Aunt Evelyn with a green bee-veil over her head [...].
The large rambling garden, with its [...] yews and sloping paths and
wind-buffeted rose arches, remains to haunt my sleep. [...] With a
sense of abiding strangeness I see myself looking down from an upper
window on a confusion of green branches shaken by the summer
breeze. In an endless variety of dream-distorted versions the garden
persists as the background of my unconscious existence. (24–5)

Sassoon's language is descriptive, and it is easy for the reader to envisage the Arcadian garden he describes. However, this passage contains
an altogether different subtext: although the white pigeons link back to
the wartime propaganda poster mentioned earlier, they are here chased
by cats that might be well-fed but that are still predators out to kill. Yew
trees are predominantly associated with church- and graveyards, and
thus point to the countless deaths that Sherston will have to witness
during the war. The use of the verb 'haunt' in this passage also adds a
more negative meaning to the text: happy memories do not, generally,
haunt but are usually welcome reminders of the past. The 'confusion
of green branches' that Sherston looks down upon from his window as
well as the 'dream-distorted versions' of the garden also point towards
the confusion of his mind: where actual memory is mixed up with
imaginative interpretation and wishful thinking, the result might be
unreliable. Sherston's recollections of his aunt's pre-war garden turn
something familiar that should inspire a 'homely' feeling into something confusing, nauseating, frightening, and consequently subverts
the initial sense of well-being.

These juxtaposed double meanings can also be seen in other instances
in the text. During a train journey back home to Butley in Kent,
Sherston ponders:

The air was Elysian with early summer and the shadows of steep
white clouds were chasing over the orchards and meadows; sunlight
sparkled on green hedgerows that had been drenched by early morning showers. As I was carried past it all I was lazily aware through
my dreaming and unobservant eyes that this was the sort of world
I wanted. For it was my own countryside, and I loved it with an
intimate feeling. (76)

Even in this idyllic depiction of the countryside, which could be read
as a declaration of love, there are ominous signs. We could of course
argue that the 'chasing' clouds herald doom. Furthermore, Sherston's

wishful declaration that this was the world he wanted immediately suggests that he no longer has it. More poignant, however, is the use of the word 'Elysian': it can indicate that the air felt 'of or like paradise'.[35] But that is only the second meaning of the adjective 'Elysian'. The primary meaning is 'relating to Elysium or the Elysian Fields, the place of Greek mythology where heroes were conveyed after death'.[36] Death is thus present again, as England's green and pleasant land is stalked by the dead.

Sherston also repeatedly refers to his own ignorance where world events are concerned.[37] He contrasts the familiar countryside of his childhood to London, the political heart of the country, and to France, that as yet foreign territory across the Channel:

> Nearly all the way we were looking, on our left-hand side, across the hop-kiln dotted Weald. And along the Weald went the railway line from London to the Coast [...]. I knew very little about London, and I had never been across the Channel, but as I watched a train hurrying between the level orchards with its consequential streamer of smoke, I meditated on the coast-line of France. (77)

The railway line thus symbolizes modernity which literally divides the familiar landscape and brings discord – the smoke – and potential disruption to Sherston's life; it is just such a train that will, later on, take him to France, and to the front.

In the second volume of the Sherston trilogy, *Memoirs of an Infantry Officer*, Sassoon is no longer content with mere hints.

> I was meditating about England, visualizing a grey day down in Sussex; dark green woodlands with pigeons circling above the tree-tops; dogs barking, cocks crowing, and all the casual trappings and twinklings of the countryside. I thought of the huntsman walking out in his long white coat with the hounds; of Parson Colwood pulling up weeds in his garden till teatime; of Captain Huxtable helping his men get in the last load of hay while a shower of rain moved along the blurred Weald below his meadows. It was for all that, I supposed, that I was in the front-line with soaked feet, trench mouth, and feeling short of sleep.[38]

The last sentence underlines the fact that Sassoon is no longer convinced by the idealized image of the England he is presenting to his readers. The interjection 'I supposed' clearly voices his doubts about his motives for fighting, as does the comment later on in the second volume: 'staring at the dim brown landscape I decided that the War was worth while if it was being carried on to safeguard this kind of thing. Was it? I wondered' (102). The juxtaposition of the familiar rural scene with 'soaked feet', 'trench mouth' and lack of sleep shows that the one is not really worth the other. Throughout the trilogy, Sassoon's character Sherston becomes more and more disillusioned with the England he *thought* he had come out to France to defend. In the first volume, he complains that 'England wasn't what it used to be' (299), and this phrase is repeated verbatim in the second volume (91). Already in the first volume, there is a sense that his own 'past was wearing a bit thin' (299). Two years later, rot and decline are as visible in rural England as they are in France: 'I visited the stables. Stagnation had settled there; nettles were thick under the apple-trees [...] saddles were getting mouldy and there were rust-spots on the bits and stirrup-irons' (94).

Throughout the Sherston trilogy, Sassoon combines romantic pastoralism with shocking war truths, with an unsettling result for his readers. As Samuel Hynes has compellingly shown, Robert Graves applied a very similar technique in his poem 'A Dead Boche' in which he depicts, in Hynes's words, 'a conventional Romantic scene: a man alone in a wood, leaning against a tree'.[39] The startling difference in Graves's poem is achieved by the fact that the 'man' is actually the bloated, rotting corpse of a German soldier: death has invaded Arcadia. Hynes asserts that 'what Graves did in "A Dead Boche" was to take a Romantic convention and thrust war into it, turning landscape into landscape-with-corpse, and making the plain words of war do the work of the coloured words of Romantic poetry'.[40] Sassoon does the same in *Memoirs of a Foxhunting Man* but in a more subtle way that requires more attention to small details on the part of his readers.

Among the wartime *Letters and Recollections* of 'Ben' Keeling (his full name was Frederick Hillersdon Keeling) one comment stands out: 'Every pleasant landscape now seems to suggest the horrors of war by contrast.'[41] Sassoon's *Memoirs of George Sherston* shows just that. Instead of being a mere nostalgic evocation of a mythical, prelapsarian Arcadia, Sassoon's pre-war English landscape is a palimpsest with very different and contradictory messages, and he thus challenges his readers who, accustomed to the pastoral poetry and writing of many of Sassoon's contemporaries, would have approached his work with entirely different expectations. Sassoon's work thus stands in direct opposition to the 'visions' of rural England that were (ab)used in the service of war-time propaganda – and that are influential to this day. The danger – then as well as now – lies in falling prey to the lure of the powerful myth surrounding the English countryside. Edwardian England is still held up by some as the halcyon days of a prelapsarian English society where a traditional social hierarchy was still intact, and the beautiful countryside as yet untainted by modernity. Blinded by this, it is easy to disregard the subversive subtext that underlies Sassoon's narrative. Read thus, the trilogy *could* – and did – once again become part of a nostalgic ideology that tried to perpetuate rural English values through generation after generation of future readers. It is only through a counter-intuitive reading that the impact of Sassoon's text is revealed. Hindsight, the cruellest of all sights, ensures that Sassoon can no longer look at England's alleged green and pleasant land without seeing in it the shadows of the dead.

Notes

1. W.J.T. Mitchell, 'Imperial Landscape', in W.J.T. Mitchell (ed.), *Landscape and Power*, 2nd edn (Chicago: University of Chicago Press, 2002), 5.
2. Paul Cloke and Nigel Thrift, 'Introduction: Refiguring the Rural', in Paul Cloke et al. (eds), *Writing the Rural: Five Cultural Geographies* (London: Paul Chapman, 1994), 3.
3. Benedict Anderson, *Imagined Communities: Reflections on the Origin and Spread of Nationalism* (London: Verso, 1983), 6–7.
4. Martin J. Wiener, *English Culture and the Decline of the Industrial Spirit 1850–1980* (Cambridge: Cambridge University Press, 1981), 5.
5. See Ian Ousby, *The Englishman's England: Taste, Travel and the Rise of Tourism* (London: Pimlico, 2002), 100–51.
6. See Wendy Joy Darby, *Landscape and Identity: Geographies of Nation and Class in England* (Oxford: Berg, 2000). John Barrell, *The Dark Side of the Landscape: the Rural Poor in English Painting, 1730–1840* (Cambridge: Cambridge University Press, 1980). One of the most popular and enduring of nineteenth-century English landscape paintings, Constable's *The Hay Wain* (1821), also bears out this point. The focus is on the picturesque scene presented by the hay wain in the river – not on the hard labour behind it. The rural worker who is driving the cart is turned away from the gaze of the observer, so as to render him anonymous and deprive him of any distinguishing features. See http://www.nationalgallery.org.uk/paintings/john-constable-the-hay-wain, accessed 10 March 2010.
7. Darby, *Landscape and Identity*, 78.
8. Cited in Keith Halfacree, 'Landscapes of Rurality: Rural Others/Other Rurals', in Iain Robertson and Penny Richards (eds), *Studying Cultural Landscapes* (London: Hodder Arnold, 2003), 143 (emphasis added).
9. Modris Eksteins, *Rites of Spring: the Great War and the Birth of the Modern Age* (London: Papermac, 2000), 119 (emphasis added).
10. Ibid., 132.
11. Brian Loughrey (ed.), *The Pastoral Mode* (London: Macmillan, 1984), 8.
12. Terry Gifford, *Pastoral* (London: Routledge, 1999), 1–2.

13. See John Barrell and John Bull (eds), *The Penguin Book of English Pastoral Verse* (Harmondsworth: Penguin, 1982).

14. Gifford, *Pastoral*, 72.

15. See Adrian Barlow, *The Great War in British Literature* (Cambridge: Cambridge University Press, 2000), 18.

16. More recently, Julian Barnes has picked up on this connection between 'land' and war sacrifice. In his short story 'Evermore' Barnes recounts the struggles of the sister of a soldier killed in action who spends her entire life in regular visits to his grave in France. She is troubled by the fact that her beloved brother, who sacrificed his life for his country, is now buried underneath 'French grass, [...] the coarser type, inappropriate for British soldiers to lie beneath'. She takes the drastic step of removing some of the offending French grass, to replace it with 'softer English turf', only to find, to her immense indignation, that, by her next visit, the French grass is back. Barnes's story thus takes the Thomas myth to the literal level, with his fictional 'Miss Moss' arguing the case that soldiers dying for England should be buried beneath English grass, thus giving extra weight to Rupert Brooke's famous lines about 'some corner of a foreign field / That is forever England'. See Julian Barnes, 'Evermore' in *Cross Channel* (London: Picador, 1996), 89–111; 108.

17. Edmund Blunden, *Undertones of War* (London: Cobden-Sanderson, 1950), 209.

18. Cited in Gifford, *Pastoral*, 1.

19. Cited ibid., 11.

20. See David Stevenson, *1914–1918: the History of the First World War* (London: Penguin, 2004).

21. Ernest Rhys (ed.), *The Old Country: a Book of Love and Praise of England* (London: J.M. Dent, 1917), viii.

22. A.G. Gardiner, 'In Praise of England', in Rhys, *The Old Country*, 149.

23. Ibid.

24. Gardiner also extols the virtues of the Malvern Hills above their European counterparts.

25. Rupert Brooke, 'If I should die', in Rhys, *The Old Country*, 320.

26. Sir Arthur Yapp, 'Introduction', in Rhys, *The Old Country*, v.

27. William Blake, 'And Did Those Feet in Ancient Time' (From the Prophetic Books), in Rhys (ed.), *The Old Country*, 17.

28. Petra Rau has made a persuasive argument linking modernity and Germany, and the threat of both to English identity. See Petra Rau, *English Modernism, National Identity and the Germans, 1890–1950* (Aldershot: Ashgate, 2009).

29. Paul Fussell, *The Great War and Modern Memory* (Oxford: Oxford University Press, 2000), 231; 235.

30. Christopher Lane, 'In Defense of the Realm: Sassoon's Memoirs', *Raritan* 14/1 (1994): 93.

31. Marsh published five volumes of Georgian poems between 1912 and 1922. Sassoon's work was included in volumes three and four, *Georgian Poetry 1916–1917* and *Georgian Poetry 1918–1919*.

32. Siegfried Sassoon, *Memoirs of a Foxhunting Man* (London: Faber and Faber, 1999), 101. All subsequent references to this edition will be cited parenthetically in the text.

33. Bernard Bergonzi, *Heroes' Twilight: a Study of the Literature of the Great War* (Manchester: Carcanet, 1996), 94.

34. Fussell, *Great War and Modern Memory*, 95.
35. *Compact Oxford English Dictionary Online* (2008), http://www.askoxford.com/concise_oed/elysian?view=uk, accessed 4 November 2009.
36. *Compact Oxford English Dictionary Online* (2008), http://askoxford.com/results/?view)dict&field.12668446=elysian&branch=138, accessed 4 November 2009.
37. See for example *Memoirs of a Foxhunting Man*, 195 or 227.
38. Siegfried Sassoon, *Memoirs of an Infantry Officer* (London: Faber and Faber, 2000), 44. All subsequent references to this edition are cited parenthetically in the text.
39. Samuel Hynes, *A War Imagined: the First World War and English Culture* (London: Bodley Head, 1990), 192.
40. Ibid.
41. Quoted in Hynes, *A War Imagined*, 200. Keeling's complete letters and recollections, edited by 'E.T.' and with a foreword by H.G. Wells, can be found at http://www.archive.org/stream/keelinglettersre00Keeluoft/Keelinglettersre00Keeluoft_djvu.txt.

2
Violence and the Pacifist Body in Vernon Lee's *The Ballet of the Nations*

Patricia Pulham

By the time hostilities broke out in 1914, the cosmopolitan writer and critic Vernon Lee was internationally recognized, and known for her often strident views on the major political and social issues of the period.[1] British by birth but resident in Italy, in August of that year Lee was in the process of paying her customary annual visit to England and found herself stranded in Britain for the duration of the war. Soon realizing, like so many others, that the war was not going to come to a swift and amicable conclusion, Lee, a staunch pacifist, began to strengthen her alliances with like-minded British intellectuals. She became an active member of the newly-formed Union of Democratic Control and publicly supported pacifist activities with her pen and her purse.[2] The circles in which she moved brought her into contact with other prominent pacifists including Charles Trevelyan, Ramsay MacDonald, Lytton Strachey and the philosopher Bertrand Russell.[3]

In 1915, Vernon Lee wrote an allegorical work, *The Ballet of the Nations*, published by Chatto & Windus as 'a Christmas book, with illustrations by Maxwell Armfield'.[4] The term 'ballet' is no doubt intentionally ironic – Lee's 'ballet' is a 'dumb-show', a 'danse macabre' that defies performance – but, as I aim to show, Lee's use of 'ballet' as a medium of expression may be of greater significance than it might at first seem.[5] *The Ballet* was never staged, but it *was* read aloud by Lee twice in 1915: once at Armfield's studio in Glebe Place, Chelsea, and again at the Margaret Morris theatre, described by Grace Brockington as 'the focal point of Chelsea's avant-garde community'; an apt location given what is, arguably, the 'avant-garde' nature of Vernon Lee's work.[6] Of *Satan the Waster* (1920), Lee's extended meditation on the First World War, which contains a revised version of *The Ballet of the Nations* embellished and bordered by a prologue, an epilogue and copious notes, Gillian Beer writes, '[t]he genre [...] does not quite correspond to any other work'.[7] The same might be said of *The Ballet* itself, the nucleus of the longer text, which combines elements of Greek tragedy and, in particular, the medieval morality play. Satan (the 'immortal Impresario') compares it to a Spanish *auto sacramental*, a dramatic genre consisting of short allegorical plays, performed at Corpus Christi, which bears a similarity to the medieval mystery play and by implication the *auto da fé*, a public spectacle of penance and punishment featuring condemned heretics.

While all of these are suggestive for a discussion of Lee's text, I want to concentrate on the ways in which *The Ballet* relates to the *auto sacramental* and the *auto da fé*. In *Satan the Waster*, *The Ballet of the Nations*, originally published at Christmas 1915, is followed by notes dated Easter 1919. Taken together, these works constitute Lee's most comprehensive intellectual response to the war, yet both texts contain visceral images that highlight the violence that war performs on the physical body. In this chapter, I argue that *The Ballet*, framed in Lee's works by Christmas and Easter, and containing allusions to Christian ritual and sacrifice, calls attention not only to the horrors of war, but also explicitly to the fragmented and ravaged national body and implicitly to the abject pacifist body.

The Ballet of the Nations

In her introduction to *Satan the Waster*, Lee describes the genesis of *The Ballet of the Nations*. She tells her readers that *The Ballet* was prompted specifically by responses to the sinking of the *Lusitania*, torpedoed by a German U-boat on 7 May 1915, which turned the tide of popular opinion against Germany, and more generally by a European war which from her point of view, was 'gigantically cruel, but at the same time needless and senseless like some ghastly "Grand Guignol" performance'.[8] On its title page, *The Ballet of the Nations* carries an epigraph from Dante Gabriel's Rossetti's sonnet, 'Vain Virtues' (1869): 'What is the Sorriest thing that enters Hell? / Not any of the Sins'. The topic of sins and 'vain virtues' is again suggested in the description of the work as 'a present-day morality' play and, indeed, it has many of the features of its medieval forerunner: it is a didactic allegory, virtues and vices are personified, and its message is conveyed in accessible language.[9] Lee's 'danse macabre' is stage-managed by the ballet-master Death at Satan's request; the dancers are the fighting nations; and the orchestra is composed of allegorical figures such as Idealism, Adventure, Fear, Panic, Suspicion, Hatred, Self-Righteousness and blind Heroism.[10] The orchestra members are mostly dressed 'in classical, mediæval, biblical or savage costumes', while two contemporary members, Science and Organization, wear modern attire (*Ballet*). The audience consists of those nations who have yet to dance, 'sundry sleepy Virtues' and the 'Ages-to-Come' (*Ballet*).[11]

In *The Ballet*, Death is only too eager to follow Satan's instructions to 're-open the Theatre of the West' (*Ballet*). He observes that the West is fast losing its taste for those Aristotelian tragedies that 'purge the world of its inhabitants by terror and pity' and, with Satan, fondly recalls former spectacular successes such as the 'French Revolution Ballet' (*Ballet*). The ballet begins and unfolds into what Brockington describes as a 'gory fable': a disturbing textual display of blood, gore and dismemberment.[12] The 'Smallest-of-all-the-Corps-de-Ballet' (easily identifiable as Belgium) is trampled by a 'Giant' (clearly Germany) who performs 'on its poor little body' a horrifying '*pas seul*' that pounds it 'out of all human shape into a dancing-mat for the others' (*Ballet*). As the colours illuminating the stage sky are blotted out 'by volumes of flamelit smoke and poisonous vapours', the other nations 'maimed' and 'bleeding' 'dance upon stumps', and, resembling 'a living jelly of blood and trampled flesh', trail themselves along providing that their Heads remain 'fairly unhurt' (*Ballet*). These 'Heads' or Governments can 'order the nation's body to put forth fresh limbs' or, if that's impossible, they can keep their stumps dancing 'in obedience or disobedience to what are called the Rules of War', pirouetting on a stage slippery with 'blood and entrails and heaps of devastated properties' (*Ballet*). As they dance, the nations lop off each other's limbs and blind one another 'with spurts of blood and pellets of human flesh' and as they continue they transform themselves into 'terrible uncertain forms, armless, legless, recognisable for human only by their irreproachable-looking heads' until they become 'mere unspeakable hybrids between man and beast' (*Ballet*). Satan enjoys the spectacle and remarks:

> Dear Creatures [...] how true it is that great artistic exhibitions, especially when they address themselves to the Group-Emotion, invariably bring home to the nations that there is, after all, a Power transcending their ephemeral existence! Indeed that is one reason why I prefer the Ballet of the Nations to any of the other mystery-plays, like Earthquake and Pestilence, which Death puts on our stage from time to time. The music is not always very pretty, at once too archaic and too ultra-modern for philistine taste, and the steps are a trifle monotonous. But it gives immense scope for moral beauty, and revives religious feeling in all its genuine primeval polytheism. It answers perfectly to what the Spaniards call an *Auto Sacramental*, a sacred drama having all the attractions of a bull-fight. (*Ballet*)[13]

Vernon Lee made no secret of her rejection of conventional religion and in particular of her aversion to the representations of violence in those Catholic displays of pain and suffering represented by the Spanish *auto sacramental* and the *auto da fé*.[14] The *auto sacramental* commonly took place in the streets during the feast of Corpus Christi, preceded by processions peopled by penitents and images or statues of the crucified Christ and the Virgin Mary in attitudes of sorrow. Lee visited Granada in January 1889 and in one of the commonplace books she kept, assessed the elements which, in her opinion, informed the Spanish imagination: 'a violence, a thirst for the exaggerated, a desire, as it were to be bruised [and] stunned, or to bruise [and] stun others'.[15]

In her preface to 'The Virgin of the Seven Daggers', a story set in Spain, published originally in 1909 and reprinted in the collection *For Maurice: Five Unlikely Stories* (1927),[16] Lee returns to the topic of Spanish violence. In it she expresses to her dedicatee, the Catholic writer Maurice Baring, her 'detestation' for the 'Spanish cultus of death, damnation, tears and wounds, "du sang, de la volupté et de la mort" as expounded by its dev-otee', the French writer and nationalist Maurice Barrès, and 'taking root in the Spanish mud half and half of *auto da fés* and bull fights'.[17] The coupling of Spanish culture with Barrès's name here refers to his travel book *Du Sang, de la volupté, et de la mort* (1893). The allusion to the *auto da fé* juxtaposes his name with a spectacle of cruelty and punishment that has implications, as we shall see, for Lee's depiction of fragmented nations and sacrificial bodies in *The Ballet*. Lee's Virgin, whose seven daggers invoke the Passion of Christ, features in a story that is itself based on one of Pedro Calderón de la Barca's *autos sacramentales*, *El Purgatorio de San Patricio* (1628) (*The Purgatory of St Patrick*). The implicit reference to Barca's *auto sacramental* in 'The Virgin of the Seven Daggers' returns us to the mention of the *auto sacramental* in *The Ballet of the Nations*: particularly the 'Theatre of the West' in which it is set resonates interestingly with the title of another of Barca's *autos*, *El gran teatro del mundo* (*The Great Theatre of the World*), a philosophical work which, like *The Ballet*, employs allegory to make its point, and shares *The Ballet*'s didactic purpose. In Lee's allegory the emphasis on 'theatre' seemingly plays with the term 'theatre of war', commonly used to describe a particular region in which a war is being fought, and simultaneously anticipates Paul Fussell's discussion of theatre as a metaphor for war in *The Great War and Modern Memory*,[18] but it also relates interestingly to the theatrical nature of the *auto da fé*.

Like the *auto sacramental* and, indeed, Lee's *Ballet*, the medieval *auto da fé* offers a spectacle of suffering which has both a didactic and a symbolic purpose. Francisco Bethencourt explains that 'the convicted individuals wearing *sambenitos* ("costumes of infamy")' had to confess, and be publicly excommunicated before being led to a place of execution 'where they were burned (or in the case of repentance, strangled first, then burned)'.[19] Bethencourt notes that, in the case of the Spanish and Portuguese Inquisitions, such spectacles became 'regular and collective events': '[i]nstead of one or just a few persons being convicted of religious crimes, hundreds every year were paraded and punished in impressive public displays'.[20] The increasing 'complexities of staging and procedure' involved in this ritual led to an understanding of the *auto da fé* as 'theatre' where the stage becomes 'a space of religious and social significance'.[21] Moreover, the nature of the prisoners' crimes was 'explicitly symbolized by the decoration on their *sambenitos*'.[22] These aspects of the *auto da fé* resonate with elements of Lee's 'ballet' which, according to Satan, 'revives religious feeling' and stages a bloody ritual of social significance (*Ballet*).

According to Maureen Flynn, the *auto da fé* also rehearses, on a symbolic level, the biblical account of the Day of Judgment, 'When the Son of man shall come in his glory [...], and before him shall be gathered all the nations', while the public plays the role of God: '[t]hese acts of faith were vivid reminders of the trial and judgment that spectators believed would confront them all at the end of their days' and '[w]atching penitents on stage, they lived through their own apprehensions of the Final Judgment'.[23] She argues that in this respect, the *autos da fé* were Aristotelian tragedies 'of the most fundamental kind', touching on those emotions of pity and fear which, for Aristotle, lie at the heart of the tragic form; tragedy permitting 'the catharsis of these two emotions' and evoking 'a cleansing upsurge' that 'discharges violent emotion to calm the soul'.[24]

The 'theatrical' nature of the *auto da fé*, its religious significance, the symbolic aspect of the penitents who function as personified sins, its representation of the Day of Judgement, and its relationship to Aristotelian tragedy, all suggest that Lee plays with, even parodies, the ritual in *The Ballet of the Nations*. Like the *auto da fé*, Lee's *Ballet* is, ostensibly, a theatrical spectacle in which sins wear human form, and in which, as on the Day of Judgement, the nations are gathered. As in the *auto da fé* and in the Aristotelian tragedy, Fear and Pity are present. However, here, 'Fear' is a 'poor slut', 'seized with delirium tremens', while Pity is 'wan like waters under moonlight [...] and also, like such waters, dangerous in her innocence' (*Ballet*). In Lee's *Ballet*, Pity and Fear offer no catharsis, contributing instead to the sense of unease, apprehension and irresolution. Moreover, the spectacle in *The Ballet* is presided over, not by God, but by Satan. In *Satan the Waster*, Lee asks the question in the minds of many of her readers: 'Why have I chosen Satan for my spokesman in a discussion of what is, or is not, right?' Her answer is typically direct: 'Because I am sick of hearing this war discussed from the point of view of God, as if the speaker or writer, English, French, German, American, or what not, held a brief from on high to "justify the ways of God to man" or rather to identify the ways of his own particular nation with the ways of God' (115). Here, Lee's stance, along with that of other pacifists, is based perhaps on disillusionment with the Christian churches which had given the war their official approval.[25] However, implicit in her statement is an issue which informs her political writings, underlies *The Ballet*, and becomes more explicitly important in the revised version of it which appears in *Satan the Waster*: patriotism.

Patriotism and national identity

In *The Making of English National Identity*, Krishan Kumar argues,

> It is common enough for nations, as for individuals, to develop a sense of themselves by a process of opposition and exclusion. What they are – French, German – is defined by what they are not – German, French. The 'content' of national identity is more often than not a counter-image of what is seen as distinctive in the culture of the other nation or nations.[26]

His point is one that preoccupied Vernon Lee in her political writings, and informed her membership of the Union of Democratic Control, billed as '[a]n organisation created to secure the control over their Foreign Policy by the British people, and for the promotion of International understanding'.[27] The desire for 'International understanding' was at the heart of Lee's political comment before, during, and after the war. In her article 'The Sense of Nationality' (1912), Lee wrote in response to the nationalist politician, Maurice Barrès, later mentioned in her 1927 preface to 'The Virgin of the Seven Daggers', who along with others had preached 'the imperative need for a *Sense of Nationality*'.[28] Lee argued that this call for unity had in fact resulted in a rise in Chauvinism, a stance she viewed as 'incompatible' with a sense of nationality:

> Chauvinism implies the preference of ourselves, *because we are ourselves*. And to prefer ourselves happens to be the one tendency [...] in which all nations resemble one another like brothers and twins, even as the quality *of being oneself* is the quality which [...] all men and all

animals [...] possess to an equal and (so far as others are concerned) equally uninteresting degree; unnatural as it seems to our feelings, and revolting to our pride, there is absolutely nothing distinguished or even distinctive in everybody being himself.[29]

She argued that '[t]he knowledge, the intuition, of *what one is besides not being somebody else, and of what someone else is besides not being oneself* is what 'constitutes the sense of nationality, one's own and other folks'; for Lee, a 'true sense of nationality' is determined by a 'sensitiveness to national qualities and differences' which makes us aware of both our virtues and our vices.[30] Lee practised what she preached and, throughout the war and beyond, disseminated her ideas of respect, empathy and tolerance between nations. As Patrick Wright shows in *Iron Curtain: from Stage to Cold War*, she was not averse to expressing such ideas in a variety of fora, ranging from open letters to *The Nation* to an article on 'Bach's Christmas Music in England and Germany' in *Jus Suffragii*, in which she describes her experience of hearing Bach at the Temple church in London:

> With the first rasping notes of the organ, tearing the veil of silent prayer, there came before my mind [...] the fact that *There* also, *There* beyond the sea and the war chasm, in hundreds of churches of Bach's own country [...]*There*, at this very moment, were crowds like this one at the Temple, listening to this self-same Christmas Music [...]. They are thinking and feeling the same, those German and these English crowds. [...] Never have we and they been closer together, more alike and akin, than at this moment when War's cruelties and recriminations, War's monstrous iron curtain, cut us off so utterly from one another.[31]

Here we see Lee's attempts to draw parallels between the German and the English experience, and one might argue that her decision to use German music as a mediator is itself a political point as four months earlier 'the *Daily Mail* had been pleased to report that German and Austrian music had been removed from Britain's Promenade Concerts'.[32] According to Wright, Lee's emphasis in this article 'on a cultural tradition that transcends national enmities [...] was particularly indebted to the thinking of Romain Rolland, the French author, socialist, and fellow European "cosmopolitan" to whom she was soon to dedicate *The Ballet of the Nations*'.[33] Written in the early stages of the war, Lee's article clearly attempted to point out the similarities between – the congruence of – the English and German peoples. Rhetorical strategies that make 'these' and 'those', 'they' and 'we' interchangeable reinforced this message. It was a message that she repeated after the war in the introduction to *Satan the Waster* in which she again debated issues of 'empathy' and 'sympathy' and in which, in a tone bordering on exasperation, she argued:

> As regards intensification and enlargement of sympathy, that has doubtless taken place towards those fighting on one's own side; but it is more than counter-balanced by the addition of anger and vindictiveness on one's own, and the utter inability to recognize the bare human nature of those to whom one's sufferings are attributed. Thus the women of every belligerent nation seemed to forget that there were mothers, wives and sisters on the enemy side; much as the air-raided Londoners crying for reprisals on the 'Baby-killers' forgot that there were babies in Rhineland towns and that Allied bombs must surely kill some of them. (xix)

This quotation demonstrates Lee's ability to see both sides and underlines the parallels between the nations that jingoism and propaganda so willingly ignored. It also draws attention to Lee's concern with the notion of 'Group-Emotion', so favoured by Satan in *The Ballet of the Nations*. As Gillian Beer has shown, Lee was sceptical and mistrustful of the 'group-mind' as expounded by early twentieth-century psychologists such as William McDougall in *Body and Mind* (1913) and *The Group Mind* (1920), and Wilfred Trotter in *Instincts of the Herd in Peace and War* (1916).[34] Beer notes that Lee resists their 'totalizing views', which emphasize 'the single herd, the tribe, the war machine, the hive', and opposes the idea of any 'anthropomorphic entity called "the nation"'.[35] Lee's annotations to Trotter's text make these views clear:

> The members of a nation, i.e. the classes and individuals do not cooperate and compete in time of peace with reference to the nation but with reference to their trade, locality etc. A bee makes honey for the hive; but a workman makes goods for anyone, for consumption or barter.[36]

In other words, for Lee, the notion of the 'nation' deployed in wartime is distinctly artificial and subject to fragmentation. In *The Ballet of the Nations*, she highlights the ways in which the 'nation', as an entity, is willing to sacrifice its members (literally and figuratively) in order to maintain power until they become 'terrible uncertain forms, armless, legless, recognisable for human only by their irreproachable-looking heads' (*Ballet*). These maimed and fragmented bodies counter any propagandistic sense of national unity. They accentuate the fact that governments often abuse citizens' bodies for political ends.

Lee is equally at pains to emphasize that the concept of 'patriotism', closely associated with a sense of national unity, is especially problematic. In the 1915 version of *The Ballet*, patriotism goes unmentioned, but in the post-war version that appears in *Satan the Waster* in 1920, patriotism plays a prominent part, and Lee devotes a key section of her notes to 'The Orchestra of Patriotism' (231). The stage directions of the 1920 *Ballet* indicate that the orchestra is separated from the stalls by 'a carved handrailing or balustrade' which bears 'in ornamental letters the words "Patriotism"' (32). Satan welcomes newcomers to the 'small but very choice and famous' amateur band known by the name of 'Patriotism' (35). In an added dialogue with Clio, the Muse of History, Satan begs her to read the list of the Passions that 'constitute the famous Orchestra of Patriotism' (38). In addition, the ballet-master Death addresses his performers in a long speech in which he continually alludes to Patriotism and makes it clear that it plays a vital part in the dynamics of war:

> Ladies and Gentlemen, Valiant Nations of my Corps du Ballet [*sic*], and ever-responsive Passions of the Orchestra so justly admired under the name of Patriotism! [...] Let me remind you that, for the satisfaction of my Lord Satan [...] you are about to take part in the vastest and most new-fashioned spectacle of Slaughter and Ruin I have so far had the honour of putting on to the World's Stage [...]. Let me remind the Passions about to take their seats in the Orchestra of Patriotism that the duration of our performance depends entirely on their activity. [...]. The members of the Orchestra of Patriotism are therefore urgently requested to replenish their energies by unstinting use of the appropriate refreshments, carefully warmed up by commonplaces and fiery dramas of eloquence, which will be handed round unceasingly by Lord Satan's lackeys of the Press and Pulpit. (41–3)

For Lee, one of the essential characteristics of patriotism is that it 'depends upon *segregation*, not to say antagonism; upon a *railing*, upon something separating those who feel it from everyone else' (234). For Lee, 'patriotism', like the 'nation', is based on the principle of exclusion. The satirical emphasis on patriotism in the later version of *The Ballet* implies that war had crystallized Lee's sense of being an outsider. As a woman, Lee is, in key ways, already an 'outsider'. As Virginia Woolf was to suggest in *Three Guineas* (1938), on the threshold of another world war, outsiderism could have positive aspects: a woman's exclusion from positions of public influence reserved for men with a public school education, allowed her a degree of independent thought untainted by the ideological structures that encouraged an unthinking patriotism.[37] However, Lee, a woman born in France, raised in Europe, and resident in Italy, was doubly an outsider, and the 'outsiderism' that allowed her a perspective lacking in those who embraced the war at times proved problematic. As Wright observes, once Britain entered the war, 'the nation' accepted the situation; even those who had previously urged caution now began to change their minds: 'Being in, we must win.'[38] Lee's awareness of the implications of 'being out' of the war, is explained in *Satan the Waster* where she tells her readers of the things which her 'not *being in*' had allowed her to see: '[c]hief among these are the circumstances and feelings by which certain facts concerning the war, or rather concerning all the belligerents engaged in it, were hidden or disguised from the recognition of those who, unlike myself, *were in*' (xix).

Nevertheless, there were consequences to not '*being in*'. In a prescient moment in 1912, Lee acknowledges that those who criticize their nations gain 'a pariah-reputation of lacking a sense of nationality'.[39] 'Group-Emotion', that feeling which brings to nations a sense of unity and permanence, seems for Lee to be at its most dangerous when it manifests itself in patriotism. It is little wonder, then, that in her 'Notes to the Ballet', Lee repeats the statement 'I have not Patriotism' a number of times and acknowledges that 'there are moments in the World's history when one is really not altogether comfortable without some little Patriotism' (244); it is a comment based on bitter experience. The outbreak of war separated Lee physically from her Italian home, but it was also to separate her spiritually and intellectually from many of her British and European friends who could not comprehend her pacifist stance, and, significantly, from her British readership as well. As the war progressed, many of the journals to which she had regularly contributed refused to publish her work: in England, only three periodicals continued to run her political articles.[40] Her views were considered 'unpatriotic'. It is therefore ironic that in his review of *Satan the Waster*, George Bernard Shaw praised Lee's pacifist integrity and her dispassionateness: 'Vernon Lee is English of the English'; by 'sheer intellectual force, training, knowledge and character, [she] kept her head when Europe was a mere lunatic asylum' and 'held her intellectual own all through'.[41] Yet it was precisely Lee's 'un-Englishness' that isolated her during the war. Her head, like those of the dancing nations, may appear to have remained intact but her European upbringing, which enabled her to see all sides, fragmented her allegiances and perhaps even the sense of her own identity. Others brutally challenged her lack of patriotism. In 1914, the French writer Augustine Bulteau, formerly a close friend, wrote:

> I have just read your shameful letter in the *Nation* [...]. I hope, if ever chance bring us together, you will refrain from greeting me. I know that you are a waif, a stray, that nothing very lasting, no regular family or friend, binds you to your country. I know that the English refuse to grant any importance to your adaptation of ideas picked up in Germany. I know that the 'thinker,' which you regard yourself, is the cause of much laughter among your countrymen. But is that, all that, enough, at such a terrible moment as this, to make you renounce the honour of being English, to make you raise your thin pretentious voice in support of the enemy of your country, your suffering country which never was so great as now?[42]

There is no doubt that Bulteau's words, like those of other former friends, caused Lee some personal suffering. In the introduction to *Satan the Waster*, she acknowledges, 'As regards myself, I own that the sorrow which war's bare fact has brought into my life is more likely to have made me misunderstood than understand it' and suggests that, unlike those who, despite personal suffering and loss, can take consolation in their faith and in victory, she, who has faith only in peace, can only 'look upon the victory of either side as the victory of war' (xviii–xix). If, as Satan claims, war 'revives religious feeling' and according to Death patriotism is its means of propulsion, then in wartime patriotism becomes a form of creed or quasi-religious dogma. If during war, patriotism becomes a 'faith', then the pacifist, by implication, becomes a 'heretic'. In this context, the maimed bodies of *The Ballet*, representing the remains of warring nations, double as the tortured bodies of heretics in the *auto da fé*, and its 'Corps du Ballet' [*sic*] suggest the Corpus Christi, the ravaged and tortured body of Christ – arguably the ultimate pacifist.

Heresy, pacifism and abjection

The long-standing link between Christ and pacifism centres on key passages from Jesus' Sermon on the Mount that preach non-resistance: 'Blessed [are] the peacemakers: for they shall be called the children of God'; 'Ye have heard that it hath been said, An eye for an eye, and a tooth for a tooth: But I say unto you, That ye resist not evil: but whosoever shall smite thee on thy right cheek, turn to him the other also'; 'Love your enemies, bless them that curse you, do good to them that hate you, and pray for them which despitefully use you, and persecute you'.[43] As Richard Horsley notes, 'These sayings provide the crucial textual basis for traditional Christian pacifism.'[44] The need to resolve the tension between active Christianity and combat was hotly debated during and after the First World War. In an essay written during the conflict, John Mecklin comments on 'the feverish attempts' made at this time to 'reconcile the ethic of Jesus with the Christian patriot's duty'.[45] In his 1918 essay 'Religion and War', Shailer Mathews states,

> [T]he pacifist claims that war is un-Christian and that he is the true representative of Christianity, [yet] Love, which is at the heart of the Christian message, cannot permit a nation or an individual to remain passive while the well-being of others is endangered. [...] The true Christian patriot at the present time is in fact saying to certain ideals, 'You must for the moment retire from the scene. I have a desperately nasty mess to clean up'.[46]

In the complicated ethical shifts demanded by the First World War, the pacifist becomes paradoxically both a 'heretic' – one who dissents from the established dogma of patriotism – and a Christ-like figure.[47] Lee's decision, as a pacifist, to present her allegory in the form of a 'ballet' may therefore have equally complex implications that require unpacking. Satan's explicit reference to the *auto sacramental* associates her ballet with traditional dances performed in Spain during Corpus Christi, some of which had 'many features of ballet'.[48] Moreover, the instruments that often accompanied such dances – the horn, the trumpet and the drum – are key instruments in the orchestra that plays for Satan's dancers.[49] The tacit presence of the Corpus Christi compels the alerted reader to re-examine Death's 'Corps du Ballet [*sic*]' composed of the dancing nations (*Ballet*). The 'nations' function as metonyms for those battling bodies, indeed, those very real corpses that litter the fields of war and, as Beer points out, on stage they 'decompose'.[50] The sufferings of Death's *corps de ballet*, performing in a dance implicitly associated with the religious feast of Corpus Christi, thus suggest the ravaged body of Christ, scourged, wounded, crucified and killed for his beliefs.[51] While seemingly representing the fragmentation of nations and the agony of their troops, *The Ballet* also quietly draws attention to the figuratively sacrificial body of the pacifist who, in wartime, inhabits the role of the martyred Christ. In doing so, it suggests that the pacifist, outcast and disowned, is an abject figure; an interpretation implied not only by the visceral images of blood, mangled flesh and dismemberment that cover the stage, but by the nature of the ballet itself as an expression of pacifist belief.

For Julia Kristeva, the corpse is 'the utmost of abjection', the expulsion of the 'I'; the abject is that which 'disturbs identity, system, order. What does not respect borders, positions, rules. The in-between, the ambiguous, the composite.'[52] Deborah Caslav Covino argues that, '[a]bjection is a supple term: it names the undesirable contents of our being – pain, disease, body waste, and death – as well as our active repudiation of these contents.'[53] It also names 'the condition or state of being both downcast and outcast, of being both burdened and outraged by our morality, and of being rejected or scapegoated as a representative of that which is undesirable'.[54] Given these definitions of abjection, Lee's *Ballet* appears to be an example of what Kristeva identifies as '"abject" literature': 'the sort that takes up where apocalypse and carnival left off'.[55] Lee's *Ballet* 'does not respect borders, positions, rules'. It is 'ambiguous': the orchestra dressed in 'classical, mediæval, biblical or savage costume' and its 'contemporary members' dressed in modern attire, challenge our ability to determine whether the ballet is set in the past or present. It is 'composite': in terms of genre, it encompasses elements of the *auto da fé*, the *auto sacramental*, sacred ballets performed at Corpus Christi, the medieval mystery play and Aristotelian tragedy. In raising images of entrails, blood, dismemberment, 'uncertain forms' and 'unspeakable hybrids' (*Ballet*), it also invokes that which, according to Kristeva, problematizes representation – the abject body. As Kristeva argues:

> The abject is not an ob-ject [*sic*] facing me which I name or imagine. [...] The abject has only one quality of the object – that of being opposed to *I*. If the object, however, through its opposition, settles me within the fragile texture of a desire for meaning, [...] what is abject [...] draws me toward the place where meaning collapses.[56]

It is perhaps, then, only fitting that Lee's 'abject' ballet is accompanied by an authorial injunction that denies the spectator a visual or aural experience of the events that take place on the stage. In the final version of *The Ballet of the Nations* included in *Satan the Waster*, Lee adds an '*Author's Note for Stage Managers (other than Satan)*':

> In the event of this play being performed, it is the author's imperative wish that no attempt be made at showing the Dancing of the Nations. The stage upon the stage must be turned in such a manner that nothing beyond the footlights, the Orchestra and auditorium shall be visible to the real spectators, only the changing illumination

which accompanies the Ballet making its performance apparent. Similarly, [...] none of the music must be audible, except the voice and drum of Heroism. Anything beyond this would necessarily be hideous, besides drowning or interrupting the dialogue. (57)

If Lee's play was never performed and, indeed, defies performance, refusing the audience any sight of its dancers and any sound of its music, what is it that *is* being staged in Lee's work? In an article entitled 'Vicarious Tragedy' she asks: 'What shall we do for the lack of the tragic element in life?' and notes that 'tragedy remains aesthetically enjoyable' only when it is not 'personally distressing', citing the recent common 'enjoyment' of the Titanic disaster as an example.[57] She acknowledges that '[a]cute sensitiveness to the cruelty and sordidness of other men's fate and surroundings is [...] a powerful instrument for diminishing, however little, the world's mass of evil and ugliness' but argues that 'it is more useful to rebel than to acquiesce in such things'.[58] Yet in *The Ballet* Lee spectrally stages her own 'acute sensitiveness' to the cruelty suffered by man at the hands of man, while a form of 'vicarious tragedy' remains at work. The tragedy represented by the maimed and mangled nations implicitly reflects Lee's own fragmented and dismembered nationalism and the abject body of the Christ-like pacifist. Indeed, the publication of *The Ballet* captures Lee 'in crisis, putting her political and artistic convictions in the firing line'.[59] It is also telling that during the war years Lee wrote a series of notes collectively entitled 'Myself' in which she 'analyses her reasons for opposing the war' and 'distinguishes her own feelings from those of other pacifists'.[60] For instance, in a note headed '*Einfühlung*!' written in 1916, she observes that her fellow pacifists are not 'isolated' as she is, but 'segregated in their own clique'.[61] They see what she calls 'war-feeling' 'entirely from the outside' and condemn it as 'odious', 'unjust' and 'childish' whereas she feels that it is entirely inevitable and comprehensible, and feels that it is *she* 'who must seem odious, unjust, childish etc.'[62] *Einfühlung* or 'empathy',[63] a concept which Lee is said to have introduced into British aestheticism, becomes increasingly problematic during the war years. She questions that selective empathy that cries for its own losses, while refusing to acknowledge that others, elsewhere, are also crying for theirs. She explains:

The thesis summed up in my allegory and brought home to me by the war's prodigious waste of human virtue, is that the world needs rather than such altruism as is expressed in self-sacrifice, a different kind of altruism which is the recognition of the other (for *alter* is Latin for *other*), sides, aspects, possibilities and requirements of things and people. (*Satan*, xlvii)

Recognizing other sides, aspects and possibilities, while commendable and often desirable, necessarily leads to a fragmentation of the self. How can one remain fully oneself, when one is constantly trying to understand, enter into, and inhabit the thoughts and actions of others? In the aftermath of its publication, in an ironic reversal, the bodily fragmentation and sacrificial violence played out in *The Ballet of the Nations*, is metaphorically enacted on its author. In advocating the permeability of national boundaries and identities, in stressing the permeability of her own sensibilities, Lee herself becomes an abject figure. *The Ballet* recalls not only the sacrifices made by each nation, but also by those pacifists, like Lee, whose international empathy caused them to be sacrificed on the altar of patriotism.

Notes

1. Vernon Lee (Violet Paget, 1856–1935) achieved literary notice in 1880 when she published a critical work on Italian culture, *Studies of the Eighteenth Century in Italy*. Over the years, she moved in social circles that included Robert Browning, Walter Pater, Henry James, Bernard Berenson, Bertrand Russell, Lady Ottoline Morrell, Ethel Smyth and Virginia Woolf, and wrote on a wide range of topics including travel, fiction, history, aesthetics, philosophy and politics.
2. Irene Cooper-Willis, 'Preface', *Vernon Lee's Letters* (London: privately printed, 1937), i–xiv; xiv.
3. See Peter Gunn, *Vernon Lee: Violet Paget 1856–1935* (London: Oxford University Press, 1964), 206 and Patrick Wright, *Iron Curtain: from Stage to Cold War* (Oxford: Oxford University Press, 2007), 110.
4. Gunn, *Vernon Lee*, 207.
5. In the later version of *The Ballet of the Nations* which appears in *Satan the Waster* (1920), Lee states that 'it is the author's imperative wish that no attempt be made at showing the Dancing of the Nations' and the text of *Satan* opens with a note stating that the 'drama is intended to be read, and especially read out loud, as *prose*'; see Vernon Lee, *Satan the Waster: a Philosophical War Trilogy with Notes and Introduction* (New York: John Lane, 1920), 57. All subsequent references to this text will be cited parenthetically in the text.
6. Grace Brockington, 'Performing Pacifism: the Battle between Artist and Author in *The Ballet of the Nations*', in Catherine Maxwell and Patricia Pulham (eds), *Vernon Lee: Decadence, Ethics, Aesthetics* (Basingstoke: Palgrave Macmillan, 2006), 143–59; 154. Gill Plain likens *Satan the Waster* to Brechtian epic theatre; see 'The Shape of Things to Come: the Remarkable Modernity of Vernon Lee's *Satan the Waster* (1915–1920)', in Claire Tylee (ed.), *Women, the First World War and the Dramatic Imagination: International Essays (1914–1999)* (Lewiston, New York, and Lampeter: Edwin Mellen Press, 2000), 5–21; 14.

7. Gillian Beer, 'The Dissidence of Vernon Lee: *Satan the Waster* and the Will to Believe', in Suzanne Raitt and Trudi Tate (eds), *Women's Fiction and the Great War* (Oxford: Clarendon, 1997), 107–31; 110.

8. Vernon Lee, Introduction. *Satan the Waster*, vii.

9. Vernon Lee, *The Ballet of the Nations: a Present-Day Morality*, illustrated by Maxwell Armfield (London: Chatto & Windus, 1915). An online version can be viewed at http://www.archive.org/stream/balletofnationsp00leev, accessed 11 March 2010. All subsequent references to this unpaginated edition will be cited parenthetically in the text as *Ballet*.

10. In her article on *Satan the Waster*, Gillian Beer suggests that 'masque-like presences called "Greed, Loyalty, Discipline, Comradeship, Jealousy, Chivalry, Egotism, Bullying, Science, Organisation, Ennuie, Discipline [*sic*], Self-Interest, Fear" form the corps-de-ballet'; Beer, 'Dissidence', 110. This is incorrect, as these are 'passions' that form part of the orchestra of patriotism. The *corps-de-ballet* is composed of the dancing nations.

11. In *Satan the Waster*, Clio (the muse of History) is invited to join Satan as he watches the play and their dialogue replaces the narrator in the 1915 version of *The Ballet*.

12. Brockington, 'Performing Pacifism', 146.

13. It is worth noting that the bullfight is often considered a form of symbolic 'passion play', and that elements of the bullfight inform Picasso's meditation on war in *Guernica* (1937).

14. In *Baldwin: Being Dialogues on Views and Aspirations* (1886), Lee included two dialogues on the topic of religion: 'The Responsibilities of Unbelief' and 'The Consolations of Belief' which outlined the reasons why she rejected the Christian concept of God in favour of what might be described as 'an evolutionary humanism'. Gunn, *Vernon Lee*, 113.

15. Vernon Lee, *Commonplace Book*, ns. 4. Special Collections, Miller Library, Colby College, Waterville, Maine, USA.

16. 1909 is the publication date of the English version of the story; a French version, under the title 'La Madone aux sept glaives' appeared in *Feuilleton du journal des débats du Samedi*, 8, 9, 11, 12, 14 February 1896.

17. Vernon Lee, Preface to 'The Virgin of the Seven Daggers', in Catherine Maxwell and Patricia Pulham (eds), *Hauntings and Other Fantastic Tales* (Peterborough, Ontario: Broadview Press, 2006), 243–8; 245.

18. 'Theatre of War', *Oxford English Dictionary*, 2nd edn (Oxford: Clarendon Press, 1989). The term was reputedly coined by Carl von Clausewitz in *On War* (1832). See also Paul Fussell, *The Great War and Modern Memory* (Oxford: Oxford University Press, 1977), 191–230.

19. Francisco Bethencourt, 'The Auto da Fé: Ritual and Imagery', *Journal of the Warburg and Courtauld Institutes* 55 (1992): 155–68; 155–6.

20. Ibid., 156.

21. Ibid., 158; 160.

22. Ibid., 158.

23. *King James Bible*, Matthew 25: 31–32. http://www.kingjamesbibleonline.org/, accessed 8 October 2009. Maureen Flynn, 'Mimesis of the Last Judgment: the Spanish Auto da Fé', *Sixteenth Century Journal* 22/2 (1991): 281–97; 282, 286, 295.

24. Ibid., 296.

25. See Martin Ceadel, *Pacifism in Britain 1914–1945* (Oxford: Clarendon Press, 1980), 34.
26. Krishan Kumar, *The Making of English National Identity* (Cambridge: Cambridge University Press, 2003), ix.
27. Vineta Colby, *Vernon Lee: a Literary Biography* (Charlottesville and London: University of Virginia Press, 2003), 296.
28. Vernon Lee, 'The Sense of Nationality', *The Nation* XII (12 October 1912): 96–8; 96. Auguste-Maurice Barrès (1862–1923) was elected to the Chamber of Deputies with the Boulangistes, a party of populist Chauvinists who encouraged anti-German feeling in France. In 1898, he ran (unsuccessfully) as a National Socialist in the city of Nancy using as a platform a manifesto rife with xenophobia and anti-Semitism.
29. Ibid.
30. Ibid., 96; 98.
31. Vernon Lee, 'Bach's Christmas Music in England and in Germany', *Jus Suffragii* 9/4 (1915): 218.
32. Wright, *Iron Curtain*, 80.
33. Ibid., 86.
34. Trotter's ideas had been disseminated earlier in two articles entitled, 'Herd Instinct and its Bearing on the Psychology of Civilized Man' (parts 1 and 2), which appeared in the *Sociological Review* in July 1908 and January 1909 respectively. See Beer, 'Dissidence', 114–15.
35. Ibid., 115–16.
36. Cited ibid., 116.
37. Eveline Kilian, 'What Does "Our Country" Mean to me an Outsider? Virginia Woolf, War and Patriotism', in Barbara Korte and Ralf Schneider (eds), *War and the Cultural Construction of Identities in Britain* (Amsterdam: Rodopi, 2002), 143–62; 143. Gillian Beer suggests that Lee's *Satan* may have informed *Orlando* (1928) and the pageant in Virginia Woolf's *Between the Acts* (1941), ('Dissidence', 128). Woolf knew Lee well and had both read and edited her work.
38. Slogan of the liberal *Daily News*, cited in Wright, *Iron Curtain*, 117.
39. Lee, 'The Sense of Nationality', 98.
40. See Colby, *Vernon Lee*, 293. Political articles in addition to those cited in this chapter include: 'The Lines of Anglo-German Agreement', *The Nation* VII (10 September 1910), supplement between pp. 838 and 839. 'Angels Fear to Tread', *The Nation* XI (7 September 1912): 828–9. 'The Policy of the Allies', *The Nation* XVI (2 February 1915): 649–50. 'Bismarck Towers', *New Statesman* V (20 February 1915): 481–3. 'Militarists against Militarism', *Labour Leader* XII, 13 (1 April 1915): 3. 'Après la Mêlée', *New Statesman* V (19 June 1915): 249–51. 'The Wish for Unanimity and the Willingness for War, France–Italy, 1911–13' [written before August 1914], *Cambridge Magazine* IV (12 June 1915): 482, 484. 'War the Grave of All Good', *Labour Leader* XII/43 (28 October 1915): 3. 'Enmity', *War and Peace* III/25 (October 1915): 11–12. 'The Heart of a Neutral', *Atlantic Monthly* CXVI (November 1915): 687.
41. Cited in Colby, *Vernon Lee*, 307.
42. Cited ibid., 205.
43. *King James Bible*, Matthew 5: 9, 38–9, 44. http://www.kingjamesbibleonline.org/, accessed 7 October 2009.

44. Richard A. Horsley, '"Love your Enemies" and the Doctrine of Non-Violence', *Journal of the American Academy of Religion* 54/1 (1986): 3–31; 3.
45. John M. Mecklin, 'The War and the Dilemma of the Christian Ethic', *American Journal of Theology* 23/1 (1919): 14–40; 14.
46. Shailer Mathews, 'Religion and War', *Biblical World* 52/2 (1918): 163–76; 171–6.
47. In the sense that Christ challenged the accepted religious tenets of his own period he, too, might be considered 'heretical'.
48. See J.B. Trend, 'The Dance of the Seises at Seville', *Music & Letters* 2/1 (1921): 10–28; 11.
49. The orchestra includes 'a woodland horn', a 'silver trumpet' and the 'drum' which accompanies Heroism's voice (*Ballet*).
50. Beer, 'Dissidence', 110.
51. See *King James Bible*, John, 19; 1–19. http://www.kingjamesbibleonline.org/, accessed 8 October 2009.
52. Julia Kristeva, *Powers of Horror: an Essay on Abjection*, trans. Leon S. Roudiez (New York: Columbia University Press, 1982), 3–4.
53. Deborah Caslav Covino, 'Abject Criticism', *Genders* 32 (2000): para. 12. http://www.genders.org/g.32/g.32_covino.html, accessed 8 October 2009.
54. Ibid.
55. Kristeva, *Powers*, 141.
56. Ibid., 2.
57. Vernon Lee, 'Vicarious Tragedy', *The Nation* XI (29 June 1912): 466–7; 466.
58. Ibid.
59. Brockington, 'Performing Pacifism', 144.
60. Cited in Gunn, *Vernon Lee*, 206.
61. Ibid.
62. Ibid.
63. For a useful discussion of Lee's understanding of 'empathy' and the theorists who influenced her thinking, see Christa Zorn, 'The Handling of Words: Reader Response Victorian Style', in Maxwell and Pulham, *Vernon Lee*, 174–92.

3
Incommensurate Histories: the Remaindered Irish Bodies of the Great War

Eugene McNulty

There is something uncanny about contemporary Ireland's relationship, on both sides of the border, to the First World War. The Great War, and Ireland's part in it, is an event that still at times has the feel of something unresolved, a touch unsettling. This is especially the case in southern Ireland. Fran Brearton, for example, on noting that as many as 200,000 Irish men enlisted for the British Army in the years 1914–18, of whom some 35,000 were killed in the war, makes the point that 'while these figures would seem able to speak for themselves, they have not done so'.[1] This problem of speech and silence, of present and absent bodies, is intimately connected with the course of Irish history in the wake of the 1914–18 conflict. Events during the Great War provided the impetus for the militarization of Irish life, with the onset first of the War of Independence (or Anglo-Irish War, 1919–21), which was followed by a civil war (1922–23). The First World War, then, was the first in a chain of conflicts that propelled Ireland towards partial independence and partition.[2] Moreover, events during 1914–18 helped shape the nature and durability of this solution. The oppositional nationalistic forces that defined this 'two Irelands' construct each found in the events of this period bodies and deaths that spoke of, and to, the mytho-poetic core of their communal identity.

In Northern Ireland the memory of those Ulstermen who died – in the trenches of the Western Front particularly – was, and remains, integral to the construction of a post-partition Unionist identity.[3] As a result remembrance of the Great War was quickly institutionalized at the level of official state discourse and ritual. For this newly formed political entity, the dead bodies of the war formed a powerful covenant with those left to defend their community. Speaking on 11 November 1922, for example, James Craig (Northern Ireland's first Prime Minister) made it clear that preserving Northern Ireland within the Union took the form of a sacred duty; this pact with the dead must not be broken because 'those who have passed away have left behind a great message [...] to stand firm, and to give away none of Ulster's soil'.[4] The palimpsestic conceit – contemporary events stand as one more layer in the 'message' of Ulster resistance – creates a symbiosis between the trenches of war and the political settlement of partition, between the bodies who must defend that settlement and those who perished in Europe. It is an image, furthermore, that conjures an uncanny return – the dead of the Great War return to stalk the territory of domestic Irish politics.

In southern Ireland the afterlife of the Great War took a quite different path. The bodies of the war in Europe – those that returned as well as those that did not – were made uncanny by their absence from official discourses of post-independence Irish identity. In Ireland's initial postcolonial moment, the Great War was 'remaindered by history'.[5] In place of official remembrance, those Irishmen – in particular those Catholics and/or nationalists – from the south who fought and died in the First World War would be relocated (relegated even) to the political unconscious. In effect these men were retrospectively read as having made the wrong choice, something which left them 'tainted with the stain of collaboration'.[6] On both sides of the border, then, the split in the body politic was reflected in the role, or absence of role, assigned in the public imaginary to Ireland's Great War dead.

This schism in remembrance, history and the politics of space, has tended to result in a rather blunt over-simplification of the intentions and decisions that sent Irishmen (north and south) to war. Particularly in Northern Ireland, where the Great War has always been 'heavily politicised', the decision to join the army is mostly presented as an uncomplicated fidelity to British sovereignty (for King and Country; in the cause of Union and Empire).[7] The truth, of course, was much more complicated. Attitudes to the war in Europe became a heavily loaded issue in terms of the internal politics of Ireland; and an extraordinarily complex web of – often conflicting – reasons sent men from all over Ireland to the theatres of European conflict.[8] For Irish Unionism, the Great War provided an opportunity to demonstrate fidelity to the Union and Empire. For Irish Republicanism, on the other hand, the war was one more imperial folly. A third position was articulated by many Irish constitutional nationalists.[9] Most famously, in 1914 the leader of the (nationalist) Irish Parliamentary Party, John Redmond, campaigned for Irishmen to enlist and join the war in Europe. Ireland could demonstrate its rightful place on the stage of nations, he argued, by playing its full part in the resolution of a European crisis with global significance. Just as importantly perhaps, the war was seen by many as a common cause which would help to resolve the internal tensions that had gathered strength in Ireland over the preceding decades. Home Rulers from all over Ireland, Redmond urged, needed to match the commitment of those (mostly) from Ulster who had signed up to mark their resistance to any break-up of the Union.[10] In other words, if some joined up to demonstrate a loyalty to Union and Empire that would make Home Rule *impossible* to carry through, many others from the nationalist community joined up to *guarantee* Home Rule.

   Against this backdrop Redmond proffered that the common experience of Irish soldiers in the war would make redundant the political divisions that impelled them towards battle: 'their union in the field may lead to a union in their home; their blood may be the seal that will bring all Ireland together in one nation, and in liberties equal and common to all'.[11] The imagery is striking: the mingling of blood on Europe's battlefields would provide the catalyst for an ideological rapprochement in the Irish body politic. Irishmen on each side of the Home Rule divide, in other words, were sent to war pre-encoded as representative bodies; their deaths would thus also be representative. The relationship between the body and ideology was for a time explicitly removed from the domain of political theory and played out at the level of actual political strategy. Where these representative bodies were imaginatively sent and where they ended up, however, were two very different things. The same is true of the deaths they experienced. The innocence of 1914 allowed for a form of chivalric imagery: these men would find 'union in the field'. Their blood sacrifice is here framed in the rhetoric and heroic ideals of warfare as they existed in a popular imagination that had not yet witnessed the onset of total war and mechanized death.

   Events in 1916 would alter Ireland's relationship to the war; they would also help shape Ireland's twentieth century. Each in their own way impacted on those, like Redmond, who read Irish Home Rule as inevitable and the Great War as an opportunity to heal domestic rifts via common experience. On 24 April 1916 the Irish rebellion known as the Easter Rising was launched. A group of determined Republicans, who had rejected the idea that Irishmen should make common cause with Britain while she retained her political domination of Ireland, seized a number of key buildings (most famously the GPO) in central Dublin and declared an independent Irish Republic. The subsequent execution of the Rising's leaders by the British authorities transformed a rather unsuccessful coup into the key event for modern Irish nationalism. Crucially, their martyred bodies would become emblems of nationalist self-sacrifice in the face of colonial oppression. Just a matter of weeks after that Easter, 1 July 1916 marked the first day's action in the Battle of the Somme. Of the 20,000 men who died on this first day alone, some 2000 came from the 36th (Ulster) Division – a Division made up almost entirely of Ulster Protestants, who sought in the European war an opportunity to demonstrate their resistance to political independence for Ireland.

The Easter Rising would become the foundational event for an independent Ireland; the losses endured by the Ulster Division on the Somme would become a key component in Ulster Unionists' argument for partition and the creation of Northern Ireland. As Edna Longley eloquently writes: 'the Somme [...] complicated the politics produced by the Rising [...]: two sacrificial shrines – the people crucified, a chosen people massacred – demanded their incompatible due'.[12] More than anything else, it was the incommensurate nature of these two events that would propel the southern Irish men who had signed up into a particularly uncompromising historical no-man's land. The nationalist MP and poet, Tom Kettle, was all too aware of his future position in history when he heard the news of the Easter Rising while in France (where he was to die in September 1916): 'Those men [...] will go down in history as heroes and martyrs; and I will go down – if I go down at all – as a bloody British officer.'[13] The poet in Kettle could read the history of this moment from an imagined future: he knew all too well that an ideological schism had just widened further – making impossible the notion of the war as a common cause – and that the resultant gap would define the nature of his disappearance.

Writing the war: re-imagining troubling bodies

Even before the end of hostilities, then, it was clear that the Great War was going to leave a fraught legacy for Ireland. At the level of cultural production, representing the Great War and the bodies who fought in it would remain a deeply problematic task for much of the twentieth century. The difficulty faced by writers reflected, of course, the general experience of the wider population. As Terence Brown puts it: 'The experience of Irish struggle and civil war were more immediate realities for many of the population than the sufferings of men who had taken a historical wrong turning that had led them to a foreign field.'[14] The man who did most to shape the nature of Irish writing in this period, W.B. Yeats, for example, refused to engage with the war in Europe in any sustained fashion, suggesting that the pity of mass warfare was not an apt subject for poetry as he imagined it.[15] Yeats was not alone in this refusal to engage; of the period immediately after the Great War, Brown suggests of southern Ireland: 'It was as if the Irish had agreed collectively, if for widely differing reasons, to dismiss from consciousness their own involvement in the greatest cataclysm ever to have befallen European civilization. And the silence of the country's writers speaks volumes.'[16]

Much of this literary silence has the feel of a self-willed disengagement – non-speech as protective shelter. But there were instances of a more active form of silencing. Most famously, in 1928, following the success of his Dublin trilogy, Sean O'Casey presented the Abbey Theatre with his *Silver Tassie*, a play that portrays the experiences of Irish men in the trenches and the impact on Dublin's working-class communities. Yeats rejected the play, suggesting it did not work well dramaturgically; he also cited as grounds for refusal the fact that O'Casey had not experienced the trenches and thus could not properly represent them or the bodies that inhabited them – a critique that seems rather more problematic. In the end the Abbey's refusal of O'Casey reveals a very specific problem for the theatre. The sight on-stage of Irish bodies dressed in British Army uniforms – bodies, moreover who are presented sympathetically and whose traumas are intended to conjure empathy in the audience – represented too much of a gamble in 1920s Dublin. The activities of British soldiers in the War of Independence, as well as their role in quelling the Easter Rising, were still a matter of first-hand memory rather than the stuff of intergenerational reporting, and this loaded signification of uniformed bodies was one that the Abbey managed to avoid by refusing O'Casey's new work.

W.B. Yeats's reluctance to address the Great War directly, and the occlusion of O'Casey's attempt to do just that, reveals much about the unreceptive conditions for producing and disseminating work that explored the experiences of the war's Irish soldiers. Not surprisingly these conditions especially affected the production of fiction and memoirs based directly on the experiences of those soldiers. Patrick MacGill's trilogy of war texts, based on his experiences in the London Irish Regiment – *The Amateur Army* (1915), *The Great Push* (1916), *The Red Horizon* (1916) – were notable exceptions to this rule in the war years.[17] That MacGill's works were relatively successful, however, was largely down to the fact that he wrote 'more as a poet of working-class solidarities than of Irish nationalist feeling', and in so doing managed to sidestep many of the political complexities that were gathering pace in Ireland.[18] The fact that his texts were written and published while the war was ongoing also meant that they did not have to engage with the tensions and paradoxes that marked out Ireland's post-war years. In this regard it is notable that Liam O'Flaherty's *Return of the Brute* (1929) is one of the few novels published in the 1920s that directly draws on the experiences of an Irish writer who had been in the trenches (O'Flaherty had been in the Irish Guards and was shell-shocked during the third Battle of Ypres). Importantly, O'Flaherty does not engage explicitly with the issue of having been an Irishman in the British Army; all the same, *Return of the Brute* was not a success either popularly or critically (one critic described it as 'one of the worst [novels] ever published'[19]).

But while it is true to say that novels recounting the *direct* experiences of the Irish combatants in the Great War were notable by their rarity, this is not to suggest a complete absence of reference to the Great War in Irish fiction during this period. Rather, Irish writers tended to engage with the war in a more oblique manner. In place of direct engagement (in terms of setting and plot), it was much more common for the Great War to form a backdrop to action set in Ireland. We can see a version of this oblique treatment in a text like Elizabeth Bowen's *The Last September* (1929), which charts the last days of an Ascendancy estate (Danielstown) during the War of Independence. The margins of Bowen's novel (the substantive – political – 'action' takes place out of view, beyond the walls of the Danielstown estate) are haunted by bodies playing out an ideological battle with its immediate roots in the 1914–18 period. This pattern is repeated later in the century in Iris Murdoch's *The Red and the Green* (1965), a novel published in the build-up to the fiftieth anniversary of the Easter Rising. Murdoch's text explores the divided loyalties experienced by a family in the war years – two cousins plan to take part in the Easter Rising, while a third is an officer in the British Cavalry posted in Dublin. The story weaves through a web of illicit desires (including incest) in a manner that reveals Irish history to be an intimate affair, a family row. Like Bowen, Murdoch uses the Great War as a contextual 'sounding-board', uniformed bodies appear back from the war and head off towards it (while others keep secret their uniforms of nascent rebellion), but its function is really to reveal the internal dynamics of Irish history at this moment of crisis.

This dialectic between Irish moments of crisis and the cultural treatment of the Great War can be seen most readily with the onset of the Northern Irish 'Troubles' in the final decades of the twentieth century. The renewed attention paid to the First World War in the context of atavistic violence on the streets of the North is wholly understandable. The re-emergence of issues left over from earlier in the century almost inevitably 'brought the Great War to the surface of the Irish literary imagination';

unresolved political questions concerning (Northern) Ireland's place in the Union, the nature of the Irish state and partition, 'stimulated memories and recognitions of a suppressed Irish experience and its contemporary pertinence. The very names in the papers are the same: Ulster Volunteer Force, Sinn Fein, the Irish Republican Army.'[20] The fact that so many parallels could be drawn between the conflicts that stood at either end of Ireland's twentieth century meant that the First World War would now finally have to be engaged with in a much more direct manner than had previously been the case. The trauma experienced by Irish bodies in the First World War (and the Irish wars that followed) now provided an amenable model for examining the underlying forces producing the traumatized bodies that haunted the North during these years.

The most obvious example of this literary re-animation is Jennifer Johnston's *How Many Miles to Babylon?* (1974), which tracks the enduring, but finally doomed, friendship between Alec, a young Protestant from an upper-class family, and Jerry, a young poor Catholic from the local village, who each join the army for very different reasons. Alec joins up because his mother goads him into it, determined as she is that her family should show the commitment to King and Country that befits their Protestant heritage; Jerry joins up because he hopes to learn about warfare and return to apply this knowledge in aid of Irish Republicanism (a paradoxical motivation that was by no means rare). The divisions of class, politics and religion follow the two boys to the Front and tragedy unfolds in the unforgiving landscape. While the horrors of the trenches are brilliantly conjured by Johnston, the novel remains fundamentally about the brutalizing impact of a divisive history on Irish bodies. This dimension is perhaps best seen in the text's melancholic denouement. To save Jerry the indignity of a firing-squad, Alec decides to shoot him in his cell and asks him to sing a song to ease the time. Knowing what is to come, Jerry closes his eyes and begins a lament recalling the history of Irish nationalist rebellion:

> The glitter of his moist unseeing eyes through the lashes. His hands lay limp on the table. I put my left hand on his. His fingers clenched around mine.
> 'I bear no hate against living thing, but I love my country above my King.'
> His eyes opened suddenly. They were blue. He smiled at me.
> 'Now Father bless me and let me go ...'
> I shut my own eyes and pulled with my finger. [...] He fell slowly away from me, his fingers pulling slowly out of my hand.[21]

In contrast to the mechanized violence that surrounds the soldiers, then, the violence with which the novel ends is of an intimate nature, erotic even, a playing out of Irish tribal loyalties and divisions against the backdrop of the Western Front. The image of violence turned inwards – one Irishman shooting another, Irish bodies divided by a history that is beyond their control or comprehension – strongly signals the novel as an exploration of the politicized violence contemporary to its publication.

Using the First World War as a lens for reviewing the complexities of the Northern Irish Troubles – and thus establishing one *historical* set of damaged bodies as a synecdoche for another *contemporary* set – is a technique that Frank McGuiness would also powerfully draw on in his extraordinary play *Observe the Sons of Ulster Marching Towards the Somme* (1985). McGuiness's work confronts its audience not just with the horror of the Somme, as experienced by the 36th (Ulster) Division, but with the continuing – and possibly dangerous – role that the mythology of sacrifice was playing in Northern Ireland.[22] The play opens with Kenneth Pyper, an Ulsterman who saw action at the Somme and is now an old man, confronting the demons left by what he had seen and done. These demons are those of his mind, but also by extension the people who sit in the audience waiting for him to recall the horrors of war:

> I do not understand your insistence on my remembrance. I'm being too mild. I am angry at your demand that I continue to probe. Were you not there in all your dark glory? Have you no conception of the horror? Did it not touch you at all? A passion for horror disgusts me. I have seen horror. There is nothing to tell you. Those willing to talk to you of that day, to remember for your sake, to forgive you, they invent as freely as they wish. I am not one of them. I will not talk, I will not listen to you. Invention gives that slaughter shape. That scale of horror has no shape, as you in your darkness have no shape. Your actions that day were not, they are not acceptable. You have no right to excuse that suffering, parading it for the benefit of others.[23]

The effect of this prologue, with its subtle shifts between past and present tenses, is to double all the action that follows on stage. Pyper wants to resist the questionable urge to replay the horrors of bodies at war; and yet despite his declared refusal the rest of the play takes place because he cannot resist returning to the scene of trauma. The bodies we encounter are thus transformed into meta-signifiers, simultaneously performing the Great War as a lived contemporary event and critiquing the version of it that was being retrospectively constructed in the context of the North's renewed violence. The prologue, moreover, leaves the audience in no doubt about this doubled frame of reference; it draws to a close with the elderly Pyper reminding the audience that 'Ulster lies in rubble at our feet' and pleading 'Save it. Save me.'[24] Later in the play we see Pyper – this time as a young man in the trenches – talking to his own blood, accusing it of signifying the unwanted horrors that lie beyond the trench, and by extension, the horrors that lie beyond the doors of the theatre. As he puts it to a comrade who observes him: 'I was telling it I hate the sight of it.'[25] It is a nuanced moment that signals a refusal, or at least a more complicated reading, of the glorification of Ulster blood spilt at the Somme. In such moments McGuiness reveals the mythologization of the Somme by Ulster Loyalism to be part of the process of 'invention' that gives 'that slaughter shape'. Moreover, it is not just Ulster Loyalism, the play seems to suggest, that is prone to this transformation of historical violence into a suspect rationale for the horrors done to contemporary bodies in the Northern Irish conflict.

Increasingly, then, as we have moved away from the event itself, the Great War has functioned for Irish writers as an imaginative territory against which to examine the inner workings of contemporary society – particularly in its moments of violent crisis or transformation. While the conflict in Northern Ireland has provided one major focus for this cultural process, a second imaginative tendency has turned its attention to the fate of southern Ireland's Anglo-Irish communities. Jennifer Johnston's work in particular has often sought out the anxieties of a once-dominant people left stranded by the historical turn around the First World War and its immediate aftermath in Ireland. In novels such as *The Captains and the Kings* (1972) and *Fool's Sanctuary* (1987), as well as the more recent *This Is Not A Novel* (2002), time and again we encounter the lost bodies of the Anglo-Irish – men and women who have been left to rattle round Big Houses as remnants (or perhaps revenants) of an alternative Irish history.

The first of J.G. Farrell's 'Empire Trilogy', *Troubles* (1970), provides another example of this tendency in Irish writing.[26] Here the crumbling Majestic Hotel becomes a final retreat for an elderly population of Anglo-Irish figures in the years immediately after the Great War. They are protected, as best he can, by Major Archer; recently returned from the Great War; but as the novel develops Archer himself begins to feel increasingly trapped in a world he struggles to comprehend. Indeed as the novel progresses the hotel's increasingly decrepit inhabitants appear evermore like internal refugees. When someone mentions the Easter Rising, for example, the proprietor of the Majestic responds to it as if to a personal (bodily) attack: '"stabbed us in the back!" Edward bellowed with a kind of pain, almost as if he had felt the knife enter between his own shoulder-blades. "We were fighting to protect them and they stabbed us in the back".'[27] As in much of Johnston's work, ageing Anglo-Irish bodies are found fading away, all the while struggling – and failing – to find a place in a historical narrative that was leaving little room for them. In this context their corporeal dissolution – as we near the text's end they are described increasingly in terms reminiscent of living corpses – becomes a marker of the death of the Anglo-Irish as a class. The fact that Farrell's novel was published in 1970 locates it additionally as a meditation on the relationship between this earlier schism in Irish history and the one that was then gathering pace in the North – the tensions he describes, and the groups involved in conflict, clearly resonate with those dominating the news reports of the early 1970s.

Writing war after the peace? Sebastian Barry and the politics of absence

As demonstrated in the quite different work of Johnston, Farrell and McGuiness, until relatively recently Irish writing's engagement with the First World War has been dominated by two major interconnected concerns – the war as a trigger for the end of Anglo-Irish hegemony, and the war as an imaginative model for unpacking those unresolved issues that drove the Northern Irish conflict. In recent years, however, a new phase has emerged in Ireland's cultural relationship with the First World War. The success of the Northern Irish Peace process (begun in the mid-1990s) has led to an ideological 'loosening' in relation to the First World War and those Irishmen who signed up to fight in the British Army. Particularly for Irish nationalism, this loosening has entailed an acknowledgement of this history as not simply the cultural concern of Irish Unionism and/or Protestantism. On 11 November 1998, for example, in Messines, near Ypres, the Irish President, Mary McAleese, and Britain's Queen Elizabeth II jointly unveiled a monument commemorating the actions of the 36th (Ulster) Division and the 16th (Irish) Division, at the place where they fought side by side in 1917 and each endured severe losses. To add to the symbolic register, the monument took the form of an Irish round tower built by workers from both sides of the border.[28] Perhaps even more significantly – in terms of Ireland's internal political landscape – in 2002 the then Sinn Fein Lord

Mayor of Belfast, Alex Maskey, laid a wreath at the City Hall Cenotaph to commemorate the dead of the First World War. Maskey commented that his actions were 'in recognition of the sorrow, hurt and suffering left behind for their relatives, friends and comrades. My objective, beyond this, is to seek to identify common ground for all of us in this generation.'[29]

This shift in political culture has been accompanied by a literary interest in those First World War Irish narratives and bodies that were not necessarily accommodated by the fixation on the fate of the Anglo-Irish and/or the recent conflict in the North. The dual impact of the First World War and the Easter Rising on Dublin's working-class communities, for example, is explored in Roddy Doyle's *A Star Called Henry* (1999) – seventy years on from Sean O'Casey's disregarded attempt to do the same thing. At the heart of the novel stands Henry Smart, a renegade Dublin street-child whose key role in the Easter Rising – as imaginatively created by Doyle – will in the end find no place in the official versions of this event. Doyle's description of the Easter Rising is also haunted at its margins by Ireland's lost bodies of the First World War: the working-class men who join the British Army to stave off starvation for their families; the women left behind to keep those families going on the meagre money provided by the army's 'separation allowance'. Indeed a group of these women arrive at the GPO in the midst of the Rising intent on collecting their money from the British government; as Henry puts it: 'They were here to collect their allowances. Their men were over in France, or dead under the muck. And the shawlies wanted their money.'[30] A little later, having been refused their allowances by the rebels now in charge of the GPO, the women make their feelings clear about an insurrection during a war that had taken their men – again we see the scene from Henry's vantage point:

– Give us our money, yeh bastards!
The glass was falling all around us, its dust like sugar on our clothes and skin.
– Fuckin' wasters! Playing at being soldiers.
– And our husbands off doing the real fighting.
– Bastards!
The officers came and hauled and kicked us off the floor.
– The Tommies'll tan your arses for yis![31]

For these people the realities of the Great War, and for that matter of the Easter Rising, are a long way from the concerns of the redundant

Big House inhabitants as encountered in Johnston's novels. They are also a long way, of course, from the narratives of self-sacrifice, national destiny and martyrdom, which will be brought to bear on this event by Irish nationalism. The presence of these voices and their resistant bodies in Doyle's text signals a desire to re-inscribe them within conceptions of this ideologically loaded period.

This same sort of desire powers the work of Sebastian Barry, although the targets which are its focus are quite different to those of Doyle. In a sense Barry's work can be seen as offering a counterpart to that of Jennifer Johnston, but instead of Johnston's concern for the fate of the Anglo-Irish in the wake of the Great War, Barry has been more interested in those elements of the Catholic population who struggled to find a place in the version of Ireland that emerged after independence. Barry has repeatedly returned to the fate of those Irish Catholics whose innate conservatism produced a loyalty to the ideas of British monarchy, Union and Empire – sometimes known (derogatively) as 'Castle Catholics'. His 1995 play *The Steward of Christendom*, for example, presents the final days of Thomas Dunne in an institution for the mentally unwell. As a younger man, Thomas had been high up in the Dublin Metropolitan Police (DMP), an organization with its base in Dublin Castle, the heart of Britain's colonial machinery in Ireland. In the years after independence this connection is a problematic one, and Thomas's harsh treatment in the care home presents his body as the target of a repressed anger. One of the orderlies (Smith) who has been directed (by Mrs O'Dea) to bath Thomas gives vent to this repressed energy, displaying a wish to obliterate bodies such as Thomas from the historical record. On this occasion Smith has been riled by the memory of the DMP's actions during the 1913 lock-out – an event that would leave many of Dublin's working-class destitute and with little option but to join the Army in 1914:

> Chief superintendent, this big gobshite was, Mrs O'Dea, that killed four good men and true in O'Connell Street in the days of the lock-out. [...] Baton-charging. A big loyal Catholic gobshite killing poor hungry Irishmen. If you weren't an old madman we'd flay you.[32]

Tellingly, Thomas is haunted in this fearful place by the ghost of his son Willie, who died in France in 1918. Willie's ghostly figure as it moves silently across the stage adds another layer of corporeal signification to the play's action. The dual fate of these two Catholic bodies in the wake of the war – one hidden in life, the other hidden by death – reveals their problematic status in an Irish society increasingly obsessed by the twin narratives of Catholicism and nationalism. Providing a form of supplement to Jennifer Johnston's lost Anglo-Irish bodies, Barry's work explores another set of excluded Irish bodies, those whose alignment of Catholicism and loyalty to Crown and Union ran counter to Irish nationalism's post-independence self-image.

In 2005 Barry would return to the figure of Willie Dunne in his novel *A Long Long Way*; but this time Barry addresses Willie's story directly. *A Long Long Way* is the most sustained attempt by a modern Irish novelist to engage with the visceral horrors endured by (southern) Irish soldiers in the trenches of Europe. It is also, moreover, a subtle exploration of the conditions that have made such a direct engagement difficult in the past. This is a novel, then, not just about Ireland's 'missing of the war', but about the processes that produced this condition of absence. *A Long Long Way* may be read as a form of meta-text, charting not just the Great War as contemporary event but the after-life of this event as it has been processed by Ireland's competing ideological formations. In this regard, Geoff Dyer invokes a special tense that he suggests comes into play when we write or think about First World War combatants. Even when we encounter them alive in images or texts, Dyer argues, these bodies will always be those *who will have died*.[33] While in the British canon of war-writing we could add that these are men *who will have died* but '*never be forgotten*', in the context of southern Irish soldiers the tense needs some adjusting – these are men *who will have died* and *will have been forgotten*.

The operation of this over-determined tense is evident right from the opening of the novel: 'He was born in the dying days. It was the withering end of 1896. [...] The new babies screeched inside the thick grey walls of the Rotunda Hospital. Blood gathered on the nurses' white laps like the aprons of butchers.'[34] Willie's birth ('in the dying days') is here not the start of a life but rather the first of a chain of events leading to inevitable death: Willie's body is born to die in the war. Again we can see the unsettling temporality – the shadow of a future erasure – inscribed onto Willie's body in the description of his diminutive size: 'He was a little baby and would be always a little boy. He was like the thin upper arm of a beggar with a few meagre bones shot through him, provisional and bare' (3). Willie's 'provisional' stature, and thus status, as a baby suggests a body that will never be fully present in the world; and this is the point of course, we already know that Willie, together with those thousands of Irishmen like him, is destined to find himself in a historical no-man's land mapped by a future silence. Theirs is a doubly complex fate – presence that leads to erasure.

As a result Barry's text seeks not simply to remember, but to acknowledge the non-remembrance, to sound out its silences. A central strategy of this project is Barry's drive to reinsert Irish bodies, like that of the loyal Catholic Willie, into the network of participants in the 1914–18 conflict:

> And all those boys of Europe born in those times, and thereabouts those times, Russian, French, Belgian, Serbian, Irish, English, Scottish, Welsh, Italian, Prussian, German, Austrian, Turkish – and Canadian, Australian, American, Zulu, Gurkha, Cossack, and all the rest – their fate was written in a ferocious chapter of the book of life, certainly. (4)

Those participants we most readily associate (remember) as key players in the First World War (English, German, French, American) are here reunited with those who have been marginalized in the canonical histories and fictions – Irish, Zulu, Cossack. In the place of separate (nationalized) histories of the war, we find an inclusive re-inscription of bodies playing their part in a single narrative. Time and again we find Willie's narrative scanning a world populated by those who would eventually fade out of common conceptions of the war. In a letter home to his girl Gretta, for example, Willie writes:

> There are Chinese diggers everywhere and black lads and the Gurkhas looking fierce, the whole Empire, Gretta. And I don't know what nation is not here, unless it is only the Hottentots and the pygmies stayed at home. But maybe they are here too, only we can't see them so low in the trenches. (38)

The implication is that a full recuperation of these marginalized narratives would have to include southern Irish soldiers in its purview. Indeed at one point Willie and his comrades are described as practically merging with those other forgotten bodies of the war: 'They ate like dogs and shat like kings. They stripped to the waist and got black as desert Arabs. The white skins were disappearing. Mayo, Wicklow, it didn't matter. They might be Algerians now, some other bit of the blessed Empire' (54). The metaphor of war's commonality of experience is thus mapped onto the skins of those from across the globe who met on the Western Front. It is a moment, of course, that also locates the Irish soldiers as imbricated in a war-machine reliant on an imperial substructure – the very systemic linkage that will complicate their histories in the post-war years.

This concern for the after-life of Ireland's Great War soldiers also shadows the novel's description of the mass graves encountered by Willie, graves dug by Chinese auxiliaries but destined for Irish bodies: 'The Chinamen dug the holes, five hundred of them. They were filled with Catholic, Protestant and Jewish Irishmen' (54). Here Irish bodies at war merge in death in a manner that resists, or refutes even, the divergent narratives that will later be applied to them. Writing in the early 1990s about the different legacies of the Great War for Ireland's various political communities, for example, Keith Jeffrey was forced to conclude that 'the sombre truth remains that the nationalist and unionist Irish casualties of the Great War became more divided in death than they had ever been in life'.[35] We could add that the literary tendency to present the First World War as a synecdoche for the Northern Irish conflict has, paradoxically, reinforced this division. Read in this light, the return to the shared mass grave in *A Long Long Way* marks a return to source, a return to an originary point in narrative that robs subsequent divisions of their sense and their material.

The ontological complexity of this period – as opposed to its neat bifurcation into politicized epistemologies in subsequent years – is explored most explicitly in those sections of the novel dealing with 1916, sections that stand at the ideological heart of the work. Crucially, Willie is granted home-leave just before Easter 1916; he thus acts as a conduit between two different political visions, between two different instances of politicized violence. More importantly, Barry brings Willie face to face with the rebels who launch the Easter Rising; at the end of his leave Willie's troop is diverted on their return to France out of Dublin and instructed to help quell the violence that has erupted. The scenes around them initially cause confusion among the returning soldiers; at first they think they are witnessing a German invasion. But as Willie comforts one of the shot rebels the misunderstanding is clarified: 'Willie knelt down to him. "I'm not going to shoot you," he said. "Are you a German?" "German?" said the man. "German? What are you talking about? I'm an Irishman. We're all Irishmen in here, fighting for Ireland"' (92). The realization that he and his fellow soldiers have been asked to subdue their fellow Irishmen haunts Willie for the rest of the novel. For the remainder of the narrative, in place of radically separate histories, Barry constantly replays the Easter Rising in its Great War context, and he does so in a way that reinforces the interconnectedness of this dual turning-point in Irish history. We are told, for example, that Willie carries the young rebel's blood back 'to Belgium on his uniform' (97), an image that locates Willie's story as understandable only in terms of a web of connected historical ruptures. It is a move that also ensures the continuing relationship between the events and bodies on the Western Front and those back in Dublin. This doubled interpretative lens frames everything that happens after the short return home of Easter 1916.

We can see this most clearly in an incident that occurs shortly after Willie's return to the Front, when he is called to bear witness to a radical rejection of all the war stood for, a rejection generated by events back in Ireland. Jesse Kirwan, whom Willie had met briefly back in their Dublin barracks, hears the news that the leaders of the Easter Rising have been executed by the British authorities. The news propels Jesse into a new reading of his situation, forcing him to conclude that he is in the 'wrong' war, wearing the wrong uniform, and fighting the wrong enemy. As he tells Willie:

> I thought it was a good thing. It seemed like a good thing. But it's not a good thing now. I'm not making a big thing out of it. [...] But I won't serve in the uniform that lads wore when they shot those other lads. I can't. I'm not eating so I can shrink, and not be touching the cloth of this uniform, you know? I am trying to disappear, I suppose. (155)

Jesse Kirwan's act of refusal, his attempt to 'disappear', foreshadows the fissures that will open up in Irish history in the wake of 1916. Kirwan's Kafkaesque act of shrinking (going on hunger strike) enacts his future historiographical erasure on his still living body. Barry presents Kirwan in a nightmarish scenario – his body is to be punished by one set of ideological imperatives (those attendant to his status as a volunteer in the British Army) because of his allegiance to another set of imperatives that have erupted into clear view in a rapidly changing Ireland. His tragedy is that he already knows he will be rejected by the historical forces that he in fact feels loyalty towards. The sense that this paradoxical position occupies a space that will become the locus of a silence is reinforced by Jesse's parting words to Willie: 'You see, what it is Willie, I want a witness to my plight, but not a witness that will say a word about it, and I know you can do that' (156).

Willie's experience of the Easter Rising is subsequently juxtaposed with the action of the Somme. Reading these events in light of each other, Willie concludes that 'the distance between the site of war and the site of home was a long one and widening. Not the ordinary pragmatic miles between, but some other, more mysterious measure of distance' (190).

Barry here allows Willie to inhabit the same kind of self-knowledge as expressed by Tom Kettle above. Like Kettle, Willie comes to realize that he will find no place in the body politic then emerging in revolutionary Ireland: 'All sorts of Irelands were no more, and he didn't know what Ireland there was behind him now. But he feared he was not a citizen, they would not let him be a citizen' (246). In such moments Barry provides Willie with a double-consciousness – a consciousness that simultaneously struggles to comprehend its present trauma and its future absence from the record. At the end of the novel, set just a month before the end of the war, Willie maps out the boundaries of his own exclusion; more than ever he senses that history has shifted and he has found himself homeless:

> How could a fella go out and fight for his country when his country would dissolve behind him like sugar in the rain? How could a fella love his uniform when that same uniform killed the new heroes, as Jesse Kirwan said? [...] What would his sisters do for succour and admiration in their own country, when their own country had gone? They were like these Belgian citizens toiling along the roads with their chattels and tables and pots, except they were entirely unlike them, because, destitute though these people were, and homeless, at least they were wandering and lost in their own land. (287)

The image of belief and purpose dissolving in the rain is one of history as trauma, of war as existential crisis; but it is also an image of the crisis enveloping the Irish bodies of the Great War. These are the war bodies that will be made radically homeless by their involvement in war – a tragic kind of catch-22. In the end Willie is killed in battle and buried near where he falls in northern France; the final image of his makeshift grave establishes his dead body as the site of a much-needed cultural archaeology. In this way Barry's novel sets out the ideological coordinates of a still current problem for Irish identity – to make at home all those 'un-homely' bodies stranded by a history that moved away from them.

Notes

1. Fran Brearton, *The Great War in Irish Poetry* (Oxford: Oxford University Press, 2000), 3.
2. See Thomas Hennessey, *Dividing Ireland: World War One and Partition* (London: Routledge, 1998).
3. For more on this see Gillian McIntosh, *The Force of Culture: Unionist Identities in Twentieth-Century Ireland* (Cork: Cork University Press, 1999).

4. Cited in Edna Longley, *The Living Stream: Literature and Revisionism in Ireland* (Newcastle upon Tyne: Bloodaxe Books, 1994), 77.
5. Edna Longley, 'The Great War, History, and the English Lyric', in Vincent Sherry (ed.), *The Cambridge Companion to the Literature of the First World War* (Cambridge: Cambridge University Press, 2005), 57–84; 57.
6. Adrian Gregory and Senia Pašeta, 'Introduction', in Adrian Gregory and Senia Pašeta (eds), *Ireland and the Great War: 'A war to unite us all?'* (Manchester: Manchester University Press, 2002), 5.
7. As Fran Brearton puts it: 'the war has been, and to some extent still remains, a taboo subject in Ireland, marginalised by history in the south and heavily politicised in the north'. *The Great War in Irish Poetry*, 9.
8. Whenever this involvement is recalled in Ireland there is a tendency to privilege in imaginative focus the Western Front – this is particularly so in Ulster where the horrific losses suffered on the Somme remain as key representative deaths in Ulster Loyalism's martyrology. But Irish soldiers saw action, and bore considerable losses, in many other of the war's key theatres (for example, in Gallipoli and Palestine). For more on this history of involvement see Myles Dungan, *They Shall Grow Not Old: Irish Soldiers and the Great War* (Dublin: Four Courts Press, 1997); Terence Denman, *Ireland's Unknown Soldiers* (Dublin: Irish Academic Press, 1992).
9. One could add a fourth position here, the call for Irish neutrality – a position that many nationalists would have adhered to but is to a certain extent written out of the histories of this politically charged period. For more on the various nationalist positions on the war, see Patrick Maume, *The Long Gestation: Irish Nationalist Life 1891–1918* (Dublin: Gill and Macmillan, 1999).
10. 'Home Rule' as it was commonly known was a bid for constitutional reform in Ireland – 'Home Rulers', or constitutional nationalists, campaigned for the devolution of powers to a more independent Ireland. The third Home Rule Bill (first presented to the Westminster Parliament in 1912) was on the statute books by 1914, but its enactment was suspended pending the end of the war – as it turned out this never happened, the end of the European conflict was followed by the onset of war in Ireland.
11. Cited in Brearton, *The Great War in Irish Poetry*, 11.
12. Longley, *The Living Stream*, 78.
13. Cited in Keith Jeffrey, *Ireland and the Great War* (Cambridge: Cambridge University Press, 2000), 61.
14. Terence Brown, 'Who Dares to Speak? Ireland and the Great War', in Robert Clark and Piero Boitani (eds), *English Studies in Transition* (London: Routledge, 1993), 226–37; 229.
15. For more on this see Brearton, *The Great War in Irish Poetry* and Brown, 'Who Dares to Speak?'
16. Brown, 'Who Dares to Speak?', 229.
17. The three texts are collected together in a recent edition: Patrick MacGill, *Rifleman MacGill's War: The London Irish Trilogy* (London: Leonaur, 2007).
18. Brown, 'Who Dares to Speak?', 230.
19. Patrick Sheeran cited in Jeffrey, *Ireland and the Great War*, 99.
20. Brown, 'Who Dares to Speak?', 230.
21. Jennifer Johnston, *How Many Miles to Babylon?* (Harmondsworth: Penguin, 1988), 155.

82   *Conflict, Nationhood and Corporeality in Modern Literature*

4
'Soft-skinned Vehicle': Reading the Second World War in Tom Paulin's *The Invasion Handbook*

Mark Rawlinson

I tried to read my evening paper. Herr Hitler had re-affirmed the principle of the Rome-Berlin collaboration. Signor Mussolini had made another speech from the balcony of the Palazzo di Venezia. The chairman of an armaments combine had announced that profits for the previous year had proved extremely satisfactory and had expressed confidence in the future of the company. Another Balkan state had gone Fascist. A Croat living in the Paris suburbs had dismembered his mistress's body with a hatchet. A banker had welcomed improved prospects for foreign lending. There were two pictures on the front page: one of two grinning and embarrassed soldiers riding on a new type of tank, the other of a famous statesman, looking like an apprehensive vulture, with a fishing-rod in one hand and a very small fish in the other. On page four was an article entitled: 'In thy strength O Britain...' by an ex-naval officer, who, I happened to know, was also a director of a naval construction yard.[1]

This briskly efficient establishing paragraph in Eric Ambler's 1938 spy-thriller, *Cause for Alarm* draws on the heterogeneous juxtapositions of the newspaper to allude to a panoramic apperception of the late 1930s (the device is similar to the choric function of radio and listener in Auden and Isherwood's *The Ascent of* F6). This chapter is about the formal potential for using the newspaper, which Marinetti, the futurist glorifier of war, called 'the synthesis of a day in the world's life' as a template for a poetic historiography of Britain's Second World War.[2]

> A whole people and more
> who're stuffed inside
> this exposed island hideout[3]

In Tom Paulin's lines a tarpaulined lorry becomes a bird-watcher's hide (a camouflage motif), then, in a cosmic and historical telescoping, the island which once had 'walls of oak', a metaphor born of naval mastery, is itself a 'soft-skinned vehicle' in which are crammed – 'like prisoners waiting to die' – myriad soft-skinned persons ('we are the shield') (172). It is largely through a capacity for a critical and inventive revision of familiar historical milestones and military icons that *The Invasion Handbook* (2002) makes a significant contribution to the re-imagination of the Second World War. In an era when the cultural reproduction of the war's legacies and traces is accelerating – the major anglophone genres of literary memorialization are supplemented now by newly emergent European and post-Imperial memory-works – *The Invasion Handbook* eschews the dominant cognitive framework of the historicized Second World War and with it the common currency of narrative. In its place, the body and the voice emerge as alternatives to historical abstractions which are aligned in the dominant narratives of the war.

The Invasion Handbook is, significantly, a product of state patronage, its author in receipt of a National Endowment for Science, Technology and the Arts (NESTA) Fellowship. But Paulin's 'looseleaf epic' (18) nevertheless plangently contests many orthodoxies of public or popular history. Additionally, Paulin seeks to reorient national historical consciousness, and rituals of memorialization, away from a cultural obsession with war as tragedy and defeat (1914–18) towards a memorial re-engagement with the victorious Britain of the Second World War.[4] Paulin 'voices' the past through a gallery of impersonations which counterpoint the story of state relations. This juxtaposition of the embodiedness of personal agents and matters of state is reflected in a further, and more familiar, opposition between the frail flesh of persons and the violent abstractions of the militarized state, between the wound and the weapon.

Paulin's approach to versifying the war is well-described by a dust-jacket puff which tells us how the poet 'sets out to recount the origins of the Second World War' with a 'simultaneous vision which proceeds by quotation and collage, catalogue and caption, prose as well as verse – a myriad staging of historical realities through [his] intense and penetrating scrutiny of the particulars of time and place'. Paulin is not the first writer to assume such historical and affective aspirations. Here is the text from another dust-jacket, protected for fifty years by the cellophane cover added by staff at Sir Jonathan North Girls School, Leicester:

> In this clear, concise account of the Second World War, written especially for young people, Katharine Savage has spread a large canvas. With confidence and authority she draws boldly and vigorously the pattern of events in every theatre of war. She suggests with remarkable insight the interaction of powerful personalities; sees with compassion the suffering of war's innocent victims the world over [...]. The result is a comprehensive, authentic picture of the war, presented simply, fluently and vividly. The reader may come to the book for its story and find at the end he has absorbed history. He will discover in its pages the war as it came to ordinary men and women, for Katharine Savage sees not only with the informed eye but with the eye of her fellow countrymen shaken out of the false security of the inter-war years into the ordeal, and often heroism, of war.[5]

The striking similarity in the way these blurbs anticipate a readerly response – 'simultaneous vision'/'pattern of events'; 'penetrating scrutiny'/'informed eye'; 'particulars of time and place'/'as it came to ordinary men and women' – is only underlined by the ostensive contrast in *style*. Paulin's (post?)modernist aesthetic – 'quotation and collage, catalogue and caption' – marks an antithesis to Savage's 'story', but the projected end is the same: through the 'staging of historical realities'/'[the reader] has absorbed history'. Can literary form really make so little difference? In the context of contemporary discourses of trauma, which figure war, memory or history as the unrecoverable or the radically inarticulable, the purported loquaciousness and fluency of these texts when it comes to re-presenting past struggle may appear a sign of historical naivety.

But at the same time we should not overstate the convergence. Frank Kermode has justly pointed out the difficulties – of a modernist kind – that lie in wait for the reader of *The Invasion Handbook*, and the way its allusive, even obscurantist presentation of its historical and literary reference can seem to require of the reader an effort of learning comparable to the author's: 'you will need to do quite a lot of research to figure out what Paulin is doing'.[6] But neither the pedagogic nor the modernist description, though each is warranted, is a wholly satisfactory account of the genre of *The Invasion Handbook*, and of just how this particular variant of the modern long aggregate poem (*The Waste Land, Autumn Journal, History: the Home Movie*) assembles and orients its component forms and voices.

The Invasion Handbook bears comparison in its range with A.J.P. Taylor's notorious *The Origins of the Second World War* (1961) or Henry Williamson's *A Chronicle of Ancient Sunlight* (1951–69), both of which were concerned to protest the 'moral validity' of the Versailles Treaty, and each of which has been criticized as an apology for Hitler.[7] Forty or more years on, with Cold War dualities no longer obligatory, the idea that Hitler was not the sole mover behind the Second World War is uncontroversial and indeed Paulin's roll-call of interwar diplomatists points up global conspiracies of class and self-interest. For instance, the self-fashioning of Australian Brendan Bracken into king-maker to Churchill is echoed by the Duke of Windsor's likely restoration to the throne, according to a primer for the conquering *Wehrmacht* in England, 'The Invasion Handbook', which also predicts the elevation of Oswald Mosley to PM and Williamson to the Laureateship (181). Another section, a poem, 'Boca di Inferno', reveals a state secret, Hitler's wedding present to the Windsors, and a solution to the Hess mystery, which resolves on the welding of the Iron Cross First Class to the Crown (175).[8] Paulin's characteristic verbal inventiveness, his eye for the uncanny as well as for antimonies, results in some perplexing juxtapositions. The playgrounds of the international rich – the Ritz and Biarritz – call forth an unspoken rhyme in a place 'far away to the east' (Auschwitz) (109). Soviet prisoners in the Kolyma gulag (the white Auschwitz beyond Siberia) have 'other things on their minds' than the fact that Goering reminds Halifax of the 'head gamekeeper at Chatsworth' (138).

Despite the increasing capaciousness of our concept of the Second World War, constantly enlarged by new ways of writing history (gender, Empire) and by the imaginative investigation of the interstices and lacunae overlooked by existing narratives (and thus constituting various secret histories), the heterogeneity of this material puts the design of *The Invasion Handbook* under some pressure. Ostensibly more integrated than a book-length collection of poems, the work is inscrutable, its movements between the global and local, the familiar and the deliberately obscure confound efforts to assimilate its procedures to existing narratives or to recognize in them a clear-cut critical or revisionist stance.

A form which clearly preoccupied Paulin (who is an essayist and broadcaster, as well as a teacher, critic and poet) during his work on the Second World War was the newspaper. *The Invasion Handbook* alludes indirectly to Hegel's widely quoted aphorism equating reading the daily paper with morning prayers – these activities are a source of security, of knowing where one stands, an orientation respectively to the world and to God. The reference also appears in 'Many Cunning Passages', a contemporary essay on T.S. Eliot and Versailles.[9] Here Paulin asserts the relations of two major voices in his poem – those of the economist J.M. Keynes and of Eliot – in a more explicit, and indeed pedagogically insistent manner. The essay's strained assertions of causality and influence are a good measure of Paulin's success in *The Invasion Handbook* in working out a formal structure (image and juxtaposition) which transcends the claims of documentary authority. With these hints, it is worth inquiring in what way might the newspaper itself be a model for understanding the form of Paulin's poem.

'Many Cunning Passages' makes the case that *The Waste Land* is 'the greatest poem of the First World War'. Paulin's thesis is that Eliot was attuned to current events as both a newspaper reader and a newspaper correspondent, and that *The Waste Land* 'aims at the immediacy of journalism (Hegel remarks that the daily newspaper is "the realist's morning prayer")'. Paulin amplifies an idea of Walter Allen's that Eliot's, as well as Whitman's, purpose was 'to seize and recapitulate history in an eternal present' with his own temporal trope echoing the Eliot of *Four Quartets*: 'that present is a type of stretched, eternal beginning – like a huge morning newspaper'.[10]

The Invasion Handbook is then both epic and newspaper, genres which are formally disjunct but functionally comparable. For Benedict Anderson, the newspaper both symbolizes and synchronizes a national consciousness.[11] In *Ulysses* Joyce writes '[o]ur national epic has yet to be written': the comedy extracted from this sense of belatedness derives in part from the 'Bullockbefriending' Stephen's efforts to place headmaster Deasy's letter about foot and mouth in the national press ('The pigs' paper').[12] Paulin himself plays on the hierarchy of genres and timescales to formulate his 'looseleaf epic' as a tissue of present beginnings, rather than a forged, historical retrospect. He earlier described John Le Carré as 'a devout and brilliant myth-maker who has raised the jargon of office politics into the terms of a national epic', anticipating his own location of the epic in the prosaic, the overlooked and the inconsequential in the procedures of *The Invasion Handbook*.[13]

These stylistic features are anticipated, on a smaller scale, in Paulin's poem 'Waftage: an Irregular Ode', which layers private and public voices. This demotic monologue of soured sex nevertheless succeeds in voicing a citation from the seventies' Le Carré (the world of George Smiley) as well as an anecdote about the poet of the found detail James Fenton (an English Kurt Schwitters in his *Exempla*), in order to point up the attributes of a mixed mode of writing, '*the subterfugue text / within the text itself*.[14] As we shall see, practices of embedding, and the practices of reading between the lines to which the reader is called upon to respond, are central to the effect of *The Invasion Handbook*.

It is in this context that 'Give Us This Day' in *The Invasion Handbook* recalls Hegel and the terms of the Eliot/Keynes essay both more explicitly, and with a reflexive twist. The stylized casualness of the citation of the idea of the secular correlative of prayer– 'so Hegel says (don't ask me where)' – counterpoints Paulin's antiquarian allusiveness with the constellation of meanings produced in daily acts of attention to the diurnal text of the newspaper.

> – i.e. the light of day
> the sun's rays
> falling on its flimsy text
> falling more like it on your reading
> of its flimsy text
> that is of course ephemeral. (150)

It is fruitful to think of the forms which evoke the ephemeral and contingent in *The Invasion Handbook* as eliciting readings mindful of their own constitutive role in suturing what is ephemerally and arbitrarily arranged (by what Anderson calls 'calendrical coincidence'):

> as you silently intone
> this new day's chapter
> of accidents
> and make it *read*
> – for *read* read *real*. (151)

By transposing the chapters of accident onto a historical and a national axis, Paulin has put a premium on the question of how to read them (make it read), and on the relationship between their imagined coalescence and the history that they annotate.

A sense of what a modern epic might owe to national newspapers is suggested by the way the papers were conceptualized as a cognitive and imaginative resource in wartime (modern epic here does not converge on Franco Moretti's rethinking of modernism, but designates something altogether more parochial, a national epic for the age of extremes).[15] In a report for the Wartime Social Survey, Louis Moss and Kathleen

Box asserted that 'about 24,000,000 civilians see morning newspapers' (the research questionnaire they were using in June and July 1943 led off by asking 'Did you see a Morning Paper yesterday?')[16] This is precisely the 'extraordinary mass-ceremony; the almost precisely simultaneous consumption ("imagining") of the newspaper-as-fiction' of which Anderson writes in *Imagined Communities*.[17] This mass of regular readers is complemented by the mass of text thereby consumed. 'Most people read a million words a year' observed Denis Thompson in 1939, as he embarked on a diagnosis of how more reading meant less exacting reading.[18] In *Between the Acts* (1941), Woolf describes Isa's generation as both 'gun-shy' and 'book-shy': 'for her generation the newspaper was a book'.[19] Thompson's book, published in the early months of the war, looked back to the role of newsprint in creating the meanings (for instance, Germans described 'as obscene animals', 'hatred and the desire for revenge') of 1914–18 which in turn shaped the peace of 1919.[20] He was offering a primer in the practical criticism of newspaper suasion: propaganda in war, advertising in peace.

Ways in which civilians are in the thick of war's communiqués and information blackouts are well-suggested by an immediately post-war text, begun in wartime: newspaper reading lies at the heart of Elizabeth Bowen's designs in describing proletarian Londoners in *The Heat of the Day* (1949). Patrician characters like Robert and Stella are formed by the long-term sedimentation of family and class repressions, but lowlier citizens are forged by more ephemeral forces and their ephemeral reactions to them. Connie, a gregarious warden, is an inveterate consumer of papers and had 'almost always been reading one just recently', embodying the Wartime Social Survey's findings concerning the cycle of consumption and reproduction of news in the workplace and home.[21] Connie is, however, a 'suspicious' reader on the model supplied by Denis Thompson, impeding or doubling her reading in a re-reading 'between the lines' (147). Her acolyte Louie, imitating Connie's 'addiction', is by contrast 'infatuated' by these daily verbal representations: 'If you could not keep track of what was happening you could at least take notice of what was said' (144). Bowen's jokes at Louie's expense provide one model of 'history in an eternal present', namely a daily condensation of contingency: 'For the paper's sake, Louie brought herself to put up with any amount of news – the headlines got that over for you in half a second, deciding for you every event's importance by the size of the print' (145). The spoof newspaper *The Onion* exploits this typographical logic in an imagined headline for 3 September 1939:

 – HEADLINE CONTINUED ON PAGE 2.[22]

Bowen's obvious enjoyment in mocking an 'imagined community' (an emergency English social order produced by wartime newsprint) is almost as exorbitant, threatening to make puppets of some of her characters, and fatally dividing them from more autonomous centres of consciousness, such as is represented by Stella Rodney. It is as if life itself is breathed into Louie only by 'true stories, which made the war seem human' (145), an irony on warfare's modern inhumanities of which she remains unaware. Bowen further surrenders the roundedness of her creature by having her regularly interpellated on the inside pages of the papers, addressed in her war-economy roles as 'a worker, a soldier's lonely wife, a war orphan, a pedestrian, a Londoner' and so on (146).

Of course, our sense of the spuriousness of such identities is revised by revelations in the patrician espionage plot, in which lover Robert turns out to be a spy (a story too far-fetched, perhaps, for the papers). Nevertheless, the broad comedy of the close reading of mass culture is unmistakeable: Louie and Connie are victim and rebel respectively in a dramatization of Denis Thompson's case that 'it is cardinal in newspaper policy that readers should not think'.[23] But the components of this per-spective- or identity-making, in particular the values of 'true stories', and the conviction that knowing 'what is said' compensates for not knowing, are given further twist in *The Invasion Handbook*. Bringing them together with our sense of the book's essentially fragmentary presentation, and mindful of Paulin's idea of 'the present' as 'a type of stretched, eternal beginning', we begin to see how *The Invasion Handbook* isn't at all what it says on the cover (a guide to a landfall never made) but is really 'like a huge morning newspaper'.[24] The fruitfulness of this model is most evident in relation to the practice of 'reading between the lines' which Paulin's form invites from us, for *The Invasion Handbook* is both spatially and temporally analogous to a newspaper. Its component poems jostle each other for front-page billing, or retire from attention, buried away on the inside pages, like the stories dispersed through the morning paper, but they are arrayed too in a historical series; in, as it were, a flickering succes-sion of headlines (Hollywood's device for indicating the 'abysm of time'). But this reading between the lines is not solely a suspicious reading.

'Myths are rare nowadays', Paulin has written, 'possibly because we have become dull positivists who mistake imaginative explanations for lies.'[25]

So rather than telling a story about the Second World War, we might think of *The Invasion Handbook* as reconfiguring, reconstellating, stories about the Second World War with 'imaginative explanations'. We are not, however, talking about the kinds of stories that are compounded into the classic Second World War narratives of multiple, emergency-coordinated lives, such as Norman Mailer's *The Naked and the Dead* (1948) or Marge Piercy's *Gone to Soldiers* (1988). Paulin's stories are historical, not fictional. And the voices of his poems are literally the voices of representatives (many unelected), not symbolically representative types. But these public figures are heard off-air or *in camera*: Paulin's origins of the Second World War is not the story recoverable from the dictionary of quotations, but a tissue of apparent ephemera. This is a further sense in which the newspaper provides us with an informative model. As Anderson notes, 'the essential literary convention of the newspaper' is 'the essential arbitrariness' of the 'inclusion and juxtaposition' of murders, coups, fossils, speeches and football results, which shows 'that the linkage between them is imaginary'.[26] This is why the newspaper is fit emblem for the imagined community, the 'community in anonymity', and why it serves Paulin as a template for an epic we have to 'imagine'.[27]

The contrivance of a sense of contingency in *The Invasion Handbook* has a number of effects. 'Looseleaf epic' works to counter the inevitability of what we all know in hindsight about victory in the Second World War (which in turn is a different thing to the inevitability that Paulin, and Keynes, and Henry Williamson, and A.J.P. Taylor see spelled out in the Versailles settlement). Crafting the obscure reference, or the imaginative explanation, into an apparently ephemeral singularity also creates a continual tension with the forms of anticipation and prolepsis which thread through the book. These compositional devices have a prominent role in Paulin's invitation to the reader to re-imagine the Second World War. Re-imagining here is not a matter of a recreation of the past, a historicizing consciousness of the war and its legacies, but of negotiating some bracing discontinuities of perspective, of scale and of value. The reader in short has to confront the distance between the arbitrariness of the newspaper and the narrative logic of epic.

An important but by no means programmatic aspect of Paulin's rendering of the war and its origins is his effort to reverse a process which a young Wilfred Owen identified compellingly in a letter from August 1914: 'bodies [...] melted down to pay for political statues'.[28] From the 1970s onwards, Paulin's poetry has mounted a pun-borne critique of precisely this usurpation of the citizen's body by the state. In the poem 'States', from his first Faber volume, with its own punning negation for a title, *A State of Justice* (1977), the machinery of government is equated, ironically, with a public convenience:

> Any state, built on such a nature,
> Is a metal convenience, its paint
> Cheapened by the price of lives
> Spent in a public service.

The juxtaposition of metal and spent flesh (sexually spent and used up in the maintenance of this public erection) is endemic to these early poems: 'security / Threatened but bodied in steel' (SP 1). In 'Under the Eyes' the symbol of justice metamorphoses into an armour that constricts its wearer to the point of bursting:

> All the machinery of a state
> Is a set of scales that squeezes out blood (2).

In the poem 'Practical Values', both the soldiers and the tarts have 'skins of sleeked steel' (a revisionary reprise of Seamus Heaney's notorious poem 'Punishment') and are equally 'servile and vicious in their uniforms' (4). The eponymous 'Monumental Mason' is presumably 'less a person / Than a function' because it is his function to make personal names public; he is a cipher of cipher-making, *RIP*. In the Audenesque *paysage moralise* 'Purity', the troop ship is softened by its 'anal colours', but its cargo is oxymoronically sharpened into a 'pink blur / Of identical features' (21). A grinning Scottish trooper in 'Desertmartin' is 'expendable / Like a brass cartridge'. Politics is an inhumane alchemy (Keith Douglas is another important predecessor here) turning flesh into base metal.

   In 'Amphion', Paulin pushes this thought further by writing a version of the violent founding myth of Thebes in which war surplus – 'nine gross of jerricans / under a pegged tarpaulin' – comes to be taken for culture, 'this new-strung form / that betters what we are' (SP 65- 6). *The Invasion Handbook* revisits this scene, with the poet supplanting the figure of the 'new government auctioneer'. Stephen Moss's *Guardian* interview with Paulin when the NESTA fellowship was announced pointed both to a long poem celebrating 'a peak of British history', and the poet's sense of the myths appropriate to a devolved, post-Union politics.[29] The idea that the crucial juncture between past and present, waste and reconstruction, history and identity is still labile, and that the surplus as well as the waste of war is open to negotiation, would seem strange if we didn't daily encounter the urgent symbolic work of accounting for the Second World War and its legacies, a leading one of which is writing history. History is a product of war, one which can work to turn waste bodies into shapely myths and national stories.

The expendable and expended body has manifold cultural and geographic locations in *The Invasion Handbook*, as it arcs from one war's aftermath to the battle that defined, for Britain, the beginning of another. For instance, the opening poem's personification of Koba (Stalin) as 'the metal Shah / the steel Tsar' turns the author's signature trope of the state-usurped, metalized body into a fantasy of power (to underscore this, Russia takes on organic form as 'a withered state') (3). This will to 'forge' a 'rigid Europe' is echoed in the determination of the authors of the Versailles Treaty to bring about a Carthaginian peace. Paulin presents the machinations of Versailles by throwing the voice of J.M. Keynes in a 'letter' from Versailles, a text heavily inflected with the imagery of *The Waste Land* and 'Gerontion' (this is effectively an additional 'imaginative explanation' of the influence of *The Economic Consequences of the Peace* on Eliot's poetry). Keynes's despatch turns inside-out a notorious 1918 electioneering slogan about squeezing reparations out of Germany 'until the pips squeak':[30] 'I can hear the pips scream. Lamp faces with puckering mouths' (11). In his next breath Keynes's humane sympathy takes on an anticipatory mode, foreshadowing the analysis of Nazism in Aimé Cesaire's post-war *Discourse on Colonialism* (1955). Keynes's private judgement on the terms of Versailles – which will put 'a white race under conditions little short of servitude' – ramify with Cesaire's analysis of Hitler's crime as monstrous to Europeans because, above all, 'it is the crime against the white man' (Hitler applied 'to Europe colonialist procedures').[31] Keynes's outrage is simultaneously amplified and qualified by this foreshadowing. The economist is granted a lonely and vatic imagination, foretelling what is being sown in the wasteland of Europe, 'I can see divisions of Freikorps rising out of it [...] like leathery eggs' (12). The poet Stephen Spender would return to the same ground in the early 1940s, reworking again and again the motif of the warriors born from the teeth of the dragon slain by Kadmus, to tell how Weimar Germany metamorphosed into Nazi Germany.[32]

'The Attack' (part of a tripartite sequence 'The Attack in the West') is a good example of how Paulin uses the short line to interweave the world-historical and the singular, state and human actors, theory and practice. Theory is represented by the Maginot Line and its 'concrete casseroles': the 'snug ovens' are 'tinpot really' (161), a statement of a strategic truism by the extension and qualification of a sensuous image. This pattern is developed in the commentary on French policy by troping the static defences and their bloated underground infrastructure (like some Ian Fleming villain's lair) as a 'half-baked idea'. This expensive system is another railway siding (echoes of the signing of the Armistice in a railway carriage near Compiègne) to which an effort to command events (Clemenceau's revenge on Germany) has been sidelined. The tissue of sensuous equivalences is, like Paulin's punning, a means of linking, shaping and pointing which falls well short of rationalizing explanation.

The materials of *The Invasion Handbook* are gargantuan; they have to coalesce in the glimpses offered by lyric concentration. Grand strategy is juxtaposed in this poem with the voice of a British serviceman, a voice in which the gift for making imaginative conjunctions is inflected with the idiom of the combat narrative. Clay 'that stuck and dried / hard as a shell' is contrasted with the pre-war remark of the French commander Gamelin that the French army could re-enter Germany like a knife through butter.[33] The attack is represented through its iconic residue in films and writings about 1940 – the swollen-uddered cow, the plane strafing French countryside, halftracks, 'name rank and number' (164), punctuated by the soldier's sense of an ending: 'I knew we were finished then' (163), 'we were goners I knew' (165). These terrifying invasions by a technology of death are as prosaic as the laconic, untriumphalist style of narration which wartime narrative and film established as a norm for negotiating world-shattering experience.[34] Paulin introduces a charged, mixed idiom to mark the soldier's getaway 'to the longest beach in Europe' where, like Aeneas, he is down among the 'living shades', in a kind of strategic limbo. The characterization of the miracle of Dunkirk is heterodox: the army, Paulin suggests, is just where appeasers would want it. An imaginary headline – 'MOSLEY FREED CHURCHILL IN TOWER' – recalls the iconoclasm of Len Deighton's alternate-history thriller *SS-GB* (1978) at the same time as it evokes radical historical contingency and, the 'worse and worse the headlines', proximity to defeat (166).[35] The over-layering of the diurnal perspective associated with the contemporary newspaper, a demythologizing example of allohistorical fiction of Nazi victory, and the historical manifestation of national character ('Dunkirk spirit'), three competing ways of understanding June 1940, clear a space for Paulin's own fashioning of a demotic icon of a British exceptionalism.

> those oily bearded faces
> helmets blasted open like metal cabbages
> ragged mackintoshes battered caps

> an army of ghost crabs
> edging out of the water
> lonely on our island
> we felt free again
> quite serenely cheerful
> like young men
> eyeing the girls
> at some thé dansant
> in a seaside town
> we became ourselves again
> ourselves alone
>
> *into the mosaic of victory*
> *I lay a pattern piece*
> *my only son*
> *into thy hands.* (167)

The transition across the Channel, from loss to finding oneself again, and from the savage displacements of 'blasted open like metal cabbages' to the sacramental order of the 'mosaic of victory' draws on a national legend of island indomitability. But Paulin's version of this almost-biblical deliverance (a pun lurking in 'mosaic') lends body to the abstraction of a nation-state standing alone (no longer encumbered by dubious allies). The lines of 'ghost crabs' (beach burrowers) are envisioned not leaving the beach, as in the widely-reproduced Granger Collection photograph, but landing 'on our island' and transformed into young men at the seaside.[36] Their serenity is balanced by a vision of victory as communal sacrifice of offspring. The implicit rejection of the imagery of generational conflict associated with the literary legacy of the First World War is a significant component in the making of this crucial motif. For the mosaic is the historical negation of the Maginot Line, with which this 230-line poem begins, and it is the affirmation of a British story. In the next poem in the book, it is Churchill who is Aeneas, gazing on his 'Latian shore', the premiership of the UK, which he gained through his studied silence, the ultimate example of wartime taciturnity, weeks earlier on the eve of the German attack in the West, in a interview with his rival Lord Halifax and the Conservative Chief Whip (Paulin dates this meeting, as Churchill himself mistakenly did, 10 May 1940).[37]

The body and the voice are then counterpoints to the historical abstractions that are lined up in the narrative of Europe from Versailles to Dunkirk (the elision of Eastern Europe is only one of them). In Paulin's longer and even denser retelling of the Battle of Britain, the poet sutures the skin of burnt airman Richard Hillary and of his film-star lover Merle Oberon with the surface technologies of fighter aviation, from airframe skins to parachutes, in a rewriting and supplement to Hillary's famous memoir, *The Last Enemy* (1942).[38] The exorbitant extrapolation of the identification of man and machine (both a desire and anxiety in wartime flying texts by Antoine de Saint Exupéry, Rex Warner and Roald Dahl) is not allowed to explode the myth of the Battle of Britain, which is encapsulated in a linguistic take-over, another usurpation like 'Lili Marlene':

> Adlertag
> their Day of the Eagle
> but it was our day
> now and ever. (194)

Like Hillary's memoir itself, Paulin's version of Hillary's life story comes down to earth. The arc of the flight of fantasy is thus congruent with the more fantastic representations of the flyer in Powell and Pressburger's *A Matter of Life and Death* (1946), with its league-of-nations heavenly court of appeal, and in the sky-voyaging couple of Lynette Roberts's *Gods with Stainless Ears: a Heroic Poem* (1951), who orbit the 'maimed cadaverous globe' prior to landfall in Wales.[39] In 'With the Setting Sun', Paulin shows he can achieve his own version of this cosmological sublime, composing a megalomaniac's dream in which the 'petit caporal' makes a parachute descent from the stars, with the map of Europe coming into focus, and Hitler himself coming into an estate 'so enormous / the world itself could not contain it'.

Denis Thompson argued in 1939 that there was no 'copy' in economic conferences: papers lived off stunts like the Schneider Trophy, the 'air epic of to-day'.[40] Paulin's 'huge morning newspaper' ranges over both, stringing out a sequence of news stories from Locarno via Ethiopia, Jarrow, Spain, Nanking, the *Anschluss*, '*Kristallnacht*', Poland to blacked-out London. The temporal sequence is knitted or knotted up by verbal and iconic equivalences. Allusions to Hans Schleger's London Transport posters, which included a 'Hands at your service' series, as well as the advice to illuminate your hand when hailing a bus, routes us back to the earlier description of Clemenceau's 'grey silk gloves' (196, 10).[41] Hence the blackout signifies as the 'immense abîme' into which the future was 'stuffed' by a punitive policy towards Germany. The phrase 'Clemenceau's revenge' is itself subjected to a relay, via Trotsky's Clemenceau Thesis (1927), which speculated on the overthrow of leaders in times of crisis, to become 'the main hinge / in the trapdoor' of Stalin's purges, a verbal talisman of dictatorial certainty (84). To more disorienting effect, the mendacious list of armaments destroyed in the fulfilment of treaty obligations by Germany, which is laid before us in 'Chancellor Hitler's Speech', is echoed in the losses at Dunkirk enumerated by the soldier in 'The Attack' (99, 165).

Data such as these signify in isolation, and again, differently, in the contexts created by repetition, variation and juxtaposition. This formal ambivalence is embodied in the slanting overprinting of headlines, straplines and small ads in the margins of the poem 'Give Us This Day', creating a cacophony of period effects and prompting the question, what do these birth notices, captions and examples of monarchical 'flunkeyism' add up to?[42] Paulin's answer is another way of describing the doubling that is occurring in *The Invasion Handbook* when we are reading the book as a newspaper: 'these paper matins are / and are not history' (150). Between that 'are / and are not' lie the senses in which Paulin's forms give a form to history, engage in a telling and retelling of the story of the Second World War.

Amongst the poems that compose the elusive meta-order of the *The Invasion Handbook* are a number that meditate on forms or the absence of form in the face of contingency, or in the aftermath of ruin. Kurt Schwitters's Dadaist collage-construction is one such model: the poem 'Merz' calls it 'art scraped / right back from the edge', an art of junk, rubble, faeces. However, Merz is not a stuff, it is an unfolding principle of composition. As Schwitters put it in 1920, 'we cannot create [the Merz composite work of art], for we would only be parts of it, in fact we would be mere material'.[43] The deferral of transcendence here speaks to the way in which Paulin's poetry of contingency constitutes another contingency, in which the writer's and the readers' semantic choices are material in further constellations of meaning (the ambiguity of 'your reading / of its flimsy text / which is of course ephemeral' (150)). This defence must, of course, be measured against the unease voiced by Kermode about Paulin's scholastic demands on the reader.

'Chaos Theory' suggests another model, which emerges from an earlier dialogue between Heideggerian and modernist architectonics ('Schwarzwald oder Bauhaus') in which a butterfly stands for Le Corbusier's nomadic machines for living:

> – its wings flicker
> and houses and buildings a thousand
> miles away

> fall flat
> or push up
> maybe they push up
> like dawn mushrooms. (92)

The apocalypse of *The Waste Land* merges with meteorologist Edward Lorenz's metaphor of the butterfly effect (a vividly poetic image for the principle of sensitivity to initial conditions in Chaos Theory) to suggest incalculable arcs of causation. In 'Chaos Theory' it is the Archduke's driver's 'wrong turning' that appears the proximal cause of a century of destruction, but another order is imposed by the repetition of dates, so that the signing of the Versailles Treaty on the same late June day as Franz Ferdinand's assassination links up with Mitterrand's political opportunism in visiting Sarajevo on another 28 June, in 1992. The effort to 'distil / from all the causes before our eyes' which incident it is that will 'begin the meltdown of all states' is thus held in suspension between on the one hand a calculus of the infinitesimal and on the other a numerological superstition, each arcing into the future to confound prediction with hindsight.

The Invasion Handbook is of course much concerned with foresight and hindsight, what could be anticipated and what now seems inevitable. This is itself inevitable given the book's form as a tissue of news which is no longer new, which is almost always already assimilated to a narrative which explains and contains. Anticipations and prolepses open up ironic perspectives on actors and their actions and reactions. 'Smart Sir Alec' (Douglas-Home) enjoys the way rhyme contrives that '*peace* / flaps its wings above *appease*' (a route chaos did not take) but is unwitting of the way in which the rhyme forecasts his future role in suppressing the anti-colonial government of Congo headed by Patrice Lumumba (134). These verbal games are at once mischievous and serious, a way of reminding us that there is no one stance from which to take the measure of events. Dowding, one of Paulin's heroes, is portrayed in just such a partial orientation to the Spanish Civil War, deliberately filtering the human and the political from his apperception of the conflict. 'A laboratory for the Luftwaffe', so too it must be for Dowding, leading RAF Fighter Command and responsible for devising Britain's future air defences 'like a scientist in a white coat':

> – he must understand the weapon,
> not the wound
> study that abstract
> adaptable weapon strategy

            with a cold eye
            and design diagrams
            to maximize the dead. (116)

The allusion in the opening pair of lines is to the Spanish Civil War poet
John Cornford (1915–36) and the single-minded rhetoric of *force majeur*
in British Communist-inspired poetry of the 1930s: 'hard as the metal
of my gun'.[44] Dowding here must be unmindful of wounds in order
to master the weapon. But in another sense he is a model of the poet
because he has to put events into a perspective, 'must make a model / of
this jittery chaos [...] still a sideshow / still a provincial history / pushed
to one side' (116). Paulin's perspective-making is provisional, requiring
a certain accountability on the part of the reader in tackling '*the subterfugue text / within the text itself*'. Perspective here is translatable as identity, and as Etienne Wenger puts it, 'a tendency to come up with certain
interpretations'.[45] *The Invasion Handbook* draws the engaged reader into
a negotiation of national identity, gives her a role in assembling the elements of the national story, a story which can involve identifying with
a national character. Unscrambling the events and symbols Paulin has
gathered means performing a perspective on them.

   Another kind of anticipation features in the shattering premonitions
experienced by the poet's mother, described in the poem 'August 39'.
These dreams of 'an open boat' with a cargo of starving figures are 'a
type of horror she hasn't met', but one which ...

            she'll learn to understand
            until years beyond
            those newsreels of the camps
            she hands her dream on
            to her eldest son

... in a nightmare relay. What is the relationship of these horrors and their
belated comprehension (the negation of trauma) to history? Alert to this,
the poem ends by asking 'if mere dreams / can weigh in the record / or
for that matter can poems?' (144). Weighing in the record implies both
permanence and an act of balancing. Elsewhere Paulin suggests that the
'civic poetry' of wartime Britain, which is exemplified in the posters of
Hans Schleger (whose mark was 'Zero'), 'will survive / our pause – yep – /
and our passing' (199). The absence of an explicit hierarchy amongst
these private and public acts, these missing and surviving cultural traces,
as they are juxtaposed with each other in *The Invasion Handbook* means

that the reader is implicated in weighing the record again. What makes the experience *like* reading a newspaper is what Anderson has identified as the imagining of linkages, which in this case means negotiating your way around an unfamiliar constellation of some familiar cultural symbols of the warrior nation.

Sartre wrote in 1947:

> The book, serving as a go-between, establishes an historical contact among the men who are steeped in the same history and who likewise contribute to its making. Writing and reading are two facets of the same historical fact.[46]

The Invasion Handbook establishes historical contact, and elicits a historical fact, through its invitation to the reader to compose an order amongst its (old news) stories. In his poem 'An English Writer on the French Revolution' (*Fivemiletown*, 1987), Paulin poked fun at one manifestation of the historicizing imagination, in the gap between the upheavals of 1789 and an inconsequential, unwittingly comic antiquarianism:

> He is building a bridge
> from here to Betelgeuse –
> a bridge of damson stones,
> tin trumpets
> and left testicles. (SP 75)

The Invasion Handbook is, from one angle, just such a collocation of minutiae, from Austen Chamberlain's 'secondhand Parker 51' (60) to the 'ME 108 – or was it a 109?' (159).[47] But the book's historical junk is so ravelled up with Paulin's personifications and symbols of the world-historical and the world-shattering that the reader does not have the option, as does the persona in 'An English Writer' to 'sit under my vine / and read him gently' (SP 75).

The Invasion Handbook co-opts the reader to the work of imagining the national emergency of Britain's Second World War through the way it articulates its component stories or vignettes aesthetically rather than ideologically or causally. Paulin has amplified Marinetti's notion of global synthesis with an account of the 'origins' of war which is not an attempt at a representative recreation of a period but a model of the determinations and contingencies which, politically and culturally, bridged the world wars. In Sarah Hall's novel *Haweswater*, a teacher brings old newspapers into remote Mardale 'so that children will become familiar with history as it passes and recognize their place within it'.[48] Paulin's project has something of the pedagogic about its (veiled) informativeness, but it is also a vivid addition to the literature of the romance of war: as one critic has owned up to recognizing, Paulin's writing about combat is 'as breathlessly exciting and shocking as any action adventure comic'.[49]

The larger project of which *The Invasion Handbook* is part remains unfinished: the work currently resolves on those British legends which have been the most potent in post-war life, both in terms of their repeated re-inscription and reproduction, and also their subjection to revisionist or debunking scrutiny: Dunkirk, the Battle of Britain (symbol of an independent deterrent), Churchill's leadership. Extending the work would involve figuring Britain's war in relation to its demographic and economic marginalization from 1941, with the emergence of a bipolar global military order. Herein lies the origins of the major context – the Cold War – of the cultural framing of Britain's story of the Second World War, the story Paulin has set out to reconfigure and reanimate. If it is possible for this ambitious work to catch up – as it begins to do with its account of Richard Hillary – with the culture of war-memorialization to which it is a supplement and critique, then we can take a larger measure of its distinctive blend of scepticism and triumphalism. At present, the achievements of formal disjunctions are mitigated by the apparent facility with which the past is cited and resuscitated, in the manner of Katherine Savage's school primer in contemporary history. 'All historic events [...] are rewritten for school use', a lawyer tells the falsely lionized Captain Trotta in Joseph Roth's 1932 novel of imperial decline, *The Radetzky March*.[50] The interrogative, literary secret history is not immune from this ideological capture.

Notes

1. Eric Ambler, *Cause for Alarm* (Harmondsworth: Penguin, 2009), 14–15.
2. F.T. Marinetti, 'Destruction of Syntax – Wireless Imagination – Words-in-Freedom', trans. Lawrence Rainey, in Lawrence Rainey (ed.), *Modernism: an Anthology* (Oxford: Blackwell, 2005), 28.
3. Tom Paulin, 'Or in a Soft-skinned Vehicle', *The Invasion Handbook* (London: Faber, 2002), 172. All references to this edition are hereafter cited parenthetically in the text.
4. Stephen Moss, 'Poetic Licence', *Guardian*, 16 May 2000, *G2*, 4.
5. Katharine Savage, *The Story of the Second World War* (Oxford: Oxford University Press, 1957), wrapper.
6. Frank Kermode, 'Reports from the not too Distant Canon', *London Review of Books*, 23 May 2002, 9.

7. A.J.P. Taylor, *The Origins of the Second World War* (Harmondsworth: Penguin, 1985), 52; and see R.J.B. Bosworth, *Explaining Auschwitz and Hiroshima: History Writing and the Second World War 1945–1990* (London: Routledge, 1993), 39–45.
8. For another imaginative attempt to reconfigure Second World War historiography via the Hess mystery, see Howard Brenton, *H.I.D. (Hess is Dead)* (London: Nick Hern Books, 1989).
9. Tom Paulin, 'Many Cunning Passages: How Maynard Keynes Made his Mark on *The Waste Land*', *Times Literary Supplement*, 29 November 2002, 14–15.
10. Ibid., 14.
11. Benedict Anderson, *Imagined Communities: Reflections on the Origin and Spread of Nationalism*, revised edn (London: Verso, 2006), 33–6.
12. James Joyce, *Ulysses*, ed. Hans Gabler (London: The Bodley Head, 1986), 158.
13. Tom Paulin, *Ireland and the English Crisis* (Newcastle: Bloodaxe, 1984), 47.
14. Tom Paulin, *Selected Poems 1972–1990* (London: Faber, 1993), 77. All subsequent references to this edition will be cited parenthetically in the text as SP. James Fenton, *The Memory of War: Poems 1968–1982* (Edinburgh: Salamander Press, 1982), 61–81.
15. Franco Moretti, *Modern Epic: the World System from Goethe to Garcia Marquez* (London: Verso, 1996), 3.
16. *Newspapers: an Inquiry into Reading amongst the Civilian Population* (Wartime Social Survey for the Publications Division of the Ministry of Information, n.s. 37a [1943]).
17. Anderson, *Imagined Communities*, 35.
18. Denis Thompson, *Between the Lines: or How to Read a Newspaper* (London: Frederick Muller, 1939), xi.
19. Virginia Woolf, *Between the Acts*, ed. Frank Kermode (Oxford: Oxford University Press, 1992), 18.
20. Thomson, *Between the Lines*, 17–18.
21. Elizabeth Bowen, *The Heat of the Day* (London: Jonathan Cape, 1949), 144. Subsequent references to this edition are cited parenthetically in the text.
22. Scott Dikkers (ed.), *Our Dumb Century* (London: Boxtree, 1999), 59.
23. Thompson, *Between the Lines*, 48.
24. Paulin, 'Many Cunning Passages', 14.
25. Paulin, *Ireland*, 47.
26. Anderson, *Imagined Communities*, 33.
27. Ibid., 36.
28. Wilfred Owen, *Selected Letters*, ed. John Bell (Oxford: Oxford University Press, 1985), 119.
29. Moss, 'Poetic Licence', 4.
30. Keith Grieves, *Sir Eric Geddes: Business and Government in Peace and War* (Manchester, Manchester University Press, 1990), 72.
31. Aimé Cesaire, *Discourse on Colonialism*, trans. Joan Pinkham (New York and London: Monthly Review Press, 1972), 14.
32. Stephen Spender, *New Collected Poems*, ed. Michael Brett (London: Faber, 2004), 164, 166, 170.
33. Ernest R. May, *Strange Victory: Hitler's Conquest of France* (London: I.B. Tauris, 2000), 214.

34. See Mark Rawlinson, 'The Second World War: British Writing', in Kate McLoughlin (ed.), *The Cambridge Companion to War Writing* (Cambridge: Cambridge University Press, 2009), 197–211.
35. See Gavriel Rosenfeld, *The World Hitler Never Made* (Cambridge: Cambridge University Press, 2005), 66.
36. Walter Lord, *The Miracle of Dunkirk* (Harmondsworth: Penguin, 1984), illustrations between 154–5.
37. For an account of the meeting, see A.J.P.Taylor, *English History, 1914–45* (Oxford: Oxford University Press, 1965), 473–4.
38. I discuss this poem at length in 'After War: Writing about World War in a Post-War Era?' in Eve Patten and Richard Pine (eds), *Literatures of War* (Newcastle upon Tyne: Cambridge Scholars, 2008), 380–400.
39. Lynette Roberts, *Collected Poems*, ed. Patrick McGuinness (Manchester: Carcanet, 2005), 68.
40. Denis Thompson, *Between the Lines*, 42–3.
41. See London Transport Museum Collection, http://www.ltmcollection.org/posters, accessed 8 August 2009.
42. Denis Thompson, *Between the Lines*, 40–1: 'the Press and cinema invest the Royal Family with semi-divine qualities'.
43. Kurt Schwitters, 'Merz' (1920), in Rainey (ed.), *Modernism*, 489.
44. John Cornford, 'Full Moon at Tierz', in *Understand the Weapon, Understand the Wound: Selected Writings*, ed. Jonathan Galassi (Manchester: Carcanet, 1976), 39.
45. Etienne Wenger, *Communities of Practice: Learning, Meaning and Identity* (Cambridge: Cambridge University Press, 1998), 153.
46. Jean-Paul Sartre, *What is Literature?* Trans Bernard Frechtman (London: Methuen, 1967), 51.
47. For an earlier version of the poem 'The Mechelen Incident' see *London Review of Books* 22/16 (24 August 2000), 8, and for correspondence about his misidentification of the aircraft flown by Reinberger and Hoenmanns, see J.G. Owen, letter to the editor, *London Review of Books* 22/17 (7 September 2000), 5.
48. Sarah Hall, *Haweswater* (London: Faber, 2002), 18.
49. Matt Bryden, 'Man Jacks and Union Jacks', review of *The Invasion Handbook* http:// www.stridemagazine.co.uk/2002/nov/paulin.htm, accessed 14 August 2009.
50. Joseph Roth, *The Radetzky March*, trans. Joachim Neugroschel (Harmondsworth: Penguin, 1995), 8.

5

'A stiff is still a stiff in this country': the Problem of Murder in Wartime

Gill Plain

My title comes from Margery Allingham's 1945 novel *Coroner's Pidgin*, and its absurd assertion of moral force is indicative of the contradictions pervading popular fiction in wartime. The words are spoken by Magersfontein Lugg, erstwhile manservant to Allingham's series detective Albert Campion, and they take the form of a reproach. Campion, who has just returned from top secret overseas war service and is en route to catch a train, has emerged from the bath in his London flat to find a body in the bedroom. The dead woman was deposited there by Lugg – now working for Heavy Rescue – who was in turn assisting a marchioness who had found the body in her son's bed. Before Campion can even begin to enquire as to the corpse's credentials, the flat is invaded by a motley collection of aristocrats, actresses and Americans whose complex interpersonal dynamics obliterate the matter of the body, turning it instead into a particularly cumbersome social faux pas. Finding himself in a setting reminiscent more of French farce than English detection, Campion understandably refuses to take things seriously – which prompts the following affronted response from Lugg:

> 'now's not the time to be funny, neither. You've 'ad your fun abroad, I dare say. This is serious. A stiff is still a stiff in this country. There'll be a lot of questions asked.'[1]

In Britain at least, Lugg implies, a line has been drawn. There may be a war on, but bodies still matter. Standards may be under threat in every aspect of life, but a corpse is still a corpse, and the rule of law has not been challenged. It is a moment of patriotic absurdity that lampoons the national trope of understatement ('you've 'ad your fun abroad'), and asserts its claim of dignity while showing no respect for the dead whatsoever.

In addition, putting these words into the mouth of Lugg, rather than his social superior Campion, further destabilizes the assertion. As if it were not enough that Lugg is an ex-criminal member of the working classes, he has just been caught showing a wanton disregard for the very law which he claims to uphold. At least to begin with, then, this is a comedy corpse, and the frivolity of its introduction situates it firmly in what might be termed a late, or even post-war, moment. In 1945, suicide, murder and international conspiracy are nothing but distractions preventing the patriotic detective from enjoying his well-earned home leave.

The cavalier treatment of the corpse in the opening chapters of *Coroner's Pidgin* raises significant questions about the meaning of murder and the representation of individual death in the face of war's priority. In his short survey, 'Murder in Wartime', Stephen Knight argues that crime fiction is perhaps the most socially responsive of literary genres, and suggests that in 'the light of acknowledged massive sales [...] it seems a positive process to explore how crime fiction mediated the notion of a nation at war'.[2] Knight addresses both the production and reception of crime fiction, and goes on to observe that it would be a mistake to dismiss its wartime consumption as an escapist phenomenon. Beginning with Agatha Christie, whose clue-puzzle fictions are too often assumed to be detached from their socio-political contexts, Knight suggests that the dislocations of crime fiction are ideally suited to symbolize, in manageable form, the alienating impact of war:

> Christie's wartime mysteries superintend contemporary battles from a distance and with an Austenesque pattern of radical displacement, not recognising the war as itself, but representing its effect in terms of disruptions to the normal balance of gender and social power.[3]

Knight is not the first to note the intersection of crime fiction and culture. Graham Greene, in *The Ministry of Fear* (1943), has his persecuted protagonist Arthur Rowe attempt to describe the modern world to his dead mother, symbol of a lost Edwardian age of innocence. Real life now, he claims, is 'like a thriller', 'it's what we've all made of the world since you died'.[4] In a bitterly ironic speech, history and fiction are yoked together to illustrate the horror of war and the expendability of human life:

> Let me lend you the History of Contemporary Society. It's in hundreds of volumes, but most of them are sold in cheap editions: *Death in Piccadilly, The Ambassador's Diamonds, The Theft of the Naval Papers, Diplomacy, Seven Days Leave, The Four Just Men* [...]. (66)

Greene suggests that life mirrors art, not so much through mimesis as through a process of becoming fantastical. The mundane and quotidian are distorted and rendered unreal by the encroachment of war's unthinkable violence: the body in the library finds its parallel in the bomb on the house. If one, why not the other? The parameters of plausibility are stretched by war and a new logic is required to make sense of unprecedented experiences.[5] Greene found the generic forms of crime fiction and the thriller to be ideal for exploring 'the new, paranoid reality of wartime',[6] but George Orwell saw things differently, fearing that such narratives were as likely to generate as to explain the violence of war.

In two powerful essays, 'Raffles and Miss Blandish' (1944) and 'The Decline of the English Murder' (1946), Orwell argues that the rise of fascism and the prosecution of the Second World War fundamentally devalued human life. 'Raffles and Miss Blandish' focuses on fiction's complicity in this process, and holds the hard-boiled novel to account for pandering to a 'cult of power'.[7] James Hadley Chase's *No Orchids for Miss Blandish* is selected as a particularly pernicious example and its attractions are denounced as 'a daydream appropriate to a totalitarian age'.[8] The success of this novel, and others like it, has been brought about, claims Orwell, 'by the mingled boredom and brutality of war'.[9] In 'The Decline of the English Murder', by contrast, Orwell proposes that it is not the law so much as its transgression that acts as an index of culture: the methods and motives of murderers are inextricably linked to the nation and its values. According to Orwell, the perfect pre-war English murderer 'should be a little man of the professional class – a dentist or a solicitor, say – living an intensely respectable life somewhere in the suburbs':

> He should go astray through cherishing a guilty passion for his secretary or the wife of a rival professional man, and should only bring himself to the point of murder after long and terrible wrestles with his conscience. [...] The means chosen should, of course, be poison. In the last analysis he should commit murder because this seems to him less disgraceful, and less damaging to his career, than being detected in adultery.[10]

This intensely English mode of murder is compared by Orwell to the actual wartime 'Cleft Chin Murder', the background to which 'was not domesticity, but the anonymous life of the dance-halls and the false values of the American film'.[11] What disturbs Orwell about this case is its lack of premeditation. Elizabeth Jones and Karl Hulten did not know their victims and seemed to kill as much for the thrill of murder as for the meagre financial rewards of their crimes. Hulten was hanged, and Jones imprisoned – an act of judicial leniency that led to a public outcry. This response provides the icing on the cake of Orwell's argument: 'It is difficult not to feel', he concludes, 'that this clamour to hang an eighteen-year-old girl was due partly to the brutalizing effects of war.'[12]

The contrasting perspectives of Orwell and Greene give some indication as to why murder is a 'problem' in wartime. It is not simply the transgression that matters, but how that act is performed and how society responds to both victim and perpetrator. Orwell's writing expresses his fear that the reader exposed to the horrors of gratuitous violence will be attracted rather than repulsed, and that war will, of necessity, construct newly callous subjectivities. This anxiety is, in microcosm, the debate about the representation of violence that has continued well beyond the parameters of the Second World War, and I do not wish to rehearse it here. What I do want to do, however, is to test Orwell's hypothesis of a brutalized society against the evidence provided by wartime fictions of murder. Although much of my focus will be on the awkward object of the corpse, I will also examine the impact of the dead upon the living, and the cultural issues that seem to be at stake in the construction of murder narratives in a time of national emergency. How crimes are investigated and who investigates them becomes newly significant in the double discourse of war and murder, and the socio-political upheavals of the period inevitably impact upon writers' representation of class and gender paradigms. Through contrasting the corpses of two well-established crime writers – Margery Allingham and Agatha Christie – with those of Graham Greene, a writer whose metaphysical preoccupations often found expression in a self-conscious deployment of genre form, I will explore a series of interrelated questions posed by the act of murder in wartime. First, what purpose is served by murder narratives in the face of the much greater social rupture of war? Second, to what extent does murder mutate across the phases of the conflict, or – to put it another way – how does the 'private' corpse relate to the public war? And third, how do the living bodies of detectives and suspects respond to domestic murder in the face of the 'legitimate' murder represented by war?

Refusing to mourn: the casual corpses of Christie and Allingham

Before examining the body in wartime, however, it is necessary to consider the state of crime fiction in the interwar years. Orwell's characterization of the typical English murder rings true for the fiction of the period, which focuses predominantly on a middle-class milieu obsessed by respectability. Keeping up appearances, after all, is essential to a genre in which every character harbours a guilty secret and is capable of murder in thought if not in deed. It is, then, an illusion to imagine that interwar murder narratives depict a prelapsarian society violated by murder and restored to harmony by the detective. For all its tidy closures and happy resolutions, this was, as Alison Light has argued, a world in which 'nothing is sacred'.[13] Light's groundbreaking study *Forever England* argues that the work of Agatha Christie can be read as a 'literature of convalescence', facilitating the recovery of a nation traumatized by the First World War. In a world of determined superficiality, corpses go unmourned, and heroic masculinity becomes an object of ridicule rather than respect.[14] Yet, as I have argued elsewhere, interwar fiction is also characterized by the satisfactions of explanation. It is not so much that justice is done, as that bodies, and what became of them, are fully and completely explained. In the aftermath of a war in which bodies were quite literally annihilated, interwar detective fiction presents a narrative in which the single corpse acquires an integrity impossible in wartime. These bodies become the subject not just of one, but of multiple competing explanations and their deaths are given a surfeit of meanings. In reconstructing the corpse-as-signifier, interwar crime fiction also consoles its readership through the presentation of death as part of a rational pattern. Victims die for a reason explicable in terms of human desire; they are not simply the collateral damage of war's mass, mechanized slaughter.[15]

The desire to give meaning to individual deaths did not disappear with the advent of the Second World War, but the evidence suggests that, in the early years of conflict at least, a new set of anxieties were addressed. Between 1940 and 1942, when the threat of invasion hung over the island and the war in the air brought devastation and death, a number of crime writers responded by raising the stakes of their fiction from the personal to the national. Detectives as diverse as Agatha Christie's Tommy and Tuppence Beresford and Allingham's Albert Campion mutated from amateur sleuths into semi-professional spy-hunters, struggling not to uncover the evidence of a past crime, but to prevent the prosecution of a future one. And the body under threat in this prospective crime was not the wealthy heiress or the greedy land-owner, but the vulnerable body of the nation itself. National security took precedence over individual concerns and the 'criminal' was configured as the 'enemy within' – the fifth columnist whose misplaced loyalties corrupt the body politic. It says much about the flexibility of the crime fiction form that familiar detective figures could be mobilized to such 'national' ends, and it also indicates the extent to which readers now desired action over explanation. Christie's *N or M?* (1941) opens with the middle-aged Tuppence's plaintive cry that 'It's bad enough having a war [...] but not being allowed to do anything in it just puts the lid on.'[16] Her sense of impotence, shared by her redundant husband Tommy, speaks to the war's disturbing removal of individual agency. In a world of conscription, evacuation, work orders and rationing, there seemed little that the individual could do to combat the vast imper-sonal forces that threatened to destroy self, community and nation. As Elizabeth Bowen observed in the preface to her wartime story col-lection *The Demon Lover*, 'life, mechanized by the controls of wartime, and emotionally torn and impoverished by changes, had to complete itself in *some* way'. Bowen draws attention to the fantasies 'with which formerly matter-of-fact people consoled themselves', and the reading of crime fiction represents a microcosmic achievement of resolution in the face of almost unbearable uncertainty.[17]

In *N or M?* the supremely ordinary Tommy and Tuppence save the nation from a fiendish fifth column plot being enacted in the improb-able surroundings of a seaside boarding house. Going undercover as middle-aged middle-Englanders, Tommy and Tuppence must try to establish which of their fellow residents is a spy, and in consequence, much of their detection focuses on a reading of bodily signifiers. Who or what is archetypally British, and whose body bears the imprint of otherness? Christie plays on all her readers' likely prejudices to throw suspicion on an Irish landlady, her firebrand daughter and a German refugee, and in this context it is perhaps unsurprising that the corpse of another refugee, Vanda Polonska, is treated with suspicion rather than respect (123). Pragmatism, not compassion, is at the forefront in the coroner's abrupt summary of the evidence: 'Polonska, according to her own story, had suffered great bereavement in her own country, and that might have turned her brain. On the other hand, she might be an enemy agent' (125). This is, emphatically, a body that does not matter. She is simply collateral damage that helps Tuppence to identify the more important living body of the spy. In this, though, Christie's vision is far from reassuring. The 'German' turns out to be British, while one spy is discovered to be the bland, neurotic mother Mrs Sprot, and the other the blustering 'hearty Englishman' Commander Haydock. As Tommy is captured by Haydock, he experiences an epiphany: 'That jovial florid face [...] was only a mask. Why had he not seen it all along for what it was – the face of a bad-tempered overbearing Prussian officer' (144). *N or M?* gives with one hand and takes away with the other, suggesting that 'little' men and women can make a difference, while fundamentally challenging concepts of a clear and legible 'national' body.

A similar fantasy of agency is enacted in Margery Allingham's *Traitor's Purse*, also published in 1941, when the threat to Britain was at its height. In this novel, as in *N or M?*, the body in peril is that of the nation, and Allingham pulls no punches in her depiction of Britain's vulnerability: 'England was such a little place. It would take so short a time to fan the poison out all over her lovely petite body.'[18] The national body is equally a female body that must be protected, and Albert Campion must save this damsel in distress from a man who thinks he alone knows what she wants: Lee Aubrey, the Principal of the Masters of Bridge. The Masters are a hereditary semi-secret society who in the name of 'custom' (62–3, 68) act as a dictatorship within the body politic, and their existence, in the heart of England, implicitly raises uncomfortable questions about the constitution of the nation and its values. Aubrey is a megalomaniac who assumes that his hereditary privilege should transform into a protofascist assumption of absolute authority (203–5); he will save the nation from the Nazis by using their methods, not the supposedly 'British' techniques of consensus, fair play, muddle and improvisation. And here lies the reassurance of Allingham's text: while her readers might be disturbed by this vein of aristocratic corruption running through the nation, they will be consoled by the fact these fascist forces can be defeated by the familiar figure of the detective. Furthermore, the detective himself is in a state of crisis: Campion has lost his memory and remembers only a pervasive sense of threat and the imperative of time. The disabled detective acts as another metaphor for Britain's imperilled state – and crucially, his ultimate success is built upon a model of class and gender cooperation. Campion, and the nation, only survive as a consequence of the support he receives from his fiancée Amanda and the ubiquitous Lugg, both of whom are depicted as being wholly committed to the nation in its hour of need. This is detection by a representative national body to save the national body in its hour of need.[19] And consequently, the attitudes exhibited towards mere individual bodies is, to say the least, utilitarian.

It is not clear quite how many people die in *Traitor's Purse*. Before the action of the book begins, a policeman has been killed, and the plot is swiftly complicated by the murder of Anscombe – a man about whom no one either knows or cares much. So far, so routine. However, the end of the novel finds Campion perched on a ledge above a cavern filled with lorries preparing to spread their criminal cargo around the nation. He is alone and unarmed, except for an experimental grenade, euphemistically described as the 'phoenix egg', which he has stolen from a research facility. Up until this point the novel remains within the parameters of British sporting amateurism, as our hero muddles through with the limited resources at hand. In a faintly absurd image, Campion throws his egg, which sails 'through the air to the goal he had chosen' (196) – at which point the novel undergoes a significant metamorphosis:

> Below him, in the bowl of the trough, there was a sea of blazing petrol and paper and the fumes of smoldering sacks. Millions of envelopes covered the place like a fall of brown snow. Injured men swore and died under their lorries, while others fought each other in their attempts to clamber onto the ledge. But the ladders which were normally used for this purpose had been smashed to matchwood and the bare sides of the rock provided no foothold. (197)

This is a conclusion beyond the scale of any of Allingham's previous novels – as Campion hurls his grenade into the cavern of trapped criminals, it implicitly becomes clear that war both breaks down the detective's habitual detachment from the crime under investigation, and eases the prohibitions of the law. The men in the cavern were not simply criminals, they were working for the enemy, and their deaths do not count as murder. Rather they serve a higher purpose in the moral balance sheet of the book.

In wartime, then, the detective is potentially licensed to kill as well as detect. He becomes judge and executioner, as well as investigating agent. The most famous wartime case of such executive power is undoubtedly Christie's *Curtain*, the final novel to feature Hercule Poirot, in which the detective solves the problem of a manipulative, untraceable murderer by killing him. However, while it is undoubtedly significant that Christie both imagined such an insoluble problem, and enabled her detective to resolve it, the novel was not published until after her death in 1976. More pertinent for the reading public at the time was *The Moving Finger*, published in 1943, which incongruously combines traditional village detection with a callous disregard for human life. As the novel ends, in typical Christie fashion with marriage and reward for the newly restored community, the narrator pauses for a brief moment of reflection:

> Just for a fleeting moment I thought of Mrs. Symmington and Agnes Woddell in their graves in the churchyard and wondered if

they would agree [that everything turns out for the best], and then I remembered that Agnes's boy hadn't been very fond of her and that Mrs. Symmington hadn't been very nice to Megan and, what the hell? we've all got to die some time! And I agreed with happy Miss Emily that everything was for the best in the best of possible worlds.[20]

The refusal to mourn here is hyperbolic to the point of comedy, and it indicates that, for all the energy expended in identifying the murderer, the main concerns of the novel lie elsewhere. It is, as Knight has suggested, a novel which 'superintends' war from a distance. The narrator, Jerry, is an injured pilot sent to recuperate with his fashionable sister Joanna in the peace and quiet of a typical English country town. Like so many of Christie's narrators, Jerry is not entirely reliable – his prejudices and preconceptions colour the narrative and facilitate Christie's deceptions – but his outsider perspective is central to the novel's exploration of mass psychology. As the anonymous letters of the Lymstock poison pen spread through the community, suspicion and paranoia begin to flourish, symbolized by the refrain 'no smoke without fire' (65). While the investigators assume the writer to be a woman, and speculate fruitlessly on the manifestations of pathological repressed femininity, the community regresses, seeking scapegoats in the non-conforming women of the village (44–5).[21] In her depiction of Lymstock under siege by the poison pen, Christie is more than usually explicit in her suggestion that the idyllic 'English' community is a fragile construct. Perhaps in response to this vulnerability, the novel also demonstrates a considerable investment in the restoration of social 'norms', with the result that *The Moving Finger* is as much a fantasy of forceful masculinity as it is a detective novel.

In a culture of wounded or absent masculinity, the marriage plot characteristic of crime fiction's resolution achieves a new significance. Nearly all of Christie's novels conform to the comedic convention of marking the restoration of social harmony through the union of lovers. *The Moving Finger* demonstrates just how far society has been destabilized by offering not one but two romances: a background one in which Jerry's wayward sister is subjugated to the will of the strong, dark and handsome local doctor, and a primary one in which Jerry restores his masculine agency through the god-like creation of woman.[22] Twenty-year-old Megan seems devoid of femininity; without training in this socially necessary condition, she remains trapped in a pre-pubescent state of liminality. Neither masculine nor feminine, for much of the novel she is described as animal: 'She looked, I decided this morning, much more like a horse than a human being. In fact she would have been a very nice horse with a little grooming' (19). Taken to London for the day and treated to just such a grooming, she is miraculously transformed into an ideal woman, leaving Jerry in awe of 'the creature [he] had created' (158). The absent femininity of Megan and the independent sexual power of Joanna act as metaphors for the war's disruption of female roles, and it is part of the novel's reassurance that both women are brought into alignment with heteronormative convention. Yet Christie struggles wholeheartedly to endorse the restoration of hegemonic masculinity, persistently undercutting events with comedy, and even allowing Megan to assert 'I don't want to be *made*' (162). Ultimately it is unclear whether Christie is making fun of the sophisticated Londoners (in a valorization of the potent myth of rural England, Jerry and Joanna decide to stay in Lymstock), or whether she feels female agency must indeed know its limits, but either way, it is not the dead who matter. As Jerry's reflections suggest, no one will mourn Mrs Symmington, while Agnes is debarred by her class from signification. Far more important is the novel's insistence upon communal health and gender normativity. *The Moving Finger* is firmly designed to assert stability in the face of change and to keep wartime trauma under control: the brutality of its almost pathological refusal to mourn may be a product of war, but it is a home-grown nihilism, not a hard-boiled American import.

The decline of the English murder?
Graham Greene's guilty pleasures

The concerns and anxieties implicit in the novels discussed so far – the question of priority, the agency of the detective, the disregard of the body – are equally the subjects of another novel published in 1943, Graham Greene's *The Ministry of Fear*. Described by its author as an 'entertainment', it combines the genres of crime fiction and the thriller to make explicit the sub-textual concerns of Allingham and Christie. This is a profoundly self-conscious novel, at all points acutely aware of the traditions it appropriates. It is, thus, a novel-length meditation on the 'problem' of murder in wartime that explores not only the ethical question of justified killing, but also the applicability of detective fiction and its conventions to a modern world in which 'it really pays to murder' (46). The protagonist of *The Ministry of Fear* is Arthur Rowe, a self-confessed murderer who cannot forgive himself for the mercy killing of his wife. Alone and unhappy, he wanders a London being blitzed beyond recognition, attempting to avoid anything that might remind him of his adult life. Imprisoned by his guilt, he wills further destruction on the landscape, hoping that 'if every street with which he had associations were destroyed, he would be free to go' (22). He is shaken from his self-obsessed torpor by stumbling into the midst of a fifth column plot to smuggle valuable documents out of the country. Beginning in a fortune teller's tent that might have been 'an impromptu outside lavatory' (11) and ending with a suicide in a public toilet (219–20), the book from the outset adopts a surreal and absurdist approach to the spy narrative. Nothing is what it seems and no one can be trusted, a situation that finds its apotheosis in the parodic version of the locked room murder that sends Rowe on the run (out of, it should be noted, another lavatory window). Not even the identity of the protagonist is stable, as Rowe is temporarily reborn as a 'happy' man after losing his memory in a bomb explosion. Renamed Richard Digby, the happy man remembers nothing of his crime, nor of the war, which – once it has been 'gently broken to him' (119) – remains as unreal as school book history (116). In this paradoxical state of innocence regained, he acquires the investigator's necessary detachment, and speculates with unwitting irony, 'do you think [...] that by any chance I was a detective before this happened?' (121).

By making his detective both a guilt-ridden murderer and an adventurer 'with the freshness of a boy' (169), Greene constantly foregrounds questions of agency and responsibility, and he also sets in train an examination of the term 'murder' itself. Ironically annoyed that someone has tried to murder him, Rowe approaches the 'Orthotex' detective agency for help. As its name suggests, this is a deeply conventional business, whose proprietor, Mr Rennit, struggles to adapt to the modern world. Indeed, Mr Rennit is so far behind the times that he does not even believe in murderers:

> Mr Rennit's calm incredulity shook Rowe. He said with resentment, 'In all your long career as a detective, have you never come across such a thing as murder – or a murderer?'
> Mr Rennit's nose twitched over the cup. 'Frankly,' he said, 'no. I haven't. Life, you know, isn't like a detective story. Murderers are rare people to meet. They belong to a class of their own.'
> [...]
> 'They are very, very seldom,' Mr Rennit said, 'what we call gentlemen. Outside of story-books. You might say they belong to the lower orders.' (35)

In linking crime solely to the lower classes, Rennit reveals a Victorian sensibility, untouched by interwar crime's insistence that the killer must be 'one of us'. This is in marked contrast to the opinions of Willi Hilfe, the novel's symbol of murderous modernity. For the inappropriately named Hilfe, an Austrian refugee, there is no such thing as a 'criminal class', and 'pleasant people, people you had sat next to at dinner' prove capable of heinous crimes (46):

> 'Your old-fashioned murderer killed from fear, from hate – or even from love, Mr Rowe, very seldom for substantial profit. None of these reasons is quite – respectable. But to murder for position – that's different, because when you've gained the position nobody has a right to criticize the means. Nobody will refuse to meet you if the position's high enough. Think how many of your statesmen have shaken hands with Hitler.' (47)

This is a more sophisticated version of the brutality described by Orwell in 'Raffles and Miss Blandish'. These people do not murder to preserve their respectability, they kill to achieve power and with it the respect born of fear. Murder, in this new world order, is not the 'English' variety – long-repressed desires mutating into an essentially romantic private scheme. Rather it is open, pragmatic, expedient and ideo-logically motivated: public, abstract murder (184). Superficially, then, Greene sets up his spy thriller along the established national lines of 'them' and 'us'. They commit murder without a qualm, we – at least in the form of Rennit – can hardly credit its existence.

However, the ethics of both murder and war are complicated in the third section of the book by the introduction of Prentice, the 'surrealist' policeman (158). Prentice is a professional detective-agent, a symbol of British modernity to counter Hilfe, but also a policeman given to 'gig-gling', who does not know how to use a gun (165–8). This ambivalence is typical of wartime representations of British national identity. In film and documentary, the contrast between the British and the Nazis is repeatedly figured in terms of bathos. J.B. Priestley's GPO Film Unit documentary *Britain at Bay* (1940), for example, juxtaposes goose-stepping Nazis in crisp uniforms against ramshackle English volunteers, drilling in baggy shorts and vests: it is a self-conscious deployment of the myth of the underdog, designed to make the Nazi war-machine seem absurdly over-blown. Faced with the impossible efficiency of the enemy, the only outlet for anxiety is humour. As Mrs Miniver, benchmark of middlebrow atti-tudes to war, observes, 'one had to laugh', and to laugh at the enemy is, psychologically at least, to deny his power.[23] Nonetheless, the war must be prosecuted in practical terms, and the character of Prentice demonstrates the contradictory forces that need to be yoked together to create a British 'agent'. He is both ruthless and infantile, merciless and gentle (160), and his introduction brings an urgency into the narrative that overrides Rowe's introspection. This is war, not 'just' murder.

As Prentice and Rowe go into action, the novel presents a complex celebration and critique of Britishness that probably finds its closest analogue in the cinema. Michael Powell and Emeric Pressburger's *The Life and Death of Colonel Blimp* (1943) is a profoundly evasive film that interrogates the question of whether the Nazis can be defeated by any methods other than their own. While the eponymous Blimp holds fast to outmoded ideals of sportsmanship and fair play, the world around him moves on to embrace a more Machiavellian doctrine in which the end justifies the means. Yet, as A.L. Kennedy has argued, the film is 'deeply ambivalent' about this new world order, and it demands respect for the values embodied in the colonel.[24] Greene's novel is equally ambivalent and difficult to 'read'. In his amnesiac state, Rowe acquires the chivalric values of Blimp. He believes in heroic ideals (162–3), justice and happy endings (176) and he must of necessity 'grow up' to acknowledge a more cruel truth (180). In bringing the two 'ages' of Rowe together, and in setting his gradual relearning of adulthood against the absolutism of war, Greene foregrounds the metaphysical cost of conflict. Discussing the fiction of Greene and Evelyn Waugh, Peter Mudford observes that 'the war not only involved the question of who survived, but also of what was being destroyed and the value of what survived'.[25] Rowe's loss of innocence is equally a national loss: in wartime the nation learns not only what it is to suffer, but also what it means to kill.

Given the conflicting discourses juxtaposed by the narrative, it is perhaps appropriate that *The Ministry of Fear* has two endings: the public and the private. Prentice and Rowe's adventure ends in 'a massacre on an Elizabethan scale' – the image of revenge tragedy suggesting a hyperbolic and incongruous accumulation of corpses. Yet the killing of the traitor Dr Forrester by his disciple, Johns, is genuinely shocking. It is one of the tonal shifts in this section of the book that sets Rowe's storybook understanding of war against a more brutal reality. It also foregrounds the moral impasse faced by the hero-worshipping but humane 'little man' Johns. Betrayed, deceived and made a passive accomplice to the murder of the innocent Stone, he can see no solution but to become himself a killer. His actions occupy a border zone between domestic murder and public war that is further complicated by the resolution of a mystery and the discovery of a 'body'. Jones, Mr Rennit's second in command, an insignificant figure who disappeared in the opening pages of the book, is eventually accounted for – but his disinterment refuses the comforts of explanation. This is not the restoration of the grievable body beloved of interwar fiction, rather it is a return to the body annihilated by war. Absurdity and moral seriousness struggle for supremacy as Greene lists the component parts that constituted Jones – his watch, his buttons, his boots: 'So is a poor human creature joined respectably together like a doll: take him apart and you are left with a grocery box full of assorted catches and buckles and buttons' (186). The uncanny signifiers of the absent body speak to the liminal state of human subjectivity in war: in time of conflict, the individual is conscripted and subsumed into a national body. But Greene's image of a corporeality known only by its remnants and traces also seems disturbingly prescient, evoking for the contemporary reader the traumatic residue of Holocaust victims.

Yet Jones's absent body is not allowed to signify for long. Rather than becoming a symbol of war's atrocity, he is swiftly assimilated into the refusal to mourn characteristic of wartime adventure narratives. This transition is achieved through the pragmatic Prentice, who offers an epitaph that undoes the seriousness of war by mischievously invoking the conventions of crime fiction:

> 'What do you think they did to Jones?'
> 'I don't suppose we shall ever know. In time of war, so many bodies are unidentifiable. So many bodies,' he said sleepily, 'waiting for a convenient blitz.' Suddenly, surprisingly and rather shockingly, he began to snore. (188)

In this image, the war does not overwrite the domestic narrative of murder; rather, the massive destructive force of the Blitz is enlisted as an accomplice – an accessory after the fact – and a blessing in disguise for the contemporary murderer.

Jones, like Rennit, Johns and Rowe himself, was a 'little man' and in Greene's bleak world there is little consolation for such figures. While in Christie's fiction, the insignificant men who are pulled into the orbit of war achieve some measure of agency, in Greene's work, they are as likely to find themselves sacrificed. The little women, meanwhile, become part of the problem rather than the solution. Greene does not envisage war as a time in which, even temporarily, women can find a public or national role, and this gives a gendered significance to the negotiation of the public and private narratives within the novel.

The final section of the book, 'The Whole Man', brings the 'private' narrative of Arthur Rowe to a close by reconciling his two identities, and making concrete his creator's belief that 'happiness should always be qualified by a knowledge of misery' (184). Yet Rowe is brought to this state not by national need – he has Hilfe at his mercy following the spy's capture by a deaf old lady – but by private obligation. Greene's novel, like Christie's *The Moving Finger*, contains a narrative of gender normativity in which Rowe, 'feminized' by his outsider status, his passivity and his existence outside time, is effectively remasculinized. 'The Whole Man' thus embraces both Greene's assertion that happiness must be qualified by pain, and the restoration of Rowe's masculinity. What separates *The Ministry of Fear* from the conventional detective narratives of Christie and Allingham, however, is that in Greene's world, masculinity is not bound to agency, but to suffering. And suffering comes, almost inevitably in Greene's fiction of the 1940s, through the figure of woman.[26] Hilfe's sister Anna puts the private above the public, as patriarchy conditions her to do. Detached from history, politics and logic, she tells Rowe: 'I don't care a damn about England. I want you to be happy, that's all' (201), before allowing her brother, the murderous spy, to escape. Hilfe predictably betrays her trust and destroys Rowe's peace of mind by telling him the truth of his past, but in so doing he also 'gifts' Arthur the opportunity of a lifetime of suffering in which he can endlessly assert his masculinity by lying to the woman he loves. The 'protection' of Anna thus becomes a means to atone for the guilt of his original murder (221).

It is a tortuous and contrived ending in which woman is scapegoated as both a danger to the nation and the root of male suffering, and it emphasizes the extent to which Greene's 'entertainment' resists the comforts and conventions of genre fiction. Yet there are similarities with the work of Christie and Allingham. Greene's bodies are displaced or disintegrated, and there is little space to mourn the wartime corpse. Grief here is reserved for the pre-war 'British' corpse of Rowe's wife Alice, and it is, in any respect, shaped less as the pain of loss than the mortifications of guilt. Greene also examines what happens when the interests of the state override the personal, and suggests that inter-war conceptions of murder – and, by Orwellian extension, national identity – are in a state of flux. Where Greene most fundamentally departs from the conventions of genre, however, is in his focus on the murderer. *The Ministry of Fear* is a fiction in which the reader is encouraged to identify not with the victim or the detective, but with the perpetrator of a crime. This is a timely refocusing given that war, in effect, turns citizens into murderers – it makes killing necessary. In his 'cardboard adventure' (178), then, Greene refuses to absolve individual or community from guilt, irrespective of the justice of the cause. In consequence, the traditional marriage plot that symbolically restores the violated community of crime fiction is here rewritten as purgatory.

Bodies that matter: the corpse's comeback

It is thus in marked contrast to the novels of the early and mid-war years that we find Lugg asserting that 'a stiff is still a stiff in this country'. As was suggested at the beginning of this chapter, attitudes to murder and the body are context-dependent. After the deprivations of the 'long haul', light relief was more urgently needed than fifth column vigilance, and consequently it is for very different reasons that *Coroner's Pidgin* struggles to care about its corpses. Through its grotesque characters and deadpan detective, the book marks the resurgence of the private and domestic, and suggests a desire to escape both from the paranoid tension of imminent threat and the grey monotony of wartime restriction. Instead, *Coroner's Pidgin* looks forward, examining the persistence of class distinction in the supposedly egalitarian 'people's war' and reassuring its readership that the core values of the British middle class have survived unchanged.

Like *The Moving Finger*, *Coroner's Pidgin* is concerned with the restoration of conventional masculine and feminine roles. Indeed, the reader cannot but be aware of a conspicuous absence. Amanda, a central character of the series since the early 1930s, a crucial helpmeet to the hero in *Traitor's Purse*, and a notably untypical woman in her penchant for aircraft design, does not appear until the final page of the book. Here, she presents Campion with her 'war work': a baby (240). The hero returning to his home to be greeted by wife and child is an iconic post-war image, and Allingham's presentation of this tableau is indicative of the national mood. Amanda's agency is sacrificed to a nostalgic vision of gender normativity, but this is not the only way in which the novel mobilizes reactionary conceptions of gender. The corpse is discovered to have been an unpopular and parasitic woman given to extra-marital affairs; the cheerful, capable working woman is found to be lieutenant to a ruthless master criminal; and the innocent Susan Shering, symbol of youth, sacrifice and a new generation, is rewarded with marriage to an American officer. The fate of Susan, though, is worth further attention, as she represents a remarkable and extreme example of woman as the object of patriarchal exchange. In a textbook instance of homosocial triangulation, Susan's first husband, a young airforce pilot, effectively leaves her to his commanding officer, who decides that marrying her is the best way to ensure her security. The commanding officer, Johnny Carados, does this out of duty, and is thus somewhat relieved when, in the American officer, he finds another man to whom he can pass the parcel of passive womanhood. Explaining his actions in a letter on the eve of a dangerous operation, he reiterates a range of culturally powerful beliefs:

> *You, Susan, will want to know if I love you. The answer to that is, of course I do, who could help it, but (if you don't understand this, Don will be able to explain it, I think) the feeling I had for old Tom Shering was different, but very, very much stronger. Since you're the girl I know you are, Susan, you won't think me unduly ungallant for this, and as for you, Don, you'll follow me, I fancy. [...]*
>
> *P.S. I took the liberty of spying out Don's reputation and reputed assets. Both are impressive. There again, Don will follow me if you don't, Susan.* (208)

The priority of the homosocial bond is evident here, as is the suggestion that women cannot understand male experience, which would become a truism of the post-war period. But also evident here is the heteronormative assumption that men have a duty to look after women, and this duty is economic as much as emotional. Susan and Don, the new generation, are thus figured from the outset in profoundly old-fashioned terms. Post-war reconstruction finds its ideological roots in the gender paradigms of the past.

Women, their roles and their bodies are thus at the centre of *Coroner's Pidgin*, but the book also contemplates post-war reconstruction through an examination of the body politic. What is at stake, as much as any investigation of the abortive Nazi plot, is the question of who will govern Britain in the new era: who will have authority, whose words will carry weight, whose bodies will matter? Like her contemporaries Nancy Mitford and Evelyn Waugh, Margery Allingham chooses in 1945 to examine the aristocracy, primarily through the figure of another woman – the marchioness Lady Carados, first seen assisting Lugg in the opening corpse-relocation scene. Lady Carados operates as a pertinent reminder that, in mid-century Britain, murder and its investigation are complicated by class. As both a woman and an aristocrat, Lady Carados believes herself outside or above the law (41–2). When her version of the truth is revealed as distorted to say the least, she falls back on the outmoded charm of the Edwardian child-woman, and this combination of irrationality and privilege makes her utterly ungovernable (122–9). To Lady Carados, the police are 'silly and officious' (129), little men beneath her notice. For the main part, Lady Carados is figured as a national monument, a symbol of the past, but her capacity to disturb the smooth operation of the law is troubling, and indicative of a sense of history that resists a clear-cut narrative of progress. The past has not been replaced by the present, nor by a vision of the future; rather times and generations coexist in an uncomfortable conjunction of nostalgia and modernity. 'It's not easy for us now', observes Susan Shering to Campion, 'there are so many different worlds, you see. We each have to live in two or three' (61).

This statement in some sense encapsulates the conflicting discourses of Allingham's *Coroner's Pidgin* – it is a novel that exists in different worlds. In its familiar detective and regulation corpse it recreates the private sphere of the interwar clue-puzzle, and its background narrative of a fifth column conspiracy to appropriate national treasures reworks, in muted fashion, the dynamic of the earlier *Traitor's Purse*. Yet now that the Nazis are not going to arrive, it is hard to accept this as a narrative of national peril, and Superintendent Oates' description of the 'men who kiss and serve and sell [...]. The men who don't know what's important' (146–7) evokes the domestic criminality of the black marketeer as much as the international concerns of espionage. Finally, though, this is also a comedy of manners, in which Allingham deploys the narratives of crime and war to analyse the curious hybrid culture of Britain in 1945. The corpse is thus a benchmark, a site of stability in the midst of flux, exposing the fractures of a changing society, and in Lugg's paradoxically disrespectful respect is found not a new brutality, but rather a nostalgic desire for certainties exploded by six years of war.

In their introduction to *The Fiction of the 1940s*, Rod Mengham and N.H. Reeve suggest that 'the anachronistic redundancy, not just of traditional methods of story-telling, but of the novel itself, is an issue for many writers faced with the Blitz'.[27] Yet crime fiction – in its interwar clue-puzzle formulation – survived the ruptures of the Blitz by revealing itself to be unexpectedly elastic, opening up from the private spaces of domestic murder to embrace the national concerns of spy fiction. Similarly, it proved its adaptability through the representation of the living, deploying women as agents when politically expedient, and sending them home to reassuring gender normativity when cultural anxieties became more pressing than economic need. In terms of the dead, however, little adjustment was required. It did not take much effort to transform interwar crime fiction's cursory depiction of the corpse into wartime crime's pragmatic, and at times brutal, dismissal.

What had changed, though, were the stakes. Where once the corpse had received the detective's full attention, it now became a distraction, its investigation and explanation subservient to higher priorities elsewhere. And here lies the ironic significance of Lugg's ludicrous assertion that 'a stiff is still a stiff in this country. There'll be a lot of questions asked' (7). For the past six years, very few questions had been asked of the body: it had become, in effect, the normative fall-out of war. In reasserting the corpse's priority, however absurdly, Allingham also asserts a return to 'normality' and to such pre-war concerns as class and convention. That the form of the clue-puzzle novel never again achieved the popularity or predominance of the interwar years, though, gives pause for thought. The desire, in the aftermath of war, to restore the known and familiar is essentially nostalgic, and in Britain in 1945 this desire for stability coexisted with a powerful will to change. The aftermath of the Second World War would be no less traumatic for the national psyche than the aftermath of the First World War, but it would not be in the clue-puzzle crime novel that culture found its 'literature of convalescence'.

Notes

Gordon McMullan read an early draft of this chapter and asked a series of perceptive questions that forced me to think again. Petra Rau then gave me the impetus to write it properly. Thanks, and a large glass of red wine to them both.

1. Margery Allingham, *Coroner's Pidgin* (London: Dent, 1987), 7. All subsequent references are to this edition and are cited parenthetically in the text.
2. Stephen Knight, 'Murder in Wartime', in Pat Kirkham and David Thoms (eds), *War Culture: Social Change and Changing Experience in World War Two* (London: Lawrence and Wishart, 1995), 162.
3. Ibid., 163.
4. Graham Greene, *The Ministry of Fear* (London: Vintage, 2001), 65. All subsequent references are to this edition and are cited parenthetically in the text.
5. A point made by Elizabeth Bowen in her short story 'Mysterious Kôr': 'This war shows we've by no means come to the end. If you can blow whole places out of existence, you can blow whole places into it. I don't see why not.' Elizabeth Bowen, *Collected Stories* (Harmondsworth: Penguin, 1983), 730.
6. Victoria Stewart, *Narratives of Memory: British Writing of the 1940s* (Basingstoke: Palgrave, 2006), 61.
7. George Orwell, 'Raffles and Miss Blandish', in *The Decline of the English Murder and Other Essays* (Harmondsworth: Penguin, 1965), 76.
8. Ibid., 78.
9. Ibid., 79.
10. George Orwell, 'The Decline of the English Murder', in *The Decline of the English Murder*, 11.

11. Ibid., 12.
12. Ibid., 13.
13. Alison Light, *Forever England: Femininity, Literature and Conservatism between the Wars* (London: Routledge, 1991), 67.
14. Ibid., 69.
15. See Gill Plain, *Twentieth-Century Crime Fiction: Gender, Sexuality and the Body* (Edinburgh: Edinburgh University Press, 2001) for a more substantial account of 'sacrificial' and 'grievable' bodies in Christie's fiction.
16. Agatha Christie, *N or M?* (London: Fontana, 1962), 6. All subsequent references are to this edition and are cited parenthetically in the text.
17. Elizabeth Bowen, 'Preface to *The Demon Lover*', in *Collected Impressions* (London: Longmans, Green & Co., 1950), 49.
18. Margery Allingham, *Traitor's Purse* (Harmondsworth: Penguin, 1954), 168. All subsequent references are to this edition and are cited parenthetically in the text.
19. I have discussed the novel's complex negotiation of class, gender and nation elsewhere, but it is worth noting that the precarious state of the male detective forms an uncomfortable parallel with the endangered nation: the patriarchal 'state' is propped up only through the cooperation of women and the working classes. See Gill Plain, '"A Good Cry or a Nice Rape": Margery Allingham's Gender Agenda', *Critical Survey* 15/2 (2003): 61–75.
20. Agatha Christie, *The Moving Finger* (London: Pan, 1948), 189. All subsequent references are to this edition and are cited parenthetically in the text.
21. Everyone assumes that the writing of anonymous letters is a 'woman's crime' and a symptom of hysteria. Naturally the truth is somewhat different – in a scenario of which Orwell would have been proud, a middle-class professional man chooses to satisfy his desires without sacrificing his respectability, poisoning his wife in the hope of marrying his children's nanny.
22. *Pygmalion* would perhaps be a more appropriate point of reference – not least because the woman in question turns out to be not quite as pliable as her creator imagined.
23. Jan Struther, *Mrs Miniver* (London: Virago, 1989), 63.
24. A.L. Kennedy, *The Life and Death of Colonel Blimp* (London: BFI, 1997), 62–3.
25. Peter Mudford, '"Quantitative judgements don't apply": the Fiction of Evelyn Waugh and Graham Greene', in Rod Mengham and N.H. Reeve (eds), *The Fiction of the 1940s: Stories of Survival* (Basingstoke: Palgrave, 2001), 188.
26. Scobie, the protagonist of *The Heart of the Matter* (1948), will be a particularly masochistic example of the masculine imperative to protect women from knowledge.
27. Mengham and Reeve, *The Fiction of the 1940s*, xii.

6
Masculinity, Masquerade and the Second World War: Betty Miller's *On the Side of the Angels*

Victoria Stewart

During the account of a wartime hospital sports day in Betty Miller's novel *On the Side of the Angels* (1945), Honor reflects on how her husband Colin, before the war a 'black-coated, pin-striped [...] rising young doctor' and now an officer in the Royal Army Medical Corps, has been transformed by the war. Then, he was 'deft and circumspect and gentle', and she wonders what has happened to erode these positive characteristics:

> She looked at him standing there in his khaki tunic, neatly belted and buttoned. It was the uniform, she felt suddenly, that had changed him. It was as if the anonymity conferred on him by uniform gave him a new sense of freedom and irresponsibility: as if he were masked, and, being masked, privileged, in a sort of carnival spirit, to conduct himself in a manner wholly alien to his normal way of life. The discipline of military life did nothing to correct this: on the contrary: being an imposed discipline, to be accepted whole and without question, it seemed to permit, in compensation, the relaxation of those personal standards, self-imposed and self-maintained, by which up till now as a private citizen he had chosen to live.[1]

The uniform here represents metonymically Colin's absorption into the corporate, masculine world of the army, to the detriment of the personal qualities that Honor has hitherto valued. The 'carnival spirit' engendered by the army does not allow for familial feelings, and is itself a mask for the violence at the heart of war. In this analysis, which is elaborated throughout the course of the novel, the uniform is much more than simply a collection of items of clothing. It is a costume that has a profound impact on the individual's relationship with those who remain, for reasons of gender or unfitness, outside the ranks.

Uniforms are the means by which the members of a fighting force can identify each other in combat, and they also serve to mark soldiers out from civilians. Within the army, the uniform is a disciplinary tool, promoting the identification of the individual with the group and therefore subduing individuality; this is necessary because the desires of the individual have to be put aside in favour of the purposes of the group, even if, as in Colin's case, this means abnegating one's own moral code. During the Second World War the uniforms of different branches of the armed forces became more widely visible and recognizable than they had been previously; for example, the Royal Naval Volunteer Reserve was known as the 'Wavy Navy' because of the distinctive braiding on the cuffs of its the uniform. Used between services, such sartorial shorthand could be less benign; Julian Maclaren-Ross recalls that, during his time in the army, 'the RAF blokes stationed next door called us Brown Jobs',[2] a not uncommon nickname with scatological implications, which further illustrates the metonymic potential of the uniform and its tendency to de-individuate. However, what promotes uniformity within the group serves as a marker of difference when individuals from that group come into contact with civilians, and, as Miller's novel illustrates, the meaning of the uniform shifts in contextually specific ways.

For an individual to don a uniform to which they are not entitled also has a disruptive effect. In order to function effectively as a soldier it is necessary to look like one, but this raises the question of whether being a soldier is simply a case of appearing and behaving in the expected way. Desertion from the army is a more common and probably more explicable crime than its opposite, the adoption of a uniform to which one is not entitled, and this latter form of deception can be undertaken for various purposes. Beginning with a consideration of some theorizations of the uniform from the 1930s and 1940s, I will outline the ways in which uniforms were used as a form of disguise for operational reasons during the Second World War. Such practices serve to foreground the already performative aspects of the wearing of uniform, which are heightened when an individual, for personal rather than militarily sanctioned reasons, adopts a uniform to which he has no entitlement.[3] Drawing examples from literary and other sources, I will argue that whether undertaken for positive, patriotic motives, or for less positive self-aggrandising ones, such abuses bring into question the significatory power of the uniform in a society at war. The oppositions of peace and war, friend and enemy, prove, in such circumstances, to be distinctly unstable.

Betty Miller's novel merits special attention. Set in and around a wartime military hospital, it focuses on how Honor, her husband Colin, her sister Claudia and Claudia's fiancé Andrew are taken in by Captain Herriot, who is not all that he appears to be. Miller's analysis of this situation is informed by her knowledge of contemporary psychoanalysis, and this is a novel that displays an acute awareness of the potential impact of war on conceptions of both masculinity and femininity. Men in uniform become the object of the female gaze, but both female and male admiration is fixed on an object – the soldier in uniform – which, beneath a patina of heroism, embodies potentially aggressive masculinity. Wartime behaviour is viewed as an expression of impulses that are kept in check during peacetime; Freud suggests that war 'strips us of the later accretions of civilization and lays bare the primal man in each of us'.[4] The paradox here is that war is nevertheless a key means by which the values of that civilization are defended. As the cynical Andrew comments in *On the Side of the Angels*, 'civilisation has become so costive that it needs a regular dose of high explosive to achieve a catharsis!' (77). Many of Miller's observations express anxiety about the effects that the valorization of violent masculinity might have both on society beyond the confines of the hospital and life beyond the confines of war. Wartime might appear to provide a contained stage for the expression of troubling emotions and impulses, but Miller and other authors of the period suggest that once in the open, these emotions will be all but impossible to sublimate.

Theorizing the uniform between the wars

The degree and nature of contact between civilians and the army varies in relation to factors such as whether the country is at war or at peace, or whether one lives in a garrison town. In *Three Guineas* (1938) Virginia Woolf focuses on the symbolic and ceremonial function of the uniform, but argues that, whilst the 'dress' uniform might be the one most often paraded in public, this cannot disguise the true purpose of the soldier: 'Obviously the connection between dress and war is not far to seek; your finest clothes are those that you wear as a soldier.'[5] She even suggests that the dress uniform can be used as a recruiting tool: 'Since the red and the gold, the brass and the feathers are discarded upon active service, it is plain that their [...] splendour is invented partly in order to impress the beholder with the majesty of the military office, partly in order through their vanity to induce young men to become soldiers' (138). Woolf can see through such displays to the barbarity beneath, but admits that refusing to don a uniform might appear to be only scratching the surface. Indeed *Three Guineas* does not stop at the question of outward appearances, whether of the army or of one of the other male-dominated professions, using this to initiate a discussion of the exclusion of women from socio-political institutions that might otherwise avert an armed conflict. Woolf does not deny that some men, having seen the horror of war, recognize that it is wrong: after quoting Wilfred Owen, she acknowledges that 'it is obvious that the same sex holds very different opinions about the same thing' (122). However, the force of *Three Guineas* rests on the forging of a connection between patriarchal tyranny at home and martial behaviour at large, a connection that depends on the assertion that 'the majority' of men are 'in favour of war' (122–3).

A powerful example, for Woolf, is a photograph that she does not reproduce in *Three Guineas* and which is, in fact, a 'verbal montage'[6] representing a particularly dangerous martial masculinity, 'Führer or Duce [...] Tyrant or Dictator' (270):

> It is the figure of a man; some say, others deny, that he is Man himself, the quintessence of virility, the perfect type of which all the others are imperfect adumbrations. [...] His body, which is braced in an unnatural position is tightly cased in a uniform. Upon the breast of that uniform are sewn several medals and other mystic symbols. His hand is upon a sword. (270)

Woolf conveys both the elements that potentially add to the figure's allure and her own disdain for these qualities: 'some say', but 'others deny', this individual's prowess; he may appear to be 'the perfect type' but his body is in an 'unnatural position'. Maggie Humm suggests that Woolf's 'choice of a verbal portrait over direct photographic evidence is [...] an ethical strategy, adopted to prevent us from identifying with the often compelling quality of fascist imagery'.[7] Refusing to reproduce an image denies it 'any published, vivid visibility'.[8] Humm's implication is that the 'compelling' photographic image would trump any verbal description; however, Woolf also takes her argument further, asserting a significance for this figure which goes beyond any specific historical example. The image of the fascist emblematizes the connection between private and public 'tyrannies and servilities [...] we cannot dissociate ourselves from that figure but are ourselves that figure' (270–1). Fascism is not merely an external, foreign concept but a force latent in the power relations that Woolf describes. This intersection of the psychical and the social was clearly of interest to Miller also. Andrew expresses a view that is similar to Woolf's, if even bleaker: 'We're not fighting something local and external, labelled Fascism – we're wrestling with our own deepest inclinations and desires' (78). The syntax here implies that it is fascism itself which is this 'deepest inclination'. Whilst militarism may be contained in democratic societies, this containment will be particularly fragile in time of war, when militarism presses at the boundaries of civil society. Fascism, in these analyses, arises when the dangerous 'inclinations and desires' cease to be regulated by social structures and are, rather, fostered and exploited by them.

Woolf's argument is partly based around the perceived duplicity of the dress uniform, which, in her view, strives to mask its military function, presenting an image of the army based on display rather than the reality of battle. Woolf's comments suggest that the dress uniform was the most visible manifestation of the uniform in the interwar period. During the First World War, however, the dress uniform was evidently not the only one to be seen by the general public. Vera Brittain reports how, home on leave in August 1915, her fiancé Roland Leighton took pride in walking through London in a uniform that bore the marks of combat:

> At that stage of the War it was fashionable for officers who had been at the front to look as disreputable and war-worn as possible in order to distinguish them from the brand-new subalterns of Kitchener's Army. [...] Modishly shabby, noticeably thinner and looking at least thirty [he was in fact only twenty], Roland on leave seemed Active Service personified.[9]

The uniform, and particularly the evidence of wear, contribute to one's credibility as a soldier. The duplicity of the dress uniform, identified by Woolf, is replaced here by an unconcealed desire to show evidence that one has seen action. Wearing his uniform allows Leighton to bond with others who have been in action, whilst distinguishing himself from those who have not. Paul Fussell comments that '[a] uniform says a great deal that you don't have to say yourself', and suggests that it can even be an antidote for loneliness.[10] These functions are much more benign than those uncovered by Woolf, reminiscent perhaps of the notion that joining the army will enable the recruit to travel the world, which masks what the purpose of those travels will really be. What is also evident from Brittain's remarks, and indeed, from Woolf's, is that, importantly, uniforms of many kinds are also legible by those who are not themselves serving in the armed forces.

Woolf finds it necessary to distinguish between the type of display represented by uniforms and women's use of dress. For women also, dress is used to attract attention, and, with any luck, a husband: 'Since marriage until the year 1919 […] was the only profession open to us, the enormous importance of dress to a woman can hardly be exaggerated' (137). For Woolf the difference between male and female display lies at least in part in the fact that in their display, in the wearing of uniforms or indeed robes of office, men are advertising their 'social, professional, or intellectual standing' (137). Women's display, in Woolf's analysis, has more limited functions, although in her description of the dictator, she admits, albeit implicitly, that male display can also be erotically charged. The relationship between male and female display, and the idea that putting on any uniform is a form of disguise, or masquerade, is further illuminated in Joan Rivière's 'Womanliness as Masquerade' (1929). Discussing this essay, Stephen Heath suggests that it is only in 'recent years that the idea of the masquerade has received significant attention and gained a certain currency'.[11] Whilst this is certainly true in terms of the emergence of this idea in film theory and gender studies, Betty Miller's work is a fascinating and much earlier example of the use of Rivière's concept of the masquerade as a means of considering interpersonal relations in time of war.

Miller's frequent use of the word 'masquerade' in *On the Side of the Angels* and her general acquaintance with psychoanalytic concepts, facilitated by the fact that she was married to a psychiatrist, make it likely that she was familiar with Rivière's work. Rivière describes the behaviour of one of her women patients, who works in a masculine professional environment, and who uses womanliness as a 'mask, both to hide the possession of masculinity and to avert the reprisals expected if she was to be found to possess it'.[12] She continues: 'The reader may now ask how I define womanliness or where I draw the line between genuine womanliness and the "masquerade". My suggestion is not, however, that there is any such difference; whether radical or superficial, they are the same thing.'[13] Heath's gloss on this often cited comment draws on *Three Guineas*, suggesting that: 'To the woman's masquerade there […] corresponds male display.'[14] Like the female masquerade, the male display serves to compensate for, or at least disguise, a sense of lack, but Mary Ann Doane reminds us that the woman's masquerade still takes masculinity as its point of orientation.[15] The structures of masquerade and display are therefore not identical, as in Rivière's analysis masquerade is about subduing masculinity and display about emphasizing it. Doane warns of the danger of over-stating the ludic possibilities of both masquerade and display as these concepts 'are not totally unreal or totally a joke but have a social effectivity that we cannot ignore'.[16]

These considerations of the relationship between male display and female masquerade are relevant to the texts I have been examining because, like Woolf, Miller seems very much aware that donning the uniform is a compensatory act, not redoubling an existing sense of masculinity but compensating for perceived deficiencies. Although my principle concern here is with men in uniform, the question of women in uniform warrants brief consideration, as the ideas I have described so far do not appear to accommodate this figure. The circumscribing of women's roles in the armed forces limited the threat that could otherwise have been posed by their incursion into a previously masculine domain. Lucy Noakes has argued that putting women in uniform posed problems for both men and women. Women did not substitute domestic for public duty by entering uniformed service but, rather, were put in a position of having to balance both: 'Women in uniform were both expected to subjugate their individual desires and identity to national needs and to maintain their individuality and femininity whilst in uniform.'[17] In this analysis, groups of men in uniform present a compounded masculinity but groups of women in uniform present a diminished femininity: they are neither one thing nor the other. The appearance of women in uniform during the First World War had threatened to 'undermine the division between home front and war front',[18] but by the Second World War, there are even greater incentives to militarize the organization of British civilians.

In an essay published in 1940 in a collection edited by Betty Miller's husband Emanuel Miller, a psychiatrist who specialized in children's developmental problems and was attached after the war to the Maudsley Hospital, Wilfred Bion considers some of the problems that might arise in a 'total war' situation. He identifies an important supplementary function of the uniform:

> The soldier is in uniform; anyone who remembers schoolboy 'shockers' will realise that he is not unused to the idea of blood and wounds on a uniformed body. The sight of blood on civilian clothes is, however, liable to be particularly unnerving.[19]

In total war, soldiers will not be the only ones to get blood on their clothes, but whilst Bion suggests that it is necessary to 'find some modification of the disciplinary framework that exists in a fighting service' through which the civilian population might be organized, thus engendering 'a corporate feeling' among civilians, he warns against 'cutting the Gordian knot' by putting everybody into a uniform of some kind.[20] This, he argues, would 'represent a complete repudiation of the stand upon which the war aims of this country are based'.[21] Bion thus advocates a limited degree of militarization as a means of accustoming civilians to being on a war footing, but is attuned to the fact that the organization of all levels of society into uniform would have fascistic overtones, as Woolf also recognized. Whilst the uniform can have a positive function as a means of distinguishing soldiers from civilians, a proliferation of uniforms would represent too explicitly the extensive militarization of society and is perceived as a potential threat to democracy. Such an argument in turn underlines the importance of policing the ways in which the uniform is used or appropriated.[22]

Uniforms and deception

The performative aspects of being a soldier, looking the part, and adopting the appropriate behaviours and language, cannot mask the fact that there is a difference between pretending to be a soldier and pretending to be in the army. Attempting to insinuate oneself into the organizational structure of the barracks or camp is more difficult than presenting oneself as a soldier within some other context. In instances of deception, the impostor relies on the recognition of his (more rarely her) belonging to a group without that group necessarily being present. The impostor also relies on those to whom he or she presents him or herself accepting, and indeed participating in, the deception, and this raises the question of what stake those who are deceived might have in believing what the impostor tells them. Before I discuss the act of imposture that is at the centre of *On the Side of the Angels*, I will briefly examine some other instances of what might be called legitimate or licensed imposture, which can themselves uncover some of the signifying power of the uniform.

Deception was an important part of Second World War strategy, its extent and significance only becoming fully apparent after the conflict had ended. Lieutenant M.E. Clifton James's impersonation of General Montgomery during visits to Gibraltar and Algiers in early 1944, for example, was intended to divert attention away from the preparations for the Normandy landings, though Michael Howard suggests that German intelligence did not appear to 'draw the appropriate conclusion' from this act of deception.[23] Notably, as Paul Fussell points out, Montgomery took a pragmatic and often casual approach to uniform, with his trademark beret often the only army issue item that he wore in action.[24] James himself was surprised to see that Montgomery's officers wore 'battle-dress trousers, suède shoes and corduroy slacks of many colours', their casual attire explained when Montgomery himself appeared in a 'grey roll-top sweater'.[25] Fussell suggests that Montgomery's informal dress served to emphasize the 'normality of war, and its proximity to familiar civilian usages' though even this apparently lax attitude towards uniform is itself a dress code, one which helped to foster the corporate identity of Montgomery and his officers.[26] James's memoir, *I was Monty's Double* (1954) describes not only the difficulties of both looking and *seeming* like Montgomery, but also the problems James faced in shaking off his role afterwards; a professional actor, James's most notable post-war role was in the 1958 film based on his memoir. James 'took the parts of both Monty and his double, thus playing himself being himself as well as playing the man he had been playing at being'.[27]

In certain circumstances members of the armed forces were required to disguise themselves as civilians. Agents of the Special Operations Executive sent to mainland Europe were warned that as they were operating in civilian guise, they could not claim army protection in the event of capture.[28] Some, such as Violette Szabo, met their deaths in Nazi concentration camps at least partly for this reason. Escapees from prisoner of war camps could face similar dangers. In Paul Brickhill's *The Great Escape* (1951), recounting the break-out from Stalag Luft III at Sagan, in March 1944, one of the recaptured escapees, Johnny Marshall, is questioned about his appearance by his Nazi captors: '"Of course you realise," said the interpreter, "you can be shot as a spy for wearing civilian clothes around Germany".'[29] Marshall tries, through his words, to undo the painstaking work that has gone into reshaping his appearance: 'Oh this is only a uniform I changed about [...] See, I recut it, put boot polish on it, and changed the buttons.'[30] His protests are unsuccessful, though he is one of the more fortunate ones; contrary to the terms of the Geneva Convention, fifty of those caught after escaping from Sagan were shot, but Marshall was returned to the camp. Many escape stories hinge on the adequacy of the disguise; having left Colditz dressed as a camp guard, Airey Neave immediately dispenses with the outer layer of his costume and claims to be a Dutch workman. When Nazi officers enter the train on which he is travelling, he becomes anxious, wondering 'whether they would recognise the colour of RAF trousers'.[31] These instances of imposture would not have been generally known about until after the war, but the dangers of disguise are highlighted in, for example, *Went the Day Well?* (1942), a film in which a group of German soldiers arrive in an idyllic village disguised in British army uniforms. In this instance, appearance cannot mask essence; suspicions are raised not only by the poor English of some of the men but by their ungentlemanly behaviour towards children and old ladies and it is not long before their cover is blown.

On the Side of the Angels

These examples of authorized imposture have strategic or political meaning, but their impact on individual subjectivity, as in the case of M.E. Clifton James, can last well beyond the term of the particular operation. In Miller's novel, the impostor's psychological disturbance, manifesting itself through his imposture, exposes to scrutiny the values and beliefs of the community he targets. The action of *On the Side of the Angels* takes place in and around a military hospital in the small town of Linfield. Honor, the mother of two young children, is married to Colin, formerly a general practitioner and now in the RAMC. Honor's sister Claudia, who works as a schoolteacher, is engaged to Andrew, a lawyer, who has been invalided out of the army with weak lungs. Claudia's ambivalent feelings towards domesticity are expressed partly through her attitude towards her sister's marriage, but also through her own unwillingness to make a full commitment to Andrew. Into this fraught network of relationships comes Captain Herriot, who is based nearby with the War Office Selection Board. Herriot is therefore on the fringes of the social circle based around the hospital, but his most important marker of difference is the fact that he is a Commando.

Graham Dawson has suggested: 'The guerrilla, the commando, the Special Operations forces, the secret agents, spies and saboteurs who operate "behind enemy lines" or in the margins of the conflict: these become the characteristic soldier heroes of twentieth-century adventure.'[32] The Commandos had a reputation for bravery, recklessness and violence that is discernible across the literature of this period. Like the fighter pilot, the Commando had an allure that marked him out from the ordinary soldier; responding to a 'War Office request for a soldier-hero to rank alongside his RAF characters',[33] Captain W.E. Johns, creator of Biggles, devised Gimlet, 'King of the Commandos'. In one series of reports first published in the *Illustrated London News*, Gordon Holman, who accompanied Commando troops on operations to Norway and France in the early 1940s, expresses the Commandos' feelings about their depiction in popular culture:

> They are most serious in their objection to anything that would put them on a different plane to other fighting units of the British army. [...] They object strongly to being 'glorified' and look with distaste on the frequent misuse of the word 'Commando' in connection with anything at all tough or out of the ordinary.[34]

Holman suggests, however, that despite these concerns, 'it may be argued that it is good for the public to have something to look up to'.[35] Holman is attempting to provide a corrective to images circulating in the popular press, but the 'over-done "Commando consciousness"'[36] that he describes characterizes well the reactions of Miller's protagonists on encountering Herriot, implying the persistence of this figure in the public's imagination.

This '"Commando consciousness"' is partly signalled in Miller's novel by reactions to two distinguishing marks: Herriot's green beret and the insignia on his sleeve. This 'flash' stands throughout the novel as a synecdoche for the type of operations in which his interlocutors (and passersby, including elderly ladies and young children) know he is likely to have participated. When Honor and Claudia first meet Herriot, their admiration is barely disguised: '[Claudia] saw the Commando flash on his sleeve: she looked at him with interest and respect. So did Honor who, smiling, spoke to him for the first time. "You're the only Commando soldier I've seen in the flesh," she said' (40). The proximity here of 'flash' and 'flesh' is notable; it is the flash that gives the flesh its status; without the flash, the flesh is just another body. Claudia and Honor are not the only ones to take note of Herriot's badge; Colin's resentment at Herriot's self-confidence also focuses on it. 'Fatuous self-satisfied fool', he reflects. 'Just because you wear a Commando flash, because you've seen active service' (58). On another occasion Claudia notes the reactions of strangers in the street: 'Women (immature girls; a wife on the arm of a husband; a middle-aged matron), recognizing the shoulder-flash, glanced boldly into his face' (213). The uniform, '[a] major force-field in [the] novel',[37] and in particular the flash, speak so clearly to his audience that Herriot has to add barely any details. Their recognition completes the imposture for him; he can rely on them to flesh out his story for themselves. Indeed, Andrew points out towards the end of the novel, after Herriot's imposture is revealed: 'We preferred the fairy-tale we ourselves helped to create' (234).

The near reverence accorded to Herriot is just one aspect of the novel; throughout, Miller grapples with the relationship between uniforms and bodies, in particular male bodies. Andrew voices a belief that what army uniforms license in particular is the eroticization of war. Early on in the novel, after being invalided out, he remarks that it will be a disappointment for Claudia not to be going out with a soldier any more: 'I want you to realize that when you agreed to marry me, you did so largely because I was in fancy dress. In uniform [...] You became engaged to the soldier, Claudia; not to me' (30). She claims that she can see beyond the uniform, but he is not so sure, and her attraction to Herriot seems to validate Andrew's suggestion. Later, Miller shows that what is at stake here is more than just which of them will be chosen by Claudia. The two men are described as being 'locked in some indefinable conflict of temperament: a conflict which because of its nature could find no overt expression, could only work itself out through the medium of a third, a separate personality' (135). Like the heroines of many classic novels, Claudia is choosing between two suitors, but Miller complicates this familiar plot by making Claudia the conduit for this 'conflict' between the two men. She has somehow to adjudicate not only between the contrary emotions that each of the men provokes in her but also between their conceptions of masculinity. Superficially, this is about the cerebral versus the physical but the moment of unspeakable conflict between the two implies the extent to which both these models of masculinity are performative. It also indicates that more is being debated here than just Claudia's happiness; implicit in this triangle are questions about fundamental social values and how the war throws these into relief.

Meanwhile, in her depiction of Colin, Miller points to the homosocial pleasures that could be afforded by army life. As a member of the RAMC, Colin is not, as his sister-in-law points out, 'an ordinary combatant soldier' (36), and the nature of his bond with his commanding officer appears to be a way of compensating for this. Honor tells Claudia that the CO 'hates wives being around' (36); when the two sisters go to meet Colin on the way home, the awkwardness of seeing him in the company of the CO is forcefully articulated:

> [Colin] wished to avoid seeing his wife. Honor understood: she knew that she humiliated him by her presence. Standing there before him, she become aware, in a moment of burning shame, of her own femininity: the fullness, the slipshod contours, of all that was inchoate, ununiformed about her: of that which was capable of giving offence, of making her innately unacceptable to the men before her. She grew suddenly pale and moved a little closer to Claudia. (39)

Honor has a new baby, but these sentiments run deeper than self-consciousness about the effects this might have had on her physical form. Confronted by these men in uniform, she identifies her own femininity as that which is 'ununiformed', unformed, and therefore unacceptable to them. Indeed, the Colonel finds Claudia, with her 'boyish form' (41) easier on the eye. He examines her 'very much as he might assess the nature and quality of an enemy's equipment' (41).

This viewing of the female form with a soldierly eye is echoed when, after Claudia resists Herriot's advances, he jokes: 'I was admiring [...] the efficiency of the de-gaussing system' (67), referring to a technique for deflecting mines from submarines. Reformulating feminine sexuality through the vocabulary of war makes it safe for these soldiers. Masculinity reaches its apogee in the uniform, it is implied; Honor, Miller suggests, is made to feel this discomfort because there is no place for her maternal femininity in their world. Not least through her description of Honor, Miller critiques the ideological devaluation of motherhood that, in her analysis, leads Claudia to think of it as a burden, something that erodes subjectivity and is to be avoided.

If the society Miller depicts in *On the Side of the Angels* is divided into separate spheres, the masculine world of war and the feminine world of domesticity, with a figure such as Claudia anxiously patrolling the border, elsewhere she gives a different analysis of how war might infiltrate the nursery. In a brief memoir published in 1946, Miller reflects on her childhood during the First World War, when the Kaiser became the object of her fascination, to the extent that she formed a secret society (consisting of herself and her sister) dedicated to endorsing this anti-establishment view. She reflects:

> The term 'Fifth Columnist' had not then been invented: nor, if it had, might it have occurred to those responsible to look for its members in the nursery. [...] [H]eresy begins at home: it is precisely in the nursery that the future victims or members of the Gestapo are busy perfecting their weapons, maturing, with regard to authority, an attitude either of compliance or rebellion.[38]

Miller here emphasizes rebellion against 'authority' as opposed to patriarchy in particular. Her secret childhood act of defiance and her later compliance with the expectations of society construct the process of acculturation as a battle, one which continues as she tries to encourage similar compliance in her own children. Whilst her use of the Gestapo as a point of comparison has an edge of bathos, it also has a serious undertow concerning the aggressive impulses in both men and women that, usually lying dormant, may be aroused and exploited in wartime. These sentiments echo those of Andrew, who asserts that: 'There's a Fifth Columnist inside every one of us' (78). This comment, like Miller's later reflections, is a means of attempting to confront what social mores would mask.

Uniforms are frequently referred to in *On the Side of Angels* as 'fancy-dress' or 'masquerade', implying that Herriot's imposture is simply a more extreme version of what all the other men are doing: dressing up.[39] Andrew teases Colin, describing his own time in the army as a 'pleasant masquerade' and suggesting that 'When the clock strikes midnight – when armistice is declared – the khaki will vanish, we'll all be clothed in humble civilian tatters again' (132). (In fact divesting one-self of the uniform will not necessarily mean a reversion to the *status quo ante*.) That Colin is particularly prone to the attractions of this opportu-nity to indulge in display is implied when Claudia remembers his 'dap-per turnout' (18) during his courtship of her sister, dismissing his care about appearances as 'male pirouetting' (18). This term implies an inap-propriate femininity on Colin's part; Claudia seems blind to the fact that Herriot's appearance in uniform is simply another version of this 'male pirouetting'. But these thoughts of Claudia's also indicate the extent to which, in this novel, the male body is placed on display. In a key scene, Honor, Colin, Claudia and Andrew go out to a restaurant to celebrate Honor's birthday. As they settle down, Honor spots a familiar face:

> 'Look – isn't that Captain Herriot over there?'
> Unanimously, they turned to look. The Captain was sitting by him-self at small table by the alcove [...] There was something unfamiliar about him: for a moment they stared at him, puzzled. Then they realized. It was his expression: the look he wore when he imagined himself alone, eating alone among strangers.
> Suddenly, he looked up. He became aware, it seemed, of the atten-tion focused on him. He turned and saw them. At once his face changed: he was familiar, recognizable again. Smiling, he waved a hand to them. (128)

This sudden change in Herriot's appearance can be understood as indi-cating the extent to which the success of his performance of the role of the Commando depends on the participation of those around him. It is notable here that Miller describes the group of four acting collectively; 'they' look, 'they' are puzzled. Their identities, it is implied, are much less fragile than his, but the true reason for this only becomes clear later. The man here is the object of the gaze, and, used to such scrutiny because of his conspicuous uniform, once Herriot is aware of it, he can respond with an appropriate word and gesture. It is in the moment before he is aware that the reader is given a further clue to the deceit he has been practising. But this scene also bears comparison to an earlier and much more trivial moment when the reaction to Claudia of her fellow train passengers is described: 'They withdrew their legs to enable her to pass: examined with open interest, now that she was about to leave them, the personality she deployed as she arose' (9–10). For a woman, according to Miller, this type of scrutiny, and the deliberate deployment of a 'personality' are quotidian.

Disguise is not confined to the men, and Miller 'uses the word to refer [...] to the way local girls make themselves up to look like film stars'.[40] The conceptualization of femininity as masquerade in Rivière's sense is more prominent in Miller's earlier novel, *A Room in Regent's Park*, published in 1942, but set on the eve of the war. Miller is here particularly concerned with the artificial augmentation of female appearance as a reflection of women's limited social roles and opportunities. Examining his wife Virginia's dressing table, a Harley Street consultant reflects that he is 'married to the aggregate of all these bottles', these items smelling 'at once fragrant and faintly stale; the composite essence of a seasoned, feminine personality'.[41] Virginia revels in her elaborate beauty regimen but she is marked as a character lacking in human warmth and spontaneity; when Robert, her step-daughter Judith's boyfriend, admires her at a party, the jealous Judith can only retort, 'She jolly well ought to look impressive, after spending the entire afternoon at Elizabeth Arden's...'[42] However, whilst the women in *On the Side of the Angels* may also be fond of their 'war-paint', the men's 'masquerade' has dangerous and violent associations beyond the confines of domesticity.

Andrew is the first to suggest that Herriot might not be what he seems, and describes the paradoxical outcome of his deception: 'He pleads guilty to murder: but what if, on investigation, he proves innocent after all, and as such, unworthy of all this social adulation?' (140). Andrew's sardonic comment strips away the wartime context of Herriot's behaviour, reminding Claudia that in peacetime, Herriot's brave deeds would seem reprehensible, and exposing a social double standard with regard to male violence. However, Andrew also places the onus on Claudia to choose between Herriot and himself; although he dismisses war as a form of escapism, the ultimate fancy-dress party, he tells Claudia: 'You've got to find out who is the reality, as far as you're concerned – Herriot or me. Which is real to you – the life Herriot stands for – or the life I can offer you?' (159). But this illusion of choice or agency is not really a choice at all, because although Claudia might be wary of being drawn into the kind of domesticity that Honor represents, it is difficult to discern what a future with Herriot would actually mean. He is not a real person, merely a conglomeration of signifiers. Claudia's escape gets no further than a rendezvous in Oxford, supposedly en route for a hotel, and a new life, in London; Herriot is arrested at the railway station and pretends they are not together in order to save her from being questioned. His denial of her effectively relegates her feelings towards him to the realm of fantasy; she returns to Andrew who forgives her for her (almost) betrayal.

When Miller's novel was published in February 1945, the war was drawing to an end, but the issues of imposture raised here continued to concern authors in the later 1940s. Claudia, the reader might feel, has a lucky escape from the object of her fantasy. Real-life imposture could be played out as farce or tragedy, but the ending was rarely happy. In his story 'Brave and Cruel' (1949) Denton Welch lightly fictionalizes his own encounter with Monté Bones, who arrived at Welch's village in 1943 claiming to be an RAF pilot. In 'Brave and Cruel', the narrator notes that Micki Beaumont, Bones's fictionalized counterpart, goes out and buys 'three symbols of his past career': a neckerchief, a record of a military march and a book about the RAF.[43] Once again, the emphasis is on the gullibility of those who are tricked; Beaumont's (and indeed Bones's) own motivations are more difficult to elucidate.[44] In a darker tone, in the creation of the confidence trickster anti-hero of *The Gorse Trilogy* (1951–55), Patrick Hamilton drew on the case of Neville Heath, who committed two sadistic murders in 1946, having told at least one of his victims that he was an RAF officer. He had been practising this deceit intermittently since being dismissed from the Air Force for impersonating an officer in the mid-1930s. The second book of Hamilton's trilogy, *Mr Stimpson and Mr Gorse* (1953) is set in the interwar years, but Gorse is able to convince his victims that he has an army record by affecting a 'military bearing', a moustache and the appropriate slang:

> In certain carefully chosen quarters he passed as one who had been on active service in the 1914–18 War. He had awarded himself the rank of Lieutenant in this war – a Lieutenant in the Royal Horse Artillery. In the quarters in which he put forth (and elaborated upon) this falsehood, he was believed.[45]

The disguise in this case is minimal, and the focus of the imposture is on creating, with the unwitting connivance of the interlocutors, a story that will be compelling to them. What is once again underlined is the extent to which, whatever its function for the impostor, the act of deception can only work within a dialogue; to accept the impostor is to license the war story that he appears to embody. In Hamilton's novel, the story itself will suffice; the uniform is no longer needed, as the mythology of wartime heroism takes on a life of its own in the post-war period.

Notes

1. Betty Miller, *On the Side of the Angels* (London: Virago, 1985), 104. All subsequent references are to this edition and are cited parenthetically in the text.
2. Julian Maclaren-Ross, 'Memoirs of the Forties' (1965), in *Collected Memoirs* (London: Blackspring Press, 2004), 183–369; 254.
3. I use the masculine pronoun here because all the examples I will be discussing involve men. For an examination of the phenomenon of women disguising themselves as soldiers, an act which, historically at least, entails cross-dressing, see Julie Wheelwright, *Amazons and Military Maids: Women who Dressed as Men in Pursuit of Life, Liberty and Happiness* (London: Pandora, 1990).
4. Sigmund Freud, 'Thoughts for the Times on War and Death' (1915), *The Standard Edition of the Complete Works of Sigmund Freud, Vol. XIV*, trans. and ed. James Strachey with Anna Freud, Alix Strachey and Alan Tyson (London: Hogarth Press and the Institute of Psycho-analysis, 1957), 273–300; 299.
5. Virginia Woolf, *Three Guineas*, in *A Room of One's Own/Three Guineas*, ed. Michèle Barrett (Harmondsworth: Penguin, 2000), 115–323; 138. All subsequent references are to this edition and are cited parenthetically in the text.
6. Maggie Humm, 'Memory, Photography and Modernism: Virginia Woolf's *Three Guineas*', in *Modernist Women and Visual Cultures: Virginia Woolf, Vanessa Bell, Photography and Cinema* (New Brunswick: Rutgers University Press, 2002), 195–216; 212.
7. Ibid., 213.
8. Ibid. The issue of the particular, and problematic, representational force of the Nazi uniform, especially the SS uniform, falls beyond the remit of this chapter, but has notably been considered by Susan Sontag in 'Fascinating Fascism' (1974), in *Under the Sign of Saturn* (New York: Farrar, Strauss, Giroux, 1980), 73–105. She offers an explanation for the 'general fantasy' about uniforms; they 'suggest community, order identity (through ranks, badges, medals, things which declare who the wearer is and what he has done: his worth is recognized), competence, legitimate authority, the legitimate exercise of violence' (99). She goes on to explain why SS uniforms in particular can be seen as emblematizing the link between sadomasochism and fascism. A blunter approach to this issue can be found in Piotr Uklański's *The Nazis* (1999), containing images from his exhibition of the same name, which reproduced enlarged stills from a variety of films and television programmes showing actors – German, American, British – in costume as Nazis (Zurich: Edition Patrick Frey, 1999). See also Laura Frost, *Sex Drives: Fantasies of Fascism in Literary Modernism* (Ithaca: Cornell University Press, 2002).
9. Vera Brittain, *Testament of Youth: an Autobiographical Study of the Years 1900–1925* (London: Virago, 1983), 178.
10. Paul Fussell, *Uniforms: Why We Are What We Wear* (Boston: Houghton Mifflin, 2002), 198, 190.
11. Stephen Heath, 'Joan Rivière and the Masquerade', in Victor Burgin, James Donald and Cora Kaplan (eds), *Formations of Fantasy* (London: Methuen, 1986), 45–61; 47.
12. Joan Rivière, 'Womanliness as a Masquerade', in Burgin, Donald and Kaplan, *Formations*, 35–44; 38.

13. Ibid.
14. Heath, 'Joan Rivière and the Masquerade', 55.
15. Mary Ann Doane, 'Masquerade Reconsidered: Further Thoughts on the Female Spectator' (1988), in *Femmes Fatales: Feminism, Film Theory, Psychoanalysis* (New York: Routledge, 1991), 33–43; 38.
16. Ibid., 43.
17. Lucy Noakes, *Women in the British Army: War and the Gentle Sex, 1907–1948* (London: Routledge, 2006), 126.
18. Ibid., 81.
19. Wilfred Bion, 'The "War of Nerves": Civilian Reaction, Morale and Prophylaxis', in Emanuel Miller (ed.), *The Neuroses in War* (London: Macmillan, 1940), 180–200; 185.
20. Ibid., 186, 189, 186.
21. Ibid., 186.
22. In an attempt to quash the activities of Oswald Mosley's Black Shirts, the 1936 Public Order Act banned the use of uniforms to signify membership of a political party; but an ordinary black shirt could not be classed, in and of itself, as a uniform and this law could therefore be circumvented by those wishing to display their allegiance to Mosley.
23. Michael Howard, *British Intelligence in the Second World War, Vol. 5: Strategic Deception* (London: HMSO, 1990), 126.
24. Fussell, *Uniforms*, 46.
25. M.E. Clifton James, *I Was Monty's Double* (London: Rider and Company, 1954), 79.
26. Fussell, *Uniforms*, 46.
27. Harry Pearson, *Achtung Schweinehund! A Boy's Own Story of Imaginary Combat* (London: Little, Brown, 2007), 34.
28. Rita Kramer, *Flames in the Field: the Story of Four SOE Agents in Occupied France* (Harmondsworth: Penguin, 1996), 124–5.
29. Paul Brickhill, *The Great Escape* (London: Cassell, 2000), 217.
30. Ibid.
31. Airey Neave, *They have their Exits* (London: Pan, 1955), 115.
32. Graham Dawson, *Soldier Heroes: British Adventure, Empire and the Imagining of Masculinities* (London: Routledge, 1994), 190.
33. Michael Paris, *Warrior Nation: Images of War in Popular Culture, 1850–2000* (London: Reaktion Books, 2000), 205.
34. Gordon Holman, *Commando Attack* (London: Hodder & Stoughton, 1942), 145.
35. Ibid.
36. Ibid.
37. Jenny Hartley, 'Warriors and Healers, Impostors and Mothers: Betty Miller's *On the Side of the Angels*', in Aranzazu Usandizaga and Andrew Monnickendam (eds), *Dressing up for War: Transformations of Gender and Genre in the Discourse and Literature of War* (Amsterdam: Rodopi, 2001), 173–82; 178.
38. Betty Miller, 'Notes for an Unwritten Autobiography', *Modern Reading* 13 (1946): 39–46; 41.
39. Quentin Crisp uses similar imagery when he describes a visit to pre-war Portsmouth: 'the whole town was like a vast carnival with, as its main attraction, a continuous performance of *HMS Pinafore*. As most of the men

were in uniform and the girls wore shorts and bras in the street, it seemed that everyone was in fancy dress.' *The Naked Civil Servant* (1968; London: Flamingo, 1977), 97.

40. Jenny Hartley, *Millions Like Us: British Women's Fiction of the Second World War* (London: Virago, 1997), 174.
41. Betty Miller, *A Room in Regent's Park* (London: Robert Hale, 1942), 38.
42. Ibid., 116.
43. Denton Welch, 'Brave and Cruel', in *Fragments of a Life Story: the Collected Short Writings of Denton Welch*, ed. Michael De-la-Noy (Harmondsworth: Penguin, 1987), 456–518; 478.
44. For a further discussion of Welch's story, and of Elizabeth Taylor's *A Wreath of Roses* (1949), in which an impostor also features, see Victoria Stewart, *Narratives of Memory: British Writing of the 1940s* (Basingstoke: Palgrave, 2006), 153–60.
45. Patrick Hamilton, *Mr Stimpson and Mr Gorse. The Gorse Trilogy* (Harmondsworth: Penguin, 1992), 271–565; 288. Notably when this book was dramatized for television in the mid-1980s, the action was moved forwards in time so that Gorse's imposture took place during the Second World War, bringing it closer into line with Neville Heath's story.

7
'One step closer to the dreamers of the nightmare': the Fascinating Fascist Corpus in Contemporary British Fiction

Petra Rau

In the 1970s and 1980s, the often eroticized representation of Nazism in film and literature caused considerable unease amongst critics and intellectuals: what could 'fascinating fascism' (as Susan Sontag called it) tell us about the mechanisms of fascist aesthetics and why did we remain susceptible to them in spite of the horrific crimes committed by the Nazis? This discomfiture has by no means abated but flares up periodically when modern art turns to the morally ambiguous territory of representing perpetrators of 'evil': more recent controversial examples are Piotr Uklański's 1998 photo-frieze *Untitled (The Nazis)* at the Photographer's Gallery in London, Norman L. Kleeblatt's exhibition *Mirroring Evil: Nazi Imagery/Recent Art* (2000) at the Jewish Museum in New York, Jonathan Littell's award-winning novel about an SS-officer on the Eastern Front, *Les Bienveillantes* (2006) and Quentin Tarantino's cinematic pastiche *Inglourious Basterds* (2009). Indeed the more remote historical Nazism becomes, the more anxious we seem to be about the rules of engagement with the fascist corpus – its iconography and aesthetics, its victims and its cultural legacy. Yet we remain fascinated on two levels: running parallel to the continued historiographical inquiry into Nazism is a critical meta-discourse about the facetious or complacent uses to which contemporary culture has put fascism. In a culture saturated with Holocaust iconography we seem to be remarkably uncertain about how to respond to images and narratives of perpetration. In fact, an ethical, respectful response to the victims of Nazism may be irreconcilable with a desire to understand fascism, to grasp its psychological hold over our imagination to this day. In this chapter I want to examine what risks are involved in adopting the perpetrator position and how these risks are addressed and 'managed' in contemporary literature. Is it possible at all to represent, even embody, the Nazi corpus without re-evoking its beguiling and abhorrent power?

It is perhaps useful, at this point, to offer a concise summary of the critical debate about fascinating fascism. In her essay Sontag interpreted the proliferation of fascist aesthetics in art, film and popular culture as the manifestation of a desire for both complete submission to and the exercise of boundless power and violence. Fascist aesthetics provided a sadomasochistic 'master scenario', a 'magnificent experience' that ordinary civil society could not deliver: in their 'preoccupation with situations of control, submissive behaviour, extravagant effort, and the endurance of pain [...] they endorse two seemingly opposite states, egomania and servitude'.[1] The sexual appeal of fascist aesthetics stemmed less from an inherent eroticism (indeed fascism sought to channel sexual energy into sacrifice and service for a community) than from its romantic ideal of the absolute triumph of power. What fascist aesthetics achieved was the dramatization of power into an 'erotic surface', an iconography and a spectacle whose citation held the promise of an extraordinary thrill.[2]

Saul Friedlander reached similar conclusions in his essay *Reflections of Nazism* (1982): Nazism offered an eroticized engagement with death as a glamorized ritual or a glorified sacrifice that neither liberal democracy nor leftist ideologies could provide. However, he located his uneasiness about the new discourse on Nazism in the dissonance between the authors' and filmmakers' declared condemnation of Nazism, the will to understand fascism and the aesthetic effect produced by the cinematic or literary narrative. For him, the manner of representation could never reduce the erotic fascination of power that had existed under Nazism. Rather, it re-evoked Nazism alongside the values its iconography embodied.[3] For this reason, any representation of Nazism was tainted. For Sontag and Friedlander, the erotic and the thanatic appeal of fascinating fascism were rooted in the manner in which Nazism staged its ideology through an erotic surface.

Laura Frost, however, has argued that this erotic surface was not an ingenious fascist invention nor even a genuine fascist fantasy[4] but had been the product of Allied projection *before* the advent of Nazism. She has traced this inventory of images back to Allied First World War propaganda. Construing German aggression as violent and sexually deviant validated non-German liberal democracy as respectable and normative.[5] In other words, 'fascinating fascism' grafted itself onto pre-existing virulent Germanophobia. As a projection of disavowed and repressed aggressive impulses it still continually bypasses historical fascism and only ever engages with its own eroticized fantasy of otherness. In constantly proclaiming 'we are not other' the liberal imagination has adopted precisely the core of an ideology that constructed absolute boundaries between an idealized, pure self and a polluted and polluting alterity that must be identified, classified, isolated, expelled and killed.[6] Fascinating fascism, then, is not merely an eroticized representation of absolute power but constitutes a fascist representation, a drama in which the self is constantly reassured about its difference from the other.[7]

The boundary between the 'liberal' self and the 'fascist' other can perhaps be more easily policed in film, where projection is literalized in the image on the screen and our vicarious enjoyment of violence depends on the allegedly secure border between reality and fantasy. Fiction does not always offer such comforts of form. In this chapter, I want to examine two novels about fascism that are formally fundamentally different but similarly demonstrate a rather ambivalent response to the Nazi corpus: Robert Harris's allohistorical noir thriller *Fatherland* and Ian McEwan's novel of ideas *Black Dogs*, both published in 1992. They belong to a spate of novels that re-engage with fascism at the very moment when it appears to fill a vacuum of alterity in a changing European political landscape after the collapse of the Soviet Union, the reunification of Germany and the signing of the Maastricht Treaty that consolidated the European Union.[8] Was the old fascism the new enemy? I am interested in the way in which both texts embody fascism and frame its cultural legacies. On a literal level, what role do fascist corporeality and iconography play? And figuratively, how do these novels situate the fascist body in the material remnants of fascist ideology (most notably the camps) that feature so prominently in our memorial landscape of fascist crime and genocide? How do these books negotiate the representation of fascism against a potential fascism of representation?

Nazi noir: uniformed men and ghostly women

Robert Harris's bestselling thriller *Fatherland* imagines the nightmare scenario of a Nazi victory in the Second World War. By 1964, the Reich has devoured most of Eastern Europe where it fights a never-ending guerrilla war against American-sponsored Soviets, while Western Europe, including Britain, has been conquered by cultural and economic German hegemony. In Albert Speer's monumental Berlin, preparations for the Führer's birthday pageant form the background to an ostensibly ordinary murder case. On the surface, this is a detective thriller in which 'regular' crime is committed to keep genocide a secret: one brutalized Nazi corpse will lead to eleven million murdered European Jews who have vanished without a trace. For the unknowing detective, the clues eventually reveal the greater 'mystery' of the Shoah. For the informed reader, the suspense consists in the interpretation of a documentary trail that retraces the process of the 'Final Solution' from the Wannsee Conference in early 1942 to the death camps in Poland, and in the question of whether the noir hero will survive to disseminate this illicit body of knowledge. The novel thus sets up two oppositions: the readable, ubiquitous Nazi bodies that populate the plot against an invisible, undetectable mountain of genocidal victims; and a material body of evidence in the form of documents about the Shoah to which the detective's vulnerable body gives access.

The plot of *Fatherland* rests on the investigative zeal and uncompromising integrity of its noir detective, SS-*Sturmbannführer* Xavier March, just as much as it depends on the reader's willingness to suspend disbelief about the plausibility of a secret Shoah. Much is made of March's difference to the police officers around him, not least because Harris has to construct a character in this corrupt Nazi state for whom the reader can root and who constitutes a credible object of desire for a female representative of democratic America, the journalist Charlie Maguire. True to the rules of noir, March must be 'the best man in his world and a good enough man for any world'.[9] Yet in a police state in which security forces proliferate (*Kriminalpolizei, Ordnungspolizei, Sicherheitsdienst* and Heinrich Müller's *Gestapo*) and their remits blur into one another, straightforward crime cannot be sharply separated from ideological transgressions, and vice versa.[10] This is precisely the point of the plot. Pitched against 'real' Nazis like the historic Artur Nebe, Joseph Bühler and Odilo Globocnik (organizer of the Operation Reinhardt death camps), March becomes that oxymoronic figure, the Good Nazi: a cynical cop whose mediocre career and failed marriage to a party faithful reassures the reader of his fundamental decency. Yet his appearance constantly undermines his position on the margins of authority where we might expect the stereotypical noir hero to operate. His menacing and dramatic SS-uniform turns him into an official embodiment of the state's power *and* constructs his body as sexually attractive. Even in a capital bustling with uniformed bodies, this is the Nazi outfit that dramatizes the hero as less ambivalently 'noir', fully implicated in the social world he polices:

His uniform was laid out in the bedroom: the body-armour of authority.
Brown shirt, with black leather buttons. Black tie. Black breeches. Black jackboots (the rich smell of polished leather).

Black tunic: four silver buttons; three parallel silvered threads on the shoulder tabs; on the left sleeve, a red-white-and-black swastika armband; on the right, a diamond enclosing the gothic letter 'K', for Kriminalpolizei.

Black Sam Browne belt. Black cap with silver death's head and Party eagle. Black leather gloves.

March stared at himself in the mirror and a Sturmbannführer of the Waffen-SS stared back. He picked up his service pistol, a 9 mm Luger, from the dressing table, checked the action, and slotted it into his holster. Then he stepped out into the morning.[11]

This reads like a more sexed-up version of the picture captions for *SS-Regalia*, that odd, fetishistic compendium of paraphernalia that Susan Sontag cites in her essay 'Fascinating Fascism' as 'a breviary of sexual fantasy': 'For fantasy to have depth, it must have detail.'[12] Unlike so many of the grotesque bodies of the Nazi leaders, March's body is indeed that of the 'Aryan superman' of Nordic race, yet it is his uniform that visibly certifies his racial superiority (96, 192). Encased in that uniform, March turns from an inconspicuous individual into a military rank; as he will tell Maguire, the armoured corporate body 'blots out the man' (208). To himself and to her, March justifies this armour of authority with the same exculpatory reasoning that became a well-worn refrain in post-war German courts of justice: 'either I am an investigator in that uniform, and try to do a little good; or I am something else without that uniform, and do no good at all' (211). Moral agency here seems to be tethered to the semiotics of power: uniformed state-empowered bodies versus an ineffectual civilian non-existence. In order to be 'the best man in his world', March must not just look like a Nazi, he must be part of the very system in which he has such bad faith.

On his path to truth March dismisses his apologia as 'bullshit' but the plot nonetheless depends on the effects of the uniform. Without the dramatization of power, March is 'barely recognisable' for his lover (208), which suggests that it is indeed the uniform that stimulates desire rather than the man or the male body inside.[13] The liaison between the American journalist and the Good Nazi in *Fatherland* bluntly literalizes the erotic attraction of democratic culture to fascism although it is meant to be read the other way round, as a redeeming feature of the Good Nazi's convertibility to democratic values: having been 'brought up to think of Germans as something from outer space', of the SS as 'murderers [...]. Sadists. Evil personified' (208–9), Maguire nonetheless goes to bed with what she purports to hate 'on sight' and explores – like the reader – the darkest secret of the fascist vision.

To be sure, March's dressing routine is much more important than taking his clothes off: getting into uniform is described three times in the novel while sex happens, coyly, off-stage. In one of the novel's most potent scenes, when March is finally arrested, interrogated and tortured, he is still in uniform. Indeed he has prepared himself for the final stage of this investigation through the dressing ritual: this 'would be the last time he wore it, one way or the other' (337). While he is violently beaten, Maguire has become the carrier of incriminating evidence; the longer he can keep his torturers occupied the greater her chances to escape over the Swiss border with crucial documents. Even before the torture scene, March's knowledge of the corrupt Nazi regime is written all over him: the sleeplessness, the poor diet and alcohol abuse, the deepening loneliness of a failed marriage and the impossibility of friendship mark his body. The torture scene, then, imprints the detective's knowledge on his body only more violently. Maguire's escape depends on March's ability to keep this intensely physical scene entirely homosocial – a punch-up between men in uniform. When the torturers punctuate their blows with the question 'Where's the girl?', the grammar of this sadomasochistic scene is predicated on a woman's absence.[14] As Gill Plain has argued in her analysis of Chandler, the hard-boiled genre reserves sensuality for the less familiar corporeality of the male. Its objectified females may in fact be the red herring in a form that, underneath frustrated heterosexual romance, may be much more interested in equally unsatisfiable homosocial dynamics.[15] In Nazi noir, *Fatherland* suggests, relationships between men are constantly betrayed for the sake of that one Big Man, the Führer, whether they are between fathers and sons, colleagues, protégés and protectors, or between war veterans.

If male friendship is unattainable, torture offers its violent, perverse replacement. In enduring pain March assumes an abject, passive position in which violence is framed like a sexual consummation: 'I have waited for this moment as a bridegroom waits for his bride' (345), whispers Odilo Globocnik before delivering the first blow. The cruelty he metes out in precise knowledge of the pain he inflicts is described with more detailed sensuousness than the coy brevity of off-stage, straight sex: the kidney punches, the hair pulling, the repeated beating and kicking, the grinding of boots into March's ear or on his hands, are foreplay to a debilitating climax in which Globocnik, having tenderly brushed the tip of a baseball bat across March's knuckles, crushes the detective's right hand to pulp. In this sadomasochistic theatre of violence, Harris makes March's body come alive in a fascist apotheosis of suffering and renunciation, superseding the little deaths in anonymous hotel rooms with those in a blood-spattered subterranean prison cell.

While he is violently beaten, March both fantasizes about his lover and shouts the names of death camps at his torturer. This confluence of violence, an elusive female body and the death camp is repeated in the novel's final scene in the ruins of Auschwitz, when March gives himself up to die in the fantasized knowledge of his lover's escape. Thus the woman is both with him in her past familiarity and irrevocably gone as a fugitive in disguise; both a spectral object of desire and a real refugee; both a distant memory and a contingent future. Already somewhat chimerical in her threadbare characterization, the female object of desire becomes a ghostly woman on the final page of *Fatherland*.

The nexus of sacrificial death, spectral and spectacular women, and unfulfillable desire on Holocaust territory is a familiar problematic that perhaps first surfaced in the controversies over Liliana Cavani's *The Night Porter* and Fassbinder's *Lili Marleen*. Ian McEwan's *Black Dogs* demonstrates the libidinal shortcomings of non-fascist ideologies vis-à-vis the continued seductions of violence in postwar Europe – a continent where the material traces of war and Holocaust elicit an uncannily sexual response in his English characters. Here too a death camp features, and here too we find the confluence of an eroticized female body, fascist violence and the material evidence of the Shoah. The narrator Jeremy first meets his wife Jenny Tremaine on a tour of Poland in the early 1980s. On this tour Jeremy is asked to accompany her to Majdanek:

> Three years before [...] I had been to Belsen and had promised myself that I would never look at another camp. One visit was a necessary education, a second was morbid. But now this ghostly pale woman was inviting me to return [...] she explained that she had never visited a concentration camp before and preferred to go with someone she could think of as a friend. As she arrived at this last word she brushed the back of my hand with her fingers. Her touch was cool. I took her hand and then, because she had taken a willing step towards me, I kissed her. It was a long kiss in the gloomy, un-peopled emptiness of the hotel corridor.[16]

The camp visit is staged as a thanatic seduction, with a woman as catalyst and prize for the sexually timid narrator. The ghostly female only becomes flesh and is only sexually fully available once she's been in a camp: after the visit to Majdanek, they immediately enter a hotel and don't leave their room for three days. As in *Fatherland*, the hotel door closes discreetly on the lovers' consummation. In her review of the novel, Kerry Fried argues that the Majdanek visit as the beginning of romance 'comes dangerously close to being obtrusive, grotesque, but McEwan is so deft a writer that again the violence does not, finally, seem gratuitous'.[17] Yet it is not the deftness of McEwan's prose that accounts for the lack of gratuitous violence of which we find plenty in his earlier fiction. While there is, in *Black Dogs*, some interest in real manifestations of violence (political, sexual and familial), it is the ubiquitous *potential* for violence that is embodied in the central metaphor of the book. If the camp visit is indeed a literalized Freudian 'morbid' return, we should perhaps ask precisely what is being repressed that so uncannily surfaces in Majdanek?

On the other side: fantasy and the perpetrator's premise

During their visit to Majdanek, Jeremy deals with two synecdochal bodies: the material remnants of the victims (masses of shoes displayed in wire cages) and the remainder of the camp as the fascist vision of 'racial cleansing'. In his encounter with this fascist corpus he rejects the moral efficacy that cultural memory of the Shoah is supposed to produce. Instead, he is 'drawn insidiously to the perpetrators' premise':

> We were strolling like tourists. Either you came here and despaired, or you put your hands deeper into your pockets and gripped your warm loose change and found you had taken one step closer to the dreamers of the nightmare. This was our inevitable shame, our share in the misery. We were on the other side, we walked here freely like the commandant once did, or his political master, poking into this or that, knowing the way out, in the full certainty of our next meal. (110)

Note the near-compulsive move, from the tourist's stroll to the commandant's stride within the psychology of identification. Obviously this passage addresses the irrational feelings of guilt in the post-memorial, post-war generation, and it raises important issues about the cultural meanings and psychological effects of memorial sites, which I will address in the next section. It is the shame of the disempowered bystander whose scrutinizing gaze seems to fix violated bodies in their victimhood and repeat the violation *ad infinitum* that ultimately makes the narrator cross to 'the other side'. In this moral transgression guilt is converted into a fantasy of domination, from whose vantage point of omnipotence the panorama of the concentrationary universe is surveyed:

> After a while I could no longer bear the victims and I thought only of their persecutors. We were walking among the huts. How well they were constructed, how well they had lasted. Neat paths joined each front door to the track we were on. The huts stretched so far ahead of us, I could not see to the end of the row. And this was only one row, in one part of the camp, and this was only one camp, a smaller one by comparison. I sank into inverted admiration, bleak wonder; to dream of this enterprise, to plan these camps, to build them and take such pains, to furnish, run and maintain them, and to marshal from towns and villages their human fuel. Such energy, such dedication. How could one begin to call it a mistake? (110f.)

This fantasy seems more in keeping with reports about lower-ranking staff in camps and ghettos who assumed godlike roles in these law-less spaces whenever they believed or knew themselves to be beyond sanction: police officers or individual camp guards.[18] Notwithstanding the evidence of such monstrous conduct, McEwan's fantasy of omnipo-tence is of a different calibre to that of the 'Evil personified' that is such a staple of the popular imagination – the sadistic torturer Globocnik in Harris's *Fatherland*, the trigger-happy psychopath Amon Goeth in Keneally's *Schindler's Ark* or Peter O'Toole's leering serial killer in *Night of the Generals*. Here the ordinary Jeremy fancies himself as Kommandant.

Jeremy's 'bleak wonder' and 'inverted admiration' is kindled by the dimensions of Majdanek as a (reconstructed) memorial site near Lublin.[19] The perpetrator's application of ordinary managerial criteria and industrial processes to the extraordinary phenomenon of exploitative genocide is the only access point to a rationalization (in both senses of the word) of the crime: to *understand* the Shoah one might have to assume the morally untenable position of the perpetrator. Even if the dreamers are still seen to produce a 'nightmare' rather than a vision, his train of thought dem-onstrates that the vision is preferable to the despair of identification or empathy with the suffering it produced. It counters Sontag's and Friedlander's explanations of 'fascinating fascism' as a Genettian drama-tization of death and violence. Rather, it implies that the focus on per-petrators we find in such genres as Nazi noir or post-Holocaust science fiction precisely *avoids* a confrontation with death:[20]

> The extravagant numerical scale, the easy-to-say numbers – tens and hundreds of thousands, millions – denied the imagination its proper sympathies, its rightful grasp of the suffering, and one was drawn insidiously to the perpetrators' premise, that life was cheap, junk to be inspected in heaps. As we walked on, my emotions died. (110)

The scale of the crime, still visible in its memorialized reconstruction, is made responsible for the visitor's confounded response. The first stage of this response echoes the sarcastic prophesy of an SS-officer, cited in Primo Levi's *The Drowned and the Saved*, that the crime is too fantastic in conception and too monstrous in proportion to be believed. McEwan's Majdanek scene explains how the move from Holocaust testimony to Nazi fantasy might be possible: 'one was drawn insidiously to the perpetrators' premise' because in that move from stunned but helpless empathy to guilt-laden awed fantasy, identification shifts from a vulnerable body, doomed to die, to a well-fed uniformed body seemingly impervious to death in its 'body armour of authority'.

Harris's *Fatherland* pushes this fantasy further since its plot demands a Nazi corpus of gargantuan proportions. Harris provides maps of the enormous expansion of the Nazi Reich and of Albert Speer's new Berlin with its megalomaniac architecture.[21] He grants the Nazis a *Reichsarchiv* with six subterranean floors and a furnace for undesirable history at its centre. The narrative is replete with historical Nazi leaders and functionaries whose biographies have been altered, but whose pronouncements are accumulated in citations and epigraphs. Remarkably, when it comes to uncovering the Shoah and turning the detective into a reluctant historian, the documentary evidence Harris marshals barely includes any Jewish testimony, only Nazi correspondence about the Wannsee Conference, rail timetables to death camps, and witness reports from functionaries' visits to camps. The more we learn about the Shoah in *Fatherland*, the more we are pushed to 'the other side', seeing it with the perpetrators' eyes: 'such energy, such dedication'.

However, for Gavriel Rosenfeld, Harris's scenario belongs to a category of counterfactual history that continues to perform an important moral function in underlining the barbarous nature of the Nazi period before books like Martin Amis's *Time's Arrow* (1991), Christoph Ransmayr's *Morbus Kitahara* (1996) and Peter Quinn's *After Dachau* (2001) ring in a more 'normalized' engagement with fascism.[22] Contemporary culture's increasing exhaustion with the cultural memory of the Holocaust manifests itself in the desire for a more 'uninhibited' relationship with the Nazis.[23] Yet is it not precisely the uninhibited imagination of Harris or McEwan that lends such fictitious Nazism its noir aesthetics and thereby reduces its moral impact (only a mind for which the historical horrors of the Nazi regime and its genocide have palled needs a worse-case scenario)? Neither critique nor irony change the associations with the Nazi system; nor do they make this representation of fascism less 'fascinating', since the detailed evocation of the fictional Nazi 'background' utilizes the same semantics as the historical original. Read thus, we would have to concur with Saul Friedlander's scepticism about the possibility of an ethical representation of Nazism. (That Harris's novel became very popular with continental neo-Nazis once a Swiss publishing house chose to translate it suggests the multivalent grammar of its scenario as well as significantly different cultural responses to 'fascinating fascism' in Europe and Anglo-America: finding this book gripping in Germany betrays right-wing leanings; finding it gripping in the UK is supposedly a reassurance of one's democratic normality.)

This representational impasse seems to have escaped Harris, whose choice of allohistorical form (in a bleak elsewhere, in another time) allows him to suggest a conflation of contemporary continental Europe with Nazi-occupied Europe: 'There are things that Germany would have achieved in 1945 which have come true in 1992, in particular the economic domination, and so on. The collapse of Bolshevism. The strength of Germany in Eastern Europe.'[24] In this paranoid reading, the Second World War may have been won on the battlefield but was subsequently lost in the corridors of Brussels. McEwan, too, concludes his novel ominously with the prediction that evil 'will return to haunt us, somewhere in Europe, in another time' (174). Thus their readers are reminded of a fascist Europe at the very moment when Britain's ties to that fateful continent become stronger (through the Maastricht Treaty of 1992), as if the fascist threat had gradually metamorphosed into the spectre of European integration.[25] *Fatherland*'s crucial body, then, may not be the fascist corpus or the vanished bodies of the Jews, but the lost integrity of a body of water: the Channel, which so fortuitously preserved British independence and democracy from continental fascist contamination. Read through its emphasis on corporeality, the novel betrays a deep uncertainty about the boundaries between liberal democracy and fascist otherness. Harris's plot consequently allows the reader to inhabit various conflicting positions all at once: to be the Aryan superman and the lonely noir hero; to engage in straight sex but yearn for male friendship; to watch Nazi sadism and be its victim; to remain a decent police officer when Himmler's secret speech in Poznan in 1943, cited in an epigraph, discredits the very notion of decency; to wear an SS-uniform and yet be 'the best man in his world'. If, as George Mosse has argued, the Western imagination principally shares one stereotype of masculinity and Nazism provides merely its most warlike manifestation,[26] then Nazi noir clearly offers the reader a safe and exciting fascist fantasy in which the Aryan protagonist with his inquisitive intelligence, bravery and rugged attractiveness invites identification despite *and* because of the ideology symbolized by the uniform. Even in pain and death March's body still conforms to aestheticized Nazi masculinity. His fate is precisely the glorified death of the Aryan soldier hero in Nazi art and propaganda, who exalts in suffering and renounces sexuality. While his body goes the way of the persecuted Jewish other – classified, hunted, arrested, tortured, forced to die in a camp – his death remains an impeccably honourable thanatic apotheosis either as a redemptive suicide or a violent fusillade that cleanses the Reich of a traitor: a luxury of ambivalence that the inmates of Auschwitz did not have.

Bodies of evidence: cultural memory and fascist representation

Auschwitz and Majdanek are of course memorial sites whose remit is the preservation of a body of evidence relating to industrial genocide and murderous inhumanity. In the 'rhetoric of ruins', as James E. Young has called it, those remnants are presented as synecdoches of historical phenomena. Our encounter with the artefacts of genocide is shaped by the manner of their presentation; indeed the latter may actually perform the task of interpretation.[27] By themselves these artefacts do not necessarily mean anything and consequently, framed in a different context, they are open to alternative appropriations. This is precisely the case with the camp sites in *Fatherland* and *Black Dogs*. In *Fatherland*, the barely recognizable foundations of brick buildings at Auschwitz have no evidentiary status without a documentary trail that gradually explains the purpose of the site. Maguire reports that survivor testimonies of atrocities are often dismissed as anti-German propaganda, hysterical outpourings of deranged people, or simply meet with indifference. In a world that has no ready-made context for industrial genocide, it remains unreadable. And yet, Harris does not seem to trust his own plot of proving the existence of the Holocaust without marshalling further evidence in the form of epigraphs that cite actual perpetrators and survivors. In such moments one does wonder whether *counterfactual* fiction really is the appropriate medium to represent historical genocide. *Black Dogs* makes an even stronger case for the multivalence of memorial sites by revealing how the victims of genocide were subsumed in an ideological narrative of national suffering and Soviet liberation. Thus they disappear three times: once as a result of the historical crime, then in the manner of commemoration in Communist Poland and finally in Jeremy's refusal to empathize and identify.

The irony of some of the camps' pastoral names (Birkenau, Buchenwald, Gross-Rosen) and the beauty of their settings have often been commented on, precisely because these signifiers cloaked their function. Their nature and size is harder to grasp, either because they are only partly reconstructed or because they were successfully destroyed, such as the Operation Reinhardt camps. Gitta Sereny, on visiting Sobibor in 1972, initially drove past the small monument that marked the site. On Treblinka, long a national memorial, she remarked:

> The Poles have spared no effort to reconstruct the whole of the camp as a national monument which, while adequately portraying the horror, can also leave one with some feeling of human dignity. But it doesn't work. All one can think of is the terrible smallness of the place. [...] the main reason why it is so difficult to visualize lies in nature itself: where there used to be huts, barbed wire, tank traps and watch towers, there are now hundreds of bushes, and young pine trees which the Germans planted to camouflage this site when, having accomplished what they set out to do, they obliterated the camp at the end of 1943.[28]

And so Sereny concludes, 'We know that more than a million human beings were killed and lie buried in these few acres, but it cannot be believed.'[29] We can only see the result of obliteration, and this means engaging unwittingly in the perpetrator's premise: to see the site with the Nazis' eyes post-genocide; to reject what we know even though monuments mark an event and museums offer us its interpretation.

Paradoxically, the material fragment makes remembering redundant and reduces it, at best, to 'a necessary education' tethered to an optional museum visit. That artefacts (like photographs or artworks) need to be framed suggests that visitors' responses are by no means self-evident. The presentation may indeed imply that the perpetrators' perspective is a more instinctual one, and might be unavoidable. As James Young argues, that a murdered people should primarily be recalled through images of their death; and that the memorial institutions utilize the very artefacts of their expropriated belongings risks 'perpetuating the very figures by which the killers themselves would have memorialized their Jewish victims'.[30] The accumulations of specific artefacts found in the camps (spectacles, suitcases, shoes, clothes, hair and so on), which are now often displayed as synecdochal exhibits of victims' bodies, are the result of the perpetrators' selections for reuse.[31] With these artefacts, museums simultaneously enshrine the perpetrators' fantasy, the vision of omnipotence and dominance. In visiting and preserving these sites, we might even, according to the Austrian survivor and writer Ruth Klüger, service our superstition about the ghosts of the victims and our own 'necrophilic desires'.[32] For Klüger, the memorial landscape of the Holocaust is about the needs of posterity: it actually distances the visitor from the Shoah and sentimentally returns him or her to self-conscious navel-gazing, thus creating a boundary between historic Jewish suffering and what one might cynically call Holocaust tourism. There is a sense here – uncomfortable as it may be – that through different modes of othering, neither Jewish suffering nor Nazi perpetration can be 'safely' represented.

Jeremy's reaction, in *Black Dogs*, to be 'insidiously drawn to the perpetrator's premise', is therefore by no means as outlandish and macabre a response as one might think, but indeed retraces the way in which the material remnants of genocide were originally intended to be seen and treated. The camp is turned from a metonymically preserved site of atrocity to a fascist body beautiful; it moves our engagement from corpses to a corpus, an ever-lasting and indestructible enterprise, a machine eternally fed by the ghosts of its victims. His 'inverted admiration' captures very neatly 'fascinating fascism' as a post-war cultural phenomenon that allows us to transgress into that morally prohibited zone of the Nazi vision that museums and memorial sites consistently deny in their rules of engagement with this body of evidence. As educational and moral spaces museums habitually disavow the psychological complexity of any encounter with atrocity.

Reflecting on the contradictory positions of liberator or survivor which the Holocaust Museum in Washington DC allows its visitor, Tim Cole questions the museum's practice of assigning the visitor victims' identities in the form of ID cards:

> Why don't they give out the cards of perpetrators and bystanders as well as victims, so that somewhere towards the end of the second floor I come to the shocking understanding that I'm a member of the German battalion which is involved in killing Jews in 1942, or

a Hungarian municipal officer involved in drawing up plans for the local ghetto in 1944?[33]

Cole inscribes a moral response to the unexpected position of perpetrator that is by no means self-evident ('a shocking understanding') and which suggests a view of history as fate rather than the collective product of individual agency (precisely the exculpatory position of many Germans taking recourse in having been the victims of Nazism as a fate beyond their control). Cole's question may be a symptom of the cultural exhaustion with official trauma discourses and ubiquitous commemorative culture that manifests itself in the desire for a more 'uninhibited' engagement with the Shoah and the Nazis alike. In contemporary museum culture, the contingency of victimhood seems to have preferable educative value to the contingency of perpetration, which we still like to confine to popular visions of 'murderers [...]. Sadists. Evil personified'. What would be the explanatory power of putting into practice Cole's suggestion, and say, handing out random *Einsatzgruppen-*IDs? There might be considerable merit in making visible how easy it is to become complicit in the abuse of power or to become habituated to committing atrocities. The unexpected and alarming perpetrator position surely requires a great deal more explanatory investigation than a metaphysical concept such as 'evil' could offer, and would therefore stimulate reflection. Yet McEwan's novel shows us that the response to atrocity cannot be easily controlled: are we too susceptible to the Kommandant's fantasy to be encouraged to inhabit it? But if we cannot be trusted, this only confirms that the (ethical) boundary between the liberal 'us' and the Nazi 'other' is one that museum culture must police and maintain.

In recent historiography the very ordinariness of the perpetrators has complemented a discourse that primarily focused on the Nazi elite. Zygmunt Bauman's *Modernity and the Holocaust* or Christopher Browning's *Ordinary Men* are not interested in the psychopathic Butcher of Riga or the fanatical ideologue. Rather, they examine the insidious sliding into opportunistic lawlessness, the gradual brutalization *process*, or the effects of a modern administrative apparatus on the sense of individual responsibility. They seemed eager to dismiss 'Evil personified' as a predictable historical vicissitude:

It is not the brutal SS man with his truncheon whom we cannot comprehend; we have seen his likes throughout history. It is the commander of a killing squad with a Ph.D. in law from a distinguished university in charge of organizing mass shootings of naked women and children whose figure frightens us.[34]

If we understood what moved the commander to sanction mass murder, we would, like McEwan's narrator, be 'on the other side' with him. In fact, there would be no 'other side', only a continuity between him and us. Therefore any encounter with atrocity must disavow the contingency of identification even if this results in a categorical prohibition to comprehend or even to represent.[35] In contrast, the brutal SS-man with a truncheon is a welcome relief despite his historical commonness, an emotionally satisfying representation of appalling alterity. Extraordinarily other in his psychopathology, the man with the truncheon is not us.

The proliferation and popular success of narratives of perpetration – from the contemporary fascination with serial killers to Nazi noir; from bestsellers of simplistic historiography such as Goldhagen's controversial *Hitler's Willing Executioners* to ubiquitous TV documentaries and films about 'the Nazis' – is a fair indicator of our need for the man with the truncheon in the tight black uniform. As Liliane Kandel suggests, the theatre of cruelty has its risks; not just of complaisance or voyeurism but of identification with the executioner.[36] The man in the SS-uniform is of course not an object of desire but a fantasy of dominance, doubly disavowed as a projection and a fascist representation: I am not other. So why is it that what lingers in the reader's mind, after putting *Fatherland* aside, is its excess: the size of the fictional buildings of Speer's Berlin, the expanse of the gigantic Reich, the scale of its undiscovered genocide, the detail of its torture scene. Harris chose his arch-villain well: the historic Odilo Globocnik was not only a convicted anti-Semitic murderer but also a fraudster, embezzler and organizer of 'Operation Reinhardt'. 'A bull in uniform' with enormous hands (138), Globocnik's size gives him the nickname Globus (globe). Outsized corporeality stands for the outsized Nazi corpus, for the grotesque megalomania of its genocidal vision. Detailed scenes of violence and torture are staple set-pieces in Nazi representations on the basis of creative contiguity: because we know of actual Nazi atrocity, fictional Nazi cruelty is presumably not pornographic but merely a plausible fictional illustration of historical fact.

McEwan's response to this strategy is to dramatize it as an eroticized fantasy that complicates the relationship between bystanders and perpetrators. Close to the end of *Black Dogs*, he offers an explanation for the evil the eponymous dogs represent throughout the story. They were trained by the Gestapo to rape their victims, in particular a pretty and independent young woman, Danielle Bertrand, who was unresponsive to some villagers' advances. The story comes several times removed, which highlights its unreliability. The rape was allegedly observed through the window by two brothers. It is then retold by the mayor with many ellipses and periphrases. His account is disputed by Mme Auriac, the female proprietor of the village inn:

> The simple truth is that the Sauvy brothers are a couple of drunks, and that you and your cronies despised Danielle Bertrand because she was pretty and she lived alone and she didn't think she owed any of you an explanation. And when this terrible thing happened to her, did you help her against the Gestapo? No, you took their side. You added to her shame with this story, this evil story. All of you, so willing to believe a couple of drunks. It gave you so much pleasure. More humiliation for Danielle. You couldn't stop talking about it. (161)

Here McEwan offers us a 'simple truth' about our fascination with fascism: it allies us to those who seem omnipotent and it isolates the victims in their shame. A veritable fictionalization of the *mise en scène* in Freud's essay 'A Child is Being Beaten', this scenario implicates the passive bystander as an active voyeur, and it replaces our fundamental ignorance of the victim's experience of physical cruelty (the nameless 'terrible thing') with a sexualized narrative: a child is being beaten (and I am watching); a woman is raped by Gestapo dogs (and I keep talking about it). For Madame Auriac, the salacious gossip that circulates long after it drove the victim from the community is a vicarious gang rape, endlessly repeatable. 'The shame is on you', she insists to the mayor, but of course her interpretation of the rumour identifies it as a way of deflecting the unbearable shame of the victim from becoming 'our inevitable shame, our share in the misery' (111). In the Majdanek scene McEwan suggests that our response to Nazism might be impossible to regulate towards the only morally appropriate position. In the Gestapo dogs story he demonstrates how (disavowed) tacit identifications are articulated in voluble tales of contiguous atrocity: identification becomes fantasy becomes projection.

There is an unresolved tension between fascism's pole position in our cultural inventory of evil alterity and its thoroughly disavowed fascination.[37] Whenever our certainty of the clear boundary between fascism's otherness and our democratic respectability is challenged, regulatory mechanisms are called upon in order to police moral landmarks. When Uklański's frieze *Untitled (The Nazis)* was shown in the Zachęta Gallery in

Warsaw in 2000, one of the actors represented in it, Daniel Olbrychski, slashed some of the images with a sword – presumably a melodramatic gesture of national pride, suitably recorded on television. Subsequently the Polish minister for culture demanded that Uklański supplement his installation with a caption that clarified his condemnation of Nazism or the exhibition would close. Close it did: if the Poles of all people were uncertain about their response to representations of Nazism, Uklański's work had made its point, however crudely. One would certainly not want to elevate fascism to the level of the ineffable. However, its ubiquitous referencing should perhaps tell us something about the way in which our culture has utilized Nazism precisely to avoid looking at it and at itself. In this defensive strategy, the representation of fascism more often than not seamlessly slides into or towards the fascism of representation. Insisting on its absolute alterity, we have created fascism as an alter ego.

Notes

1. Susan Sontag, 'Fascinating Fascism', in *Under the Sign of Saturn* (London: Vintage, 1980), 73–109; 91, 103.
2. Ibid., 102.
3. Saul Friedlander, *Reflections of Nazism: an Essay on Kitsch and Death*, trans. Thomas Weyr (Bloomington: Indiana University Press, 1993), 20; 77.
4. This is a point Klaus Theweleit makes in his compendium *Male Fantasies* about the erotic inventory of images of *Freikorps* fighters, right-wing nationalists who formed the grass-roots movement of Nazism after the First World War. One needs to make a distinction here between the unconscious life of fascists and how fascism was represented. Klaus Theweleit, *Männerphantasien*, 2 vols (Frankfurt am Main: Roter Stern, 1977.)
5. Laura Frost, *Sex Drives: Fantasies of Fascism in Literary Modernism* (Ithaca: Cornell University Press, 2002), 1–37.
6. For an incisive analysis of fascism as a technology of projection to which my argument owes a great debt, see Rey Chow, 'The Fascist Longings in our Midst', *Ariel* 26/1 (1995): 23–51.
7. Michel Foucault's critique was much broader: contemporary culture's use of the label 'fascism' was indicative of 'a general complicity in a refusal to analyse what fascism really was'. He argued that such dismissal reduced fascism to a 'floating signifier' with which any form of power and any desire for it could be summarily denounced. The effect, I would argue, is actually the same: the 'fascist' thus denounced has been denounced in a fascist way. 'Power and Strategies', in *Power/Knowledge: Selected Interviews and Other Writings, 1972–1977*, ed. Colin Gordon (Brighton: Harvester, 1980), 139.
8. For example, Kazuo Ishiguro's *The Remains of the Day* (1989; London: Faber & Faber, 1994), Philip Kerr's *Berlin Noir* series (1989–92; Harmondsworth: Penguin, 1993), and Martin Amis's *Time's Arrow* (1991; Harmondsworth: Penguin, 1992).

9. Raymond Chandler, 'The Simple Art of Murder', *The Simple Art of Murder* (New York: Vintage, 1988), 18.
10. All levels of police were implicated in implementing racial laws, ideological reliability and persecution from the very early days of the Third Reich, when political dissidents were spirited away into 'protective custody', and SA thugs could terrorize opponents and abuse Jewish citizens without police interference or legal sanction. See Gerhard Paul (ed.), *Die Täter der Shoah: Fanatische Nationalsozialisten oder ganz normale Deutsche* (Göttingen: Wallstein, 2002); Raul Hilberg, *Perpetrators, Victims, Bystanders* (New York: Harper Perennial, 1993), 36–50; and Christopher Browning, *Ordinary Men: Reserve Police Battalion 101 and the 'Final Solution' in Poland* (London: Penguin, 2001).
11. Robert Harris, *Fatherland* (London: Arrow, 1993), 45. All subsequent references are taken from this edition and are cited parenthetically in the text.
12. Sontag, 'Fascinating Fascism', 100.
13. In the 1930s, it had been the other way around for British observers of Nazi pageantry. While tourists came to inspect the new Germany, it was the splendidly regenerated German body that validated the new Nazi state as a success. Among the physical evidence was Germany's strong performance at the 1936 Olympics, the exhibition of the national labour service at the annual party rallies and the physical fitness of German youth. See Petra Rau, *English Modernism, National Identity and the Germans, 1890–1950* (Aldershot: Ashgate, 2009), 149–83.
14. The same homosocial triangulation of female absence informs the torture scenes in Philip Kerr's *March Violets* in *Berlin Noir* and Robert Wilson's *A Small Death in Lisbon* (London: Harper, 2002).
15. Gill Plain, *Twentieth-Century Crime Fiction: Gender, Sexuality and the Body.* (Edinburgh: Edinburgh University Press, 2001), 62.
16. Ian McEwan, *Black Dogs* (London: Vintage), 1992, 108. All subsequent references are to this edition and are cited parenthetically in the text.
17. Kerry Fried, 'Criminal Elements', *New York Review of Books* 40/1–2 (1993): 36–7; 37.
18. See for instance Klaus-Michael Mallmann, '"Mensch, ich feiere heut' den tausendsten Genickschuss": Die Sicherheitspolizei und die Shoah in Westgalizien', in Paul, *Die Täter der Shoah*, 109–37.
19. Before the implementation of 'Operation Reinhardt', Majdanek was conceived as the largest camp in the *General-Gouvernement*, accommodating up to a quarter of a million prisoners and PoWs on 500 hectares (at twice the population density of nearby Lublin's pre-war population), all working for the German war machine and the SS textile industry. For a map of the original gargantuan scale of Majdanek see Tomasz Samek, *In the Middle of Europe: Konzentrationslager Majdanek*, exhibition catalogue (Münster & Lublin: Stadtmuseum Münster/Państwowe Muzeum na Majdanku, 2001), n.p. The camp was scaled back to less than a quarter of its original conception. For a painstaking analysis of Majdanek's evolution from a work and prisoner camp to a site of extermination see Barbara Schwindt, *Das Konzentrations- und Vernichtungslager Majdanek: Funktionswandel im Kontext der 'Endlösung'* (Würzburg: Königshausen and Naumann, 2005).
20. On the habitual omission of the Holocaust from the Hitler-wins scenario see Joan Gordon, 'Utopia, Genocide, and the Other', in Veronica Hollinger and

Joan Gordon (eds), *Edging into the Future: Science Fiction and Contemporary Cultural Transformation* (Philadelphia: University of Pennsylvania Press, 2002), 204–17; 207.

21. For a comparison between Harris's map, Hitler's new Berlin and Speer's model see Frederic Spotts, *Hitler and the Power of Aesthetics* (London: Pimlico, 2003), 357. Much of the detail and the anecdotes for Hitler's architectural vision come from Speer's bestselling memoir *Inside the Third Reich* (1970; London: Phoenix, 2003).

22. Gavriel D. Rosenfeld, 'Alternate Holocausts and the Mistrust of Memory', in Jonathan Petropoulos and John K. Roth (eds), *Gray Zones: Ambiguity and Compromise in the Holocaust and its Aftermath* (New York: Berghahn, 2005), 240–52; 242.

23. Gavriel D. Rosenfeld, *The World Hitler Never Made: Alternate History and the Memory of Nazism* (Oxford: Oxford University Press, 2005), 292.

24. Cited in Bardo Fassbender, 'A Novel, Germany's Past, and the Dilemmas of Civilised Germans', *Contemporary Review* 265 (1994): 236–46; 243. And the cat comes out of the bag in a long article in the *Sunday Times*: 'One does not have to share the views of Nicholas Ridley or Margaret Thatcher to note the similarity between what the Nazis planned for western Europe and what, in economic terms, has come to pass.' Robert Harris, 'Nightmare Landscape of Nazism Triumphant', *The Sunday Times*, Section 2: News Review, 10 May 1992, 1 & 6; 1. He made the same point, if more subtly, in an interview with the *New York Times*: Craig R. Whitney, 'Inventing a World in Which Hitler Won', *New York Times*, Section C: The Arts, 3 June 1992, 17 & 19.

25. John Sutherland reads several bestselling 1970s novels that imagined Britain invaded (*SS-GB, The Eagle Has Landed*) or believed that despite the Allied victory in 1945 fascism was ineradicable and merely dormant (*Marathon Man, The Odessa File, The Fourth Protocol*) as a response to Britain's entry into the Common Market. *Bestsellers: Popular Fiction of the 1970s* (London: Routledge, 1981), 179 & 242.

26. George Mosse, *The Image of Man: the Creation of Modern Masculinity* (Oxford: Oxford University Press, 1996), 180.

27. James E. Young, *The Texture of Memory: Holocaust Memorials and Meaning* (New Haven: Yale University Press, 1993), 128.

28. Gitta Sereny, *Into that Darkness: from Mercy Killing to Mass Murder* (London: Pimlico, 1995), 145.

29. Ibid.

30. Young, *Texture*, p. 133.

31. For the problematics of exhibiting *bodily* remnants such as hair as opposed to material possessions see Erna Paris, 'Who Will Own the Holocaust', *Long Shadows: Truth, Lies and History* (London: Bloomsbury, 2000), 312–53; 340–42.

32. Ruth Klüger, *Landscapes of Memory: a Holocaust Girlhood Remembered* (London: Bloomsbury, 1992), 68–70.

33. Tim Cole, *Selling the Holocaust* (New York: Routledge, 1999), 164; 157.

34. Omer Bartov, *Murder in Our Midst: the Holocaust, Industrial Killing, and Representation* (New York: Oxford University Press, 1996), 67. See also Hannah Arendt's comment on 'such types of which every city has more than we would like to believe' in *Elemente und Ursprünge totaler Herrschaft* (Munich: Piper, 2005), 920.

35. On this point see in particular Saul Friedlander, 'The "Final Solution": on the Unease of Historical Interpretation', in *Memory, History and the Extermination of the Jews of Europe* (Bloomington: Indiana University Press, 1993), 111, and Gillian Rose, 'Beginnings of the Day: Fascism and Representation', in Bryan Cheyette and Laura Marcus (eds), *Modernity, Culture and 'the Jew'* (Cambridge: Polity, 1998), 242–50.
36. Liliane Kandel, 'La lettre volée de Daniel J. Goldhagen', *Les temps modernes* 592 (1997): 38–55; 53. For a perspicacious reading of Goldhagen's narrative ventriloquism of the perpetrator position see Nancy Wood, *Vectors of Memory: Legacies of Trauma in Postwar Europe* (Oxford: Berg, 1999), 79–111.
37. For an (inevitably controversial) exhibition demonstrating just this tension see Norman L. Kleeblatt, *Mirroring Evil: Nazi Imagery/Recent Art* (New York: Jewish Museum; New Brunswick: Rutgers University Press, 2001).

8
'Resentments': the Politics and Pathologies of War Writing

Marina MacKay

> Remembering and resenting are, or may be, siblings,
> like their opposites, forgiving and forgetting.
> (Ruth Klüger, 'Forgiving and Remembering'[1])

Late in his famous memoir *If This is a Man/Survival in Auschwitz*, Primo Levi recounts how he finally had the opportunity to exercise his expertise as a chemist, which may have saved his life by sparing him hard labour in the deadly cold of a Polish winter. His chemistry examination over, Levi is returning to the camp with the *Kapo* Alex, a German career criminal:

> The steel cable of a crane cuts across the road, and Alex catches hold of it to climb over: *Donnerwetter*, he looks at his hand black with thick grease. In the meanwhile I have joined him. Without hatred and without sneering, Alex wipes his hand on my shoulder, both the palm and the back of the hand, to clean it; he would be amazed, the poor brute Alex, if someone told him that today, on the basis of this action, I judge him and [the chemist] Pannwitz and the innumerable others like him, big and small, in Auschwitz and everywhere.[2]

Methodically, obliviously and humiliatingly, Alex wipes his filthy hand on a convenient human rag: a deeply characteristic Nazi act in its evidencing of what by this stage is an instinctive contempt for a Jewish man, even (or especially) one who has just demonstrated abilities far above those of the thug Alex. Yet the act is less obviously chilling than most of the enormities Levi and his generation recounted. Indeed, when Levi ends the anecdote with the declaration that 'on the basis of this action, I judge him', not only does he nail Alex and his kind to their old crimes but also dares the reader to categorize 'the poor brute' Alex's crime as a petty instance of Nazi guilt, and the 'judgment' as driven by resentment. But what would be so bad about resentment?

Resentments are not morally suspect but morally obligatory, argued another former Auschwitz prisoner, reviewing his Holocaust experience twenty years later. Born in Austria as Hans Maier in 1912, 'Jean Améry' was the unreligious son of a Catholic mother and a Jewish father who had died fighting for the Austro-Hungarian Empire in the First World War. Having fled his homeland after the *Anschluss*, Améry became a member of a Belgian Resistance group and was arrested by the Gestapo in July 1943. First incarcerated and tortured at the Nazi-appropriated Belgian fortress of Breendonk, he spent the rest of the war in a number of concentration camps, among them Auschwitz-Monowitz, Buchenwald and Bergen-Belsen. It was as Jean Améry, a Romance-language remaking of his Germanic name, that he became famous for his writings on current affairs, on nationalism, on ageing, on suicide (Améry committed suicide in 1978) and, with what remains his most widely read essay, on the enduring effects of torture.

'Whoever was tortured, stays tortured', Améry wrote in that essay, making a claim that helps to explain why the troubled temporality of trauma – once tortured, always tortured – might equally be understood as the temporality of resentment.[3] By this I mean that the traumatic paradigm has become so familiar in discussions of mid-century writing that we readers of crisis representation have tended to forget that there are alternative ways of thinking about the persistence of past violence, and about the transformation of time it both enables and requires.[4] Persecuted as a Jew and punished as a resistance activist in occupied Europe, Améry is both Holocaust witness and war writer, and this chapter asks what his treatment of damage reveals about the role of 'resentments' in narrative representations of violence, taking his mid-century essays as an opportunity to consider the relationships between temporality and violence, and between the political and the psychoanalytic in understandings of modern crisis writing.

Amnesty: a West German journey

'Sometimes it happens that in the summer I travel through a thriving land' is the deceptively unassuming opening of Améry's 1966 essay 'Resentments':

> It is hardly necessary to tell of the model cleanliness of its large cities, of its idyllic towns and villages, to point out the quality of the goods

to be bought there, the unfailing perfection of its handicrafts, or the impressive combination of cosmopolitan modernity and wistful historical consciousness that is evidenced everywhere.⁵

This 'peaceful lovely land, inhabited by hard-working, efficient, and modern people' is Germany, and the disarmingly laudatory opening swiftly proves ironic (R, 63). Améry's tone mimics that of a tour guide, gliding over cultural surfaces, bridging (West) Germany's exemplary present of outward-looking cosmopolitanism and its venerable past of traditional handicrafts and charming historic settlements. As if to re-assure us that Germany is indeed safe for the modern traveller, the nar-rator affirms that this country 'offers the world an example not only of economic prosperity but also of democratic stability', and although it 'has certain territorial claims to make and is struggling for the reunifica-tion with that part of its national body that was unnaturally separated from it [...] its behavior in these questions is commendably discreet' – and then comes Améry's punch line: 'as has long been proved, its happy people want no part of national demagogues and agitators' (R, 62–3).

As has *long* been proved? 'Long' here means the twenty years that have passed since the war's end. Germany is again the charming and cosmopolitan country it always was, and it is as if the Nazi years never happened. Indeed, Germany and the urbane narrative advocate it finds in Améry's introduction seem so tactfully to have sidelined recent his-tory that it might seem coarsely undiplomatic to recall the catastrophic German embrace of 'national demagogues and agitators'. Indeed, it is as if to draw attention to that Nazi past would to be to 'cut a poor figure', to put yourself and not Germany in the wrong (R, 63). And this is Améry's point: that by the mid-1960s the rehabilitation of Germany had so suc-cessfully sutured the fissure between Germany's post-Nazi present and its pre-Nazi past that a refusal to play along resembled a moral failure on the speaker's part, merely a 'retrospective grudge' (R, 63). And, as Améry acknowledges late in the same volume of essays, readers might well see him 'as a monster, if not of vengeance, then at least of bitterness'.⁶

But single-mindedly Améry courts that accusation in 'Resentments', recalling how triumphantly he enjoyed the vilification of Germany when the full magnitude of its crimes became apparent. Alluding to the rejected Morgenthau Plan, which, dismantling the country's industrial capability, would have turned Germany into the potato field of Europe in perpetuity, Améry writes that even the most vindictive and vengeful of international responses were absolutely fine with him – indeed, married perfectly with his own subjective feelings about Germany. Thus he took the indiscriminate denunciation of a collective German guilt as an accurate reflection of his personal experiences, for 'I had experienced their crimes as collective ones':

> I had been just as afraid of the simple private in his field-grey uniform as of the brown-clad Nazi official with his swastika armband. I also could not rid myself of the sight of the Germans on a small passenger platform where, from the cattle cars of our deportation train, the corpses had been unloaded and piled up; not on a single one of their stony faces was I able to detect an expression of abhorrence. (R, 65)

Civilians, conscripts and card-carrying functionaries of the Nazi state were all the same to him, and all the same to those who initially decried a collective culpability encompassing every German.

But global outrage dies away. Between them the willed amnesia of the Cold War and the inevitable amnesia of the historical process do their work to let German guilt fade into oblivion, while the ongoing pursuit and trial of Nazi war criminals implicitly exculpated all but the most flagrantly guilty.[7] Améry argues that as early as 1946 the term 'collective guilt' was 'forbidden', and there was a 'hushing up, shame for ever having coined such a seemingly ill-considered term' (R, 72). Now it is *he* and not Germany that is 'burdened with collective guilt [...] The world, which forgives and forgets, has sentenced me, not those who murdered or allowed the murder to occur' (R, 75). And yet Améry's own outrage lives on, rooted in the persistence of a shared past in private memory ('I could not rid myself of the sight'). What he experienced personally becomes the basis of a paralegal justice that could pass no test of disinterestedness (because the fact that he experienced so many German crimes does not prove their universality) or magnanimity (more humane, surely, to believe in those good Germans so rarely encountered). But that is precisely Améry's point. Public morality points in the direction of acquiescent forgetfulness, but there is another morality that dictates bitter remembrance: 'I preserved my resentments [...] I neither can nor want to get rid of them' (R, 67).

According to Améry, common sense and conventional morality ask you to surmount your own suffering and to allow time to obscure further the murky pasts of others, and he stresses that in refusing to submit to those demands he is not merely trying to dignify a covert lust for revenge.[8] After all, he speculates, what could constitute revenge when one has only to put into words the eye-for-an-eye fantasy of executing six million non-Jewish Germans for the utter irrelevance of ideas of 'revenge' to become apparent; and no one, he supposes, would want even the most evil of convicted perpetrators to die the same hideous deaths as their victims (R, 77). However, he reserves his harshest words for those who did not simply submit to time's rehabilitating power but attempted to hasten its work. As soon as the war was over, there were 'Jews who in this hour were already trembling with the pathos of forgiveness and reconciliation', and the essay singles out the English leftwing publisher Victor Gollancz and the German philosopher Martin Buber, who had emigrated to Jerusalem in 1938, as if to say that those self-appointed Jewish spokesmen most forcefully urging reconciliation were those with only second-hand knowledge of the extremes of anti-Semitic persecution (R, 65). Yet even Primo Levi was a 'forgiver', Améry is reported to have claimed, and although Levi rejected the label outright in his belated argument with Améry in *The Drowned and the Saved* (1986), he would criticize Améry there for a refusal to 'search for peace', and – implying a causal link between Améry's 'resentments' and his suicide – for adopting 'positions of such severity and intransigence as to make him incapable of finding joy in life, indeed of living'.[9]

Although Améry never denied the self-burdening, even self-destructive qualities of resentment, the essays are deeply suspicious of the moral and political interests its abandonment would best serve, satirically ventriloquizing the 'forgiving' viewpoint as the supposition that only 'totally obstinate, morally condemnable hate, already censured by history [...] clings to a past that was clearly nothing other than an operational mishap of German history and in which the broad masses of the German people had no part' (R, 67). But even in the face of disapproval and a loneliness that can only have been exacerbated by the spectacle of fellow-victims disavowing their resentment, Améry takes it as his 'personal task [...] to justify a psychic condition that has been condemned by moralists and psychologists alike. The former regard it as a taint, the latter as a kind of sickness' (R, 64).

Resentment as 'taint': Améry and Nietzsche

When Améry speaks of a 'moral' condemnation of resentment, he clearly has in mind those who wanted to temper the demonization of a broken Germany. There were many such, especially in view of 'the monstrous peace settlement now being forced on Germany' of which George Orwell – no pro-German apologist by nature – wrote in the 1945 essay 'Revenge is Sour', in which he meditated on the pathos and the pointlessness of taking revenge on a defeated country.[10] However, a very different morality is evoked in Améry's essay by the echo of Nietzsche, first, in the title of the essay itself, which in its original form reprises Nietzsche's famous *ressentiment*, and, second, in the title of the volume in which the essay appears. What is translated into English as *At the Mind's Limits* is, in its original German, *Jenseits von Schuld und Sühne*, 'Beyond Guilt and Atonement', surely an intentional echo of Nietzsche's *Jenseits von Gut und Böse* or *Beyond Good and Evil*. If the Olympian Nietzsche is writing, as his subtitle declares, the 'prelude to a philosophy of the future', Améry is writing against futurity itself; his is an anti-progressive philosophy that refuses to succumb to what he characterizes as the alluring amorality – indeed, 'anti-morality' (R, 71) – of the time process, which tends towards mitigation and eventual annihilation of guilt.

Notoriously, Nietzsche's appropriation by Nazism would prove the grim untruth of *Beyond Good and Evil*'s argument that 'harshness, violence, enslavement [...] everything evil, frightful, tyrannical' elevates the human species; and would cast a vicious irony over its identification of Judaism with slave morality.[11] However, it was in his amplifying sequel, *On the Genealogy of Morals*, that Nietzsche raised explicitly the problem of *ressentiment*, here the mark of the morally benighted because, incapable of acting but only of *reacting*, the sufferer compensates for his weakness and disempowerment with fantasies of revenge against the oppressor (or, Nietzsche thought more likely, against an emblem or effigy of the oppressor). A lower animal, the resentful person represents the voice of the powerless herd that clings to its wrongs because it has no power to escape its suffering in self-asserting, transcendent forgetfulness, and instead bides its time to take an oblique revenge or to voice its resentment via what Nietzsche considered the self-deceiving reversal of values made possible by the Jewish 'slave revolt in morals' whereby weakness is more moral than strength, suffering holier than happiness.

For Nietzsche, *ressentiment* is a mark of squinting inferiority, a sub-human misshapenness: 'the man of *ressentiment* is neither upright nor naïve in his dealings with others, nor is he honest and open with himself. His soul *squints*; his mind loves bolt-holes, secret paths, back doors.'[12] In the notorious next section of *Genealogy*, Nietzsche identified the aristocratic code, the very reverse of *ressentiment*, with the predatory supremacy of the 'blond beast', 'noble races' and the obsolete Aryan. To be sure, the philosophically well-versed Améry likely read Nietzsche well enough to notice his assertion that modern Germans have next to nothing in common (culturally, let alone in ethnic or 'racial' terms) with 'the blond Germanic beast'; that Nietzsche's representative of 'the *noble ideal as such*' was the French Napoleon ('this synthesis of the *inhuman* and the *super-human*'); and that he identified *ressentiment* with the real-world anti-Semitism that he appears to have loathed, as well as with Jewish morality.[13] (All of which is only to suppose that Améry would read Nietzsche more attentively than Nazi admirers did.) Even so, Améry proposed that there is no way of arguing with Nietzsche's worship of force other than to see it in the context of its twentieth-century deployment. *Ressentiment* as inferiority and forgetfulness as strength? 'Thus spake the man who dreamed of the synthesis of the brute with the superman', Améry writes: 'he must be answered by those who witnessed the union of the brute with the subhuman; they were present as victims when a certain humankind joyously celebrated a festival of cruelty, as Nietzsche himself expressed it' (R, 68).

In Améry's account, Nietzsche's *Übermensch* is no *Mensch*, his morality beyond good and evil no morality at all. When Améry describes how he continues to 'preserve' his resentments ('I neither can nor want to get rid of them'), he argues that the only meaningfully moral response to injustice is, contra Nietzsche, to refuse to rise above what has been done to you, to continue to relive the offence. And this is, emphatically, a reliving, as the French-by-adoption Améry would have been well aware. Derived from the Latin prefix *re* (back, again) and the infinitive *sentire* (to feel), *ressentiment* explicitly bears with it a particular temporality whereby the past is not past but intermittently present. The phenomenologist Max Scheler made this rejection of linear time central to his influential 1912 extension of Nietzsche's argument. *Ressentiment* is 'the repeated experiencing and reliving of a particular emotional response reaction against someone else', Scheler insisted: 'not a mere intellectual recollection of the emotion and of the events to which it "responded" – it is a re-experiencing of the emotion itself, a renewal of the original feeling'.[14] This explicit 'time-lag between offenses suffered and displeasure or indignation expressed' is what the English 'resentment' misses out, Richard Ira Sugarman notes in his book on the phenomenology of *ressentiment*, the aptly titled *Rancor against Time*: for Sugarman, the resenting person is 'out of joint with the times and with time'.[15] Sugarman is writing about Dostoevsky's Underground Man, but this is a useful characterization of Améry's rage against both the rehabilitation of Germany ('the times') and the anaesthetic or curative passage of years that makes it possible ('time').

Yet the discourse of healing has to be used advisedly in view of how easily moral fault shades into the language of pathology, to the effect that the resenting person becomes not only morally flawed but also ill and deformed. This is what Améry means when he writes that resentments may be dismissed as 'sickness' as well as 'taint', and the slippage is already evident in Nietzsche's characterization of resentment as an ability to walk 'upright', to see without 'squinting', and, a little later on in *Genealogy of Morals*, the man who cannot forget becomes the man who cannot 'digest' what has happened to him and what he himself has done. 'A stronger man with a better constitution digests his experiences [deeds, misdeeds included], as he digests his meals, even when the food is tough.'[16] Perhaps needless to say, the strong man who can forget his own 'experiences [deeds, misdeeds included]' evokes precisely the sinister strength Améry attributes to the 'peaceful lovely land' where the essay on 'Resentments' opens. And when, in his essay on torture, Améry realizes that the 'strong' man who tortured him at Breendonk has likely 'digested' his crime, he makes a point of naming him – of literally spelling out his name:

> But why, really, should I withhold his name [...]? Perhaps at this very hour he is faring well and feels content with his healthily sunburned self as he drives home from his Sunday excursion. I have no reason not to name him. The Herr Leutnant, who played the role of a torture specialist here, was named Praust. P – R – A – U – S – T. (T, 32)

Resentments constitute not an involuntary reappearance of the past in the present but rather a determined refusal to put the past behind you: what Améry proposes here is a rethinking of what psychoanalytic understandings of trauma would register as a compulsive, unwilling return to the source of the traumatic experience. That trauma entails repetition does not mean that all repetitions must – or should – be seen in terms of trauma.

Resentment as illness: Améry and Freud

That is to say, the return to the site of the injury is, according to Freud's classic formulation of trauma in *Beyond the Pleasure Principle*, something that happens *against* the conscious will of the traumatized subject, and belongs among the 'mysterious masochistic trends of the ego'.[17] Freud's trauma patient, shell-shocked soldier or damaged civilian, is compelled to relive in the present events that a 'healthy' mind would merely remember as past. In response to the 'new and remarkable fact' that 'the compulsion to repeat also recalls from the past experiences which include no possibility of pleasure', Freud concluded that the traumatic return to the horrifying scene is 'endeavouring to master the stimulus retrospectively, by developing the anxiety whose omission was the cause of the traumatic neurosis'.[18] The readiness is all, because there is 'something about anxiety that protects its subject against fright and so against fright-neuroses', and fright, origin of trauma, 'is caused by lack of any preparedness for anxiety'.[19]

If 'Resentments' is explicitly an argument with Nietzsche on *ressentiment*, the essay on 'Torture' is implicitly an argument with Freud on trauma. This essay is full of critical echoes of Freud, as when Améry proposes the sheer irrelevance of that protective 'preparedness'. He had spent much of his time with the Belgian Resistance anticipating what was in store for him on arrest: 'so many reports by former Gestapo prisoners had reached my ears that I thought there could be nothing new for me in this area':

> What would take place would then have to be incorporated into the relevant literature, as it were. Prison, interrogation, blows, torture; in the end, most probably death [...]. 'Rien n'arrive ni comme on l'espère, ni comme on le craint,' Proust writes somewhere. Nothing really happens as we hope it will, nor as we fear it will. But not because the occurrence, as one says, perhaps 'goes beyond the imagination' (it is not a quantitative question), but because it is reality and not phantasy. (T, 25)

Améry argues that it is simply impossible to prepare yourself – and thus protect yourself – in the way Freud seems to have supposed: all proleptic imaginings fall short simply because they *are* imaginings. And consider how the essay reprises Freud's quasi-organic model of trauma, rendering literally corporeal Freud's bodily metaphor. As early as *Studies in Hysteria* (1895), Freud and Josef Breuer were presenting trauma as the violation of a bodily boundary, 'a foreign body which must still be regarded as a present and effective agent long after it has penetrated', and the same figuration persists through *Beyond the Pleasure Principle*: '*Protection against* stimuli is an almost more important function for the living organism than *reception of* stimuli', Freud writes here, and what constitutes the 'traumatic' are 'any excitations from outside which are powerful enough to break though the protective shield'.[20] Compare Améry's account of the first blow from a Gestapo policeman's fist, a destruction of 'trust in the world', trust that 'the other person will [...] respect my physical, and with it also my metaphysical, being. My skin surface shields me against the external world. If I am to have trust, I must feel on it only what I *want* to feel' (T, 28). Freud's 'protective shield' is an unnecessary form of figuration, Améry implies, when there is the perfectly visible but no less woundable membrane of your own fearful skin. (Freud had supposed, of course, that suffering a physical trauma made psychological trauma less likely.)

Giving these local arguments with Freud their point is Améry's desire to ward off an account of his time-troubling resentments that would trivialize them, render them morally and politically irrelevant as a form of mental illness, 'the unwitting reenactment of an event that one cannot simply leave behind', as Cathy Caruth summarizes Freud in her now classic work of trauma theory, *Unclaimed Experience*.[21] 'Twenty-two years later I am still dangling over the ground by dislocated arms', Améry writes of his torture in Breendonk, in an obliteration of linear time easily reducible to that very model of trauma (T, 36). It is almost axiomatically true that what is at stake in trauma is *time* ('hysterics suffer for the most part from reminiscences', Freud had famously claimed in *Studies in Hysteria*).[22] Caruth argued that belatedness is the very origin of the trauma itself: 'not simply [...] the literal threatening of bodily life, but the fact that the threat is recognized as such by the mind *one moment too late*'.[23] And then there is the belatedness known as latency, the gap between an experience and its appearance as symptom (think of Freud's railway passengers walking unhurt from the scene of the accident). But what psychoanalysis understands as latency may be understood differently if we see it as a resentment that grows as – 'as' in the double sense of *while* and *because* – the rest of the world forgets. 'The experience of persecution was, at the very bottom, that of an extreme *loneliness*', Améry concluded, and surely it is this 'loneliness' that is exacerbated by the incremental temporality of global forgetting. Indeed, this renewal of loneliness may be what gives resentments their trauma-like but acutely political untimeliness (R, 70). Because the world has moved on 'I am alone, as I was when they tortured me' (O, 96).

The political significance of that sense of sheer abandonment falls away in Caruth's suggestion that such high suicide rates obtain among camp survivors and veterans (and Améry would count as one of those suicides) because 'the history of the traumatized individual is nothing other than the determined repetition of the event of destruction'.[24] Retrospectively this helps us to see why Améry's essays are so critical of a therapeutic model of 'trauma' that he presents as not only a missing of the political point but even as a form of coercion, an ironic repetition of the torturer's dehumanizing objectives. Hanged with his arms twisted behind his back until they became dislocated from their sockets, he was whipped while dangling from those twisted, dislocated limbs (the word 'torture', he explains, originates in the Latin *torquere*, to twist: 'What visual instruction in etymology!' [32–3]). His provocation is this: that the condition of 'twistedness', 'distortion' or 'warpedness' is the very diagnosis of those who would present survivors as trauma victims, as mental cases.

> I read in a recently published book about 'Delayed Psychic Effects After Political Persecution' that all of us are not only psychically but mentally damaged. The character traits that make up our personality are distorted. Nervous restlessness, hostile withdrawal into one's own self are the typical signs of our sickness. It is said that we are 'warped'. That causes me to recall fleetingly the way my arms were twisted high behind my back when they tortured me. (R, 68)

Thus he ridicules psychiatric approaches to political violence that cannot see withdrawal and mistrust as utterly reasonable responses to a torture that was not simply harrowing in its own right but also *socially sanctioned*. In presenting the mental condition of survivors as bent out of shape, those who outline normatively (and prescriptively) what constitutes health symbolically become torturers themselves.

'Am I perhaps mentally ill [...]?' Améry asked in 'On the Necessity and Impossibility of Being a Jew', his autobiographical essay about how anti-Semitism turned into a self-identifying Jew a lifelong atheist who had grown up celebrating Christmas:

> I have long since provided myself with a fully conclusive answer. I know that what oppresses me is no neurosis, but rather precisely reflected reality. Those were no hysteric hallucinations when I heard the Germans call for the Jews to 'die like a dog!' [...] I am thus forced to conclude that I am not deranged and was not deranged, but rather that the neurosis is on the part of the historical occurrence. The others are the madmen, and I am left standing around helplessly among them, a fully sane person who joined a tour through a psychiatric clinic and suddenly lost sight of the doctors and orderlies. But since the sentence passed on me by the madmen can, after all, be carried out at any moment, it is totally binding, and my own mental lucidity is entirely irrelevant. (O, 96)

But then he retracts that explanatory pseudo-medical discourse used so often in post-war Germany to diagnose Nazism as an aberrant condition – a pervasive language of national 'health' and 'illness' ironically taken over, Jennifer Kapczynski has recently argued, from Nazism itself – on the grounds that it scarcely matters whether or not Nazi anti-Semitism is best understood as a pathological condition.[25] The point, rather, is that it is 'a historical and social fact': 'I was, after all, in Auschwitz and not in Himmler's imagination' (O, 98). His lasting condition of fear and mistrust is a wholly appropriate response to a world in which anti-Semitic force, cruelty and the will to destroy can take over at any time: 'I am not "traumatized"', he insists: 'rather my spiritual and psychic condition corresponds completely to reality' (O, 99).

Améry, then, offers a way of thinking about the temporally unbounded destructiveness of political violence beyond the model of trauma now conventionally used to explain those acts of violence that, from the sufferer's point of view, will not stop happening. Like Nietzsche's sublime fantasy of transcendent forgetfulness, the discourse of 'healing' becomes anti-moral, a surrender to the time process that ought to be resisted rather than hastened. Those who let time heal their wounds, as the cliché has it, have given up on morality, their 'time sense is not dis-ordered [...] it has not moved out of the biological and social sphere into the moral sphere' (R, 71). By 'biological sphere', he is thinking of the healing of a wound, and of the animal finitude of victims and perpetrators alike; by 'social sphere', he means that it is in society's interests that victims renounce their resentment and grief (as in our own time South Africa's post-Apartheid 'Truth and Reconciliation Commission' aimed to put the past behind it): 'The social body is occupied merely with safeguarding itself and could not care less about a life that has been damaged' (R, 70).[26] Against biological inevitabilities and social imperatives, a truly moral consciousness would try to make time stop, to chain the present to the time of the catastrophe. 'The moral power to resist contains the protest, the revolt against reality, which is rational only as long as it is moral. The moral person demands annulment of time' (R, 72).

'Stubbornly, I held against Germany its twelve years under Hitler', he writes: 'I "stuck out," as I once had in the camp because of poor posture at roll call; I attracted the disapproving attention [...] of my former fellows in battle and suffering, who were now gushing [...] about reconciliation' (R, 67). In a climate of reconciliation his intransigence makes him 'stick out', and his moral posture, so to speak, reminds him of his literal posture at roll call in the concentration camp. The end result is wilfully antagonistic: those who would redeem Germany become symbolically equivalent to those who persecuted him, the 'forgivers' who make Améry's intransigence so visible become the Nazis who policed his position at roll call in the concentration camp.

Nor was this enraged collapsing of past and present, so different from 'delayed psychic effects of political persecution', unique to Améry, as he seems to have feared. In a brief contribution to a 2002 *PMLA* symposium on 'forgiveness' Ruth Klüger, another Austrian-Jewish survivor of Auschwitz, spoke up for resentments, and her compelling, uncompromising memoir of her 'Holocaust girlhood' offers some Améryesque provocations. Early in *Still Alive*, for example, Klüger writes about the small size of her extended family as she grew up in late 1930s Vienna, which reminds her in turn of how Jewish families of her acquaintance count their Holocaust dead, which leads ultimately to thoughts of the work of the Holocaust archives 'doing the counting for us':

> I won't register with them as a survivor. The form lies where my son has put it for me, gathering dust in a corner of my desk. I can't over-come my *resentful* reluctance to fill it out, as if it were one more roll call in the shivering hours of the morning, or the merciless heat of noon, on the *Appellplatz* of some last concentration camp.[27]

Here as in Améry the time of the narration and the time of the narrated events collapse into one another with the rhetorically stunning effect of conflating people who are notionally on your side (those who would 'cure' you, those who would register you) with those who wanted you dead.

Official remembrance, what Klüger calls the 'worldwide museum cul-ture of the Shoah, nowhere more evident than in Germany', is deeply suspect in *Still Alive*, and though Klüger writes that it is surely a good thing that Germany came to confront what was long ignored she under-cuts the point with mordant irony when she explains that the Germans, 'once they started, did so with the proverbial German thoroughness', reminding us thus of the 'proverbial German thoroughness' that made their acts of Holocaust memorialization necessary.[28] As the heated debates leading up to the 2005 inauguration of Berlin's Holocaust memo-rial in Berlin attest, that 'thoroughness' of memorialization continues unabated – though not unquestioned.[29] The memorial monument is our culture's default mode for making the past present in contemporary life, and thus presumably preferable to the obliviousness, in retrospect extraordinary, of the 1960s. Yet the memorial also paradoxically works to delineate the past as past, as over, because it is only by virtue of being understood as a completed event that any happening can be 'commem-orated' at all. The time of resentment, in contrast, keeps the past open.

Modernist temporalities and the uses of 'resentment'

Although Améry is careful to outline important distinctions between prisoners and front-line soldiers – the soldier could be the carrier of death as well as its victim; the soldier was meant to live, the prisoner to die – his evoking of resentment as a *necessary* temporal disruption offers a suggestive way of rethinking twentieth-century crisis representation more generally, where, again, the break with linear time has proved too easily assimilated into the pathological paradigm. Améry requires the reader to interpret what superficially reads as symptom – a private time out of joint – in terms that are morally and politically more urgent and protesting.

To remark the transformation of time in the representation of modern violence is to recall the writing of earlier decades, and the whole body of modernist work dealing with the subjectivity and malleability of temporal experience in the aftermath of the First World War. Consider, for example, such classic representations of shell-shock as Rebecca West's *The Return of the Soldier* (1918), where the veteran hero obliterates from his memory fifteen years' worth of experience in order to forget the war; T.S. Eliot's *The Waste Land* (1922), where a speaker in the London of the roaring twenties suddenly finds himself back in 'rat's alley, where the dead men lost their bones'; and in Virginia Woolf's *Mrs. Dalloway* (1925), where the suicidal veteran Septimus Smith encounters a dead comrade in post-war London as he makes his way to a psychiatrist's appointment. For the victim of violence the march of time has stopped, and considering these 'shell-shocked' flashbacks in terms of resentment, specifically, strengthens the connections between 'war neurosis' and anti-war protest suggested by historians of Great War culture.

For example, Elaine Showalter argues that the 'epidemic' of shell-shock constituted a large-scale form of protest against the obligations of pre-war 'manliness' and the passivity of trench disempowerment.[30] Instructive here would be the transformation of Siegfried Sassoon's written protest against the war, his 1917 'A Soldier's Declaration', into a symptom of 'shell-shock', as if political and somatic protest were indeed ironically interchangeable. (And, speaking of the long persistence of the past, might not Sassoon's lifelong project of reprising his Great War experience be understood as anger rather than trauma?) Likewise, Eric Leed claims that war neurosis was 'a flight from an intolerable, destructive reality' and 'the logical and necessary outcome of the realities of modern combat'.[31] Strikingly, from the fact that shell-shock was more prevalent after the war he infers not the obvious psychoanalytic point about 'latency' but an implicit denunciation of post-war conditions, when 'the most lasting pathologies of war represented the consequences that result when the individual loses his sense of himself as an autonomous actor in a manipulable world'.[32]

So a 'trauma' reading does not *necessarily* entail an escape from politics, and certainly many modernist writers were finely attuned to the oppositional politics implied by the mad veteran's lonely rejection of a post-war cultural consensus. Famously, Woolf had written of *Mrs Dalloway* that her aim was 'to criticize the social system & to show it at work, at its most intense', and central to that critique is a medical establishment callously advising the broken Septimus to cultivate a 'sense of proportion', as if he and not the war were to blame for ruining his life: 'Health we must have; and health is proportion', thinks Woolf's complacent Dr Bradshaw.[33] And if there is elegiac pathos in Woolf's treatment of a past that makes its way into the present through the memories of Clarissa Dalloway, there is also bitterness at the political forces (in which the heroine is complicit) that try to drive it back. 'The War was over', thinks Clarissa, 'it was over; thank Heaven – over'; while her Tory politician husband thinks *en passant* 'of the war, and thousands of poor chaps, with all their lives before them, shovelled together, already half forgotten', but *Mrs. Dalloway* is nothing if not an indictment of a culture that has put recent history too quickly behind it.[34] The temporal disruptions of modernism – of trauma *and* of resentment – keep that past narratively present.

Améry and modernist temporality come together very explicitly at the other end of the century in the work of the German writer W.G. Sebald. Améry is an important presence in two of Sebald's major late works: *On the Natural History of Destruction* (2003), his sometimes controversial essays on the alleged gaps and failures of German war representation,[35] and *Austerlitz* (2001), about a Welshman who comes to know himself as a child survivor of the Holocaust, taken from his native Czechoslovakia in the *Kindertransport*. Améry is to Sebald's final novel as the canonical modernists Franz Kafka and Joseph Conrad are to *Vertigo* (1990) and *The Rings of Saturn* (1995) respectively, and Rebecca Walkowitz has recently written of Sebald's 'revival of modernist strategies', singling out his debts to Woolf ('diversion'), Joyce ('renaming') and Conrad ('emphasis on reputation and patterns of recognition').[36] To these very specific tactics we might add the most easily recognizable and generally applicable of modernist techniques, the refiguring of temporal experience by which the past achieves various forms of presence.

Not surprisingly, an interest in non-linear time occupies much of the essay on Améry, the essay 'Against the Irreversible' in *On the Natural History of Destruction*, even if, rather curiously, these temporal disruptions are sometimes read in the psychotherapeutic terms that Améry rejected. Thus, for example, Sebald writes:

> For the victims of persecution [...] the thread of chronological time is broken, background and foreground merge, the victim's logical means

of support in his existence are suspended. The experience of terror also dislocates time, that most abstract of all humanity's homes.[37]

The final clause echoes the title of Améry's essay on exile, 'How Much Home Does a Person Need?', but there are other, odder echoes of the essay on torture, especially of Améry's description of his tortured body hanging from dislocated arms: 'the thread [...] is broken', Sebald writes, 'the victim's logical means of support [...] are suspended'. The passage is uncomfortably close to Améry's fear of a psychoanalytic discourse that depoliticized his protest by presenting him as 'warped' (and one notes the echo of the despised treatise 'Delayed Psychic Effects After Political Persecution' in Sebald's 'victims of persecution'). And what Améry called his 'resentments' become, in Sebald's strangely perverse diagnosis, 'an almost pathological hypermnesia'.[38] Compounding the strangeness of Sebald's misprision is how well he 'gets' Améry in other respects, particularly in their shared consciousness of, as Sebald put it, 'the outrage of supposing that history could proceed on its way afterwards almost undisturbed, as if nothing had happened'.[39]

Shortly after meeting the title character of *Austerlitz*, the architectural historian Jacques Austerlitz, the narrator visits the fortress of Breendonk where Améry was tortured. Preserved as it was between 1940 (when the Germans occupied Belgium) and 1944 (when the Allies arrived at what by then was a deserted camp), Breendonk was made a national memorial to the Resistance in 1947. When the novel returns to Breendonk at the end the reader has now learned to recognize it as one among many time capsules in the novel. There is the drowned Welsh village of Llanwddyn, flooded to make the Vyrnwy reservoir; there is a billiards room in an English country house left unopened for a century and a half; there is the forgotten waiting room at Liverpool Street Station where Austerlitz falls into his past again; lastly, there is his old nanny's flat in Prague, 'where everything was just as it had been almost sixty years ago'.[40] Less plausible than the permafrost-preserved body that shows up after seventy-two years in Sebald's *The Emigrants* ('so they are ever returning to us, the dead'), these time capsules gesture towards the impossible: a fully visitable past.[41] 'In what way do objects immersed in time differ from those left untouched by it?' Austerlitz wonders as he and the narrator visit the Greenwich Observatory, arbitrary home of the world's standard time:

I have always resisted the power of time out of some internal compulsion which I myself have never understood, keeping myself apart from so-called current events in the hope, as I now think, [...] that

> time will not pass away, has not passed away, that I can turn back and
> go behind it, and there I shall find everything as it once was. (100–1)

Like Améry's knowingly futile protest against the time process, this
fantasy of a past that remains present (we have only to look in the right
place) is used, to borrow from 'Against the Irreversible', as 'a principle of
solidarity with victims and as a deliberate affront to those who simply
let the stream of history sweep them along'.[42]

What Sebald takes from Améry, above all, is that resistance to 'the
stream of history' and to those whose culpability it washes away. His
Austerlitz embarks on a journey through Germany that recalls the tour-
istic opening of 'Resentments':

> wherever I looked I saw trim towns and villages, neat yards around
> factories and industrial buildings, lovingly tended gardens, piles of
> firewood tidily stacked under cover, level asphalted cart tracks run-
> ning through the meadows, roads with brightly colored cars purring
> along them at great speed, well-managed woodland, regulated water-
> courses, and new railway buildings [...]

What disturbs Austerlitz has disturbed Améry: 'I could not see a crooked
line anywhere, not at the corners of the houses or on the gables,
the window frames or the sills, nor was there any other trace of past
history' (100–1).

But bracketing the narrative just as the narrator's two trips to
Breendonk do are two historical artefacts that attest to the impossibility
of the clean break, of ending and starting over. The first is a sixteenth-
century painting of a skating scene in which a woman has fallen:

> I feel as if the moment depicted by Lukas van Valckenborch had never
> come to an end, as if the canary-yellow lady had only just fallen
> over or swooned, as if the black velvet hood had only this moment
> dropped away from her head, as if the little accident, which no doubt
> goes unnoticed by most viewers, were always happening over and
> over again, and nothing and no one could ever remedy it. (13–14)

This narrative of atemporal persistence is reprised much later in the
novel when Austerlitz stands in what used to be the murderous ghetto
of Theresienstadt and sees in the window of a junk-shop a porcelain
statuette of 'a hero on horseback turning to look back, as his steed rears
up on its hindquarters, in order to raise up with his outstretched left

arm an innocent girl already bereft of her last hope, and to save her from a cruel fate not revealed to the observer': the rescue, like the fall depicted on van Valckenborch's painting is 'timeless [...] but forever just occurring' (196–7). Iteration rather than completion dominates Sebald's reading of these artworks.

Although one is an exemplary work of high art and the other probably nothing more than kitsch, these artistic objects that open and close Sebald's novel allegorize the novel's own status as a record of ongoingness rather than as a monument to a completed past. This narrative ongoing-ness is, I would like to conclude, the aesthetic counterpart of resent-ment. Resentment does not feature among the 'ugly feelings' discussed at length in Sianne Ngai's book of that title, but there are important implications for modern war writing in Ngai's linking of the uncertain status, even impotence, of literature in modernity and the anti-social or dysphoric affects modern writing takes as its subject.[43] As Améry continu-ally acknowledges, the time process is unstoppable, and, with its wholly futile, even absurd protest, modern war writing takes as its justification a morality that would speak for political victims, emerging at those moments when public redress is impossible and private resignation a new defeat. This is why Améry's modernist – resentful – temporality offers such an important way of de-pathologizing and re-politicizing the ruined lives populating the literature of war: 'defining anew our *warped* state, namely as a form of the human condition that morally as well as historically is of a higher order than that of healthy straightness' (R, 68).

Notes

1. Ruth Klüger, 'Forgiving and Remembering', *PMLA* 117/2 (March 2002): 311.
2. Primo Levi, *Survival in Auschwitz: the Nazi Assault on Humanity*, trans. Stuart Woolf (New York: Touchstone, 1996), 106.
3. Jean Améry, 'Torture', in *At the Mind's Limits: Contemplations by a Survivor on Auschwitz and its Realities*, trans. Sidney Rosenfeld and Stella P. Rosenfeld (Bloomington: Indiana University Press, 1980), 34. Subsequent references are cited parenthetically as 'T' followed by page number.
4. The Holocaust and the Second World War were central to discussions of trauma and temporal disruption from the beginning, in such founding texts of 'trauma studies' as Shoshana Felman and Dori Laub's *Testimony: Crises of Witnessing in Literature, Psychoanalysis, and History* (New York: Routledge, 1992); Cathy Caruth's edited collection *Trauma: Explorations in Memory* (Baltimore: Johns Hopkins University Press, 1995) and monograph *Unclaimed Experience: Trauma, Narrative, and History* (Baltimore: Johns Hopkins University Press, 1996). More recent and more traditionally literary critical works deploying their insights about time and trauma to discuss war writing include Anne Whitehead,

Trauma Fiction (Edinburgh: Edinburgh University Press, 2004), Victoria Stewart, *Women's Autobiography: War and Trauma* (Basingstoke: Palgrave, 2004), Robert Hemmings, *Modern Nostalgia: Siegfried Sassoon, Trauma and the Second World War* (Edinburgh: Edinburgh University Press, 2008), and Paul Crosthwaite, *Trauma, Postmodernism and the Aftermath of World War II* (Basingstoke: Palgrave, 2009).

5. Jean Améry, 'Resentments', in *At the Mind's Limits*, 62. Subsequent references are cited parenthetically as 'R' followed by page number.
6. Jean Améry, 'On the Necessity and Impossibility of Being a Jew', in *At the Mind's Limits*, 100. Subsequent references are cited parenthetically as 'O' followed by page number.
7. The rehabilitation of Améry's native Austria was still more expeditious, as Ruth Beckermann has shown in her discussion of how post-war Austria swiftly rewrote its recent past – no longer Hitler's homeland but his first victim – in such a way as to explain why Améry's alienation from the culture of his birth and formation proved permanent. See her 'Jean Améry and Austria', in Dagmar C.G. Lorenz and Gabriele Weinberger (eds), *Insiders and Outsiders: Jewish and Gentile Culture in Germany and Austria* (Detroit: Wayne State University Press, 1994), 73–86.
8. Nancy Wood's *Vectors of Memory: Legacies of Trauma in Postwar Europe* (Oxford: Berg, 1999) includes a consideration of Améry's resentments that betrays some of the difficulties of distinguishing between meaningful remembrance and the kind of vengeful clinging to the past that would pre-emptively legitimize retribution. Wood describes extremely incisively how the reference point of the Holocaust has elicited passively empathic memorializing rather than actively interventionist responses to such abominations as ethnic cleansing, and yet she ends with an anecdote from Sarajevo about a young man dreaming 'on purpose' about his murdered father, which she takes to be 'an ominous foreshadowing of Europe's memorial future' – as if, contra Améry, to cling to past wrongs is always wrong-minded, ultimately a demand for vengeance after all (75).
9. Primo Levi, *The Drowned and the Saved*, trans. Raymond Rosenthal (New York: Vintage, 1989), 127, 136. In an interesting although necessarily speculative argument about the relationship between the two writers, the moral philosopher Arne Johan Vetlesen has suggested that Levi's sense of himself as 'above' resentment might properly be understood as a self-protective pose. Arne Johan Vetlesen, 'A Case for Resentment: Jean Améry versus Primo Levi', *Journal of Human Rights* 5/1 (March 2006): 27–44.
10. George Orwell, 'Revenge is Sour', *Collected Essays, Journalism, and Letters of George Orwell: Volume 4, 1945–50*, ed. Sonia Orwell and Ian Angus (London: Secker & Warburg, 1968), 5. Reporting on the Nuremberg Trials the following year, Rebecca West (no more a dove on these matters than Orwell himself) wrote in similar terms of the ambivalences of 'revenge', her point being that in defeat even those who (she had no doubt) richly deserved to suffer no longer appear as evil as they and their crimes are known to have been. Rebecca West, 'Greenhouse with Cyclamens I', in *A Train of Powder: Six Reports on the Problem of Guilt and Punishment in Our Time* (Chicago: Ivan R Dee, 2000), 3–72.
11. Friedrich Nietzsche, *Beyond Good and Evil: Prelude to a Philosophy of the Future*, trans. Marion Faber (Oxford: Oxford University Press, 2008), 41, 83.
12. Friedrich Nietzsche, *On the Genealogy of Morals*, trans. Douglas Smith (Oxford: Oxford University Press, 2008), 24.

13. Nietzsche, *Genealogy of Morals*, 26, 36. On anti-Semitism as *ressentiment* see 54 and 103.
14. Max Scheler, *Ressentiment*, trans. Lewis B. Coser and William W. Holdheim (Milwaukee: Marquette University Press, 1994), 25.
15. Richard Ira Sugarman, *Rancor against Time: the Phenomenology of 'Ressentiment'* (Hamburg: Verlag, 1980), x, 3.
16. Nietzsche, *Genealogy of Morals*, 108. Brackets in original.
17. Sigmund Freud, *Beyond the Pleasure Principle*, trans. James Strachey (New York: Norton, 1961), 12.
18. Ibid., 21, 37.
19. Ibid., 11, 36.
20. Sigmund Freud and Josef Breuer, *Studies in Hysteria*, trans. Nicola Luckhurst (Harmondsworth: Penguin, 2004), 10; Freud, *Beyond the Pleasure Principle*, 30, 33.
21. Caruth, *Unclaimed Experience*, 2.
22. Freud and Breuer, *Studies in Hysteria*, 11.
23. Caruth, *Unclaimed Experience*, 61–2.
24. Ibid., 63.
25. Jennifer M Kapczynski, *The German Patient: Crisis and Recovery in Postwar Culture* (Ann Arbor: University of Michigan Press, 2008).
26. On the relevance of Améry to transitional justice, particularly in relation to the heart-sickeningly coercive rhetorical practices of the TRC in pursuit of 'forgiveness' and 'reconciliation', see Thomas Brudholm *Resentment's Virtue: Jean Améry and the Refusal to Forgive* (Philadelphia: Temple University Press, 2008). Margaret Urban Walker's *Moral Repair: Reconstructing Moral Relations after Wrongdoing* (Cambridge: Cambridge University Press, 2006) reads Améry (and other post-Holocaust writers) alongside the problems of transitional justice in Cambodia and South Africa.
27. Ruth Klüger, *Still Alive: a Holocaust Girlhood Remembered* (New York: The Feminist Press, 2001), 19; emphasis added.
28. Ibid, 63.
29. For an extended treatment of those debates, see Peter Carrier's *Holocaust Monuments and National Memory Cultures in France and Germany since 1989* (Oxford: Berghahn, 2005). Dagmar Barnouw set the Holocaust Memorial in the wider context of a German culture of 'remorse' and what she understood as its political exploitation in *The War in the Empty Air: Victims, Perpetrators, and Postwar Germans* (Bloomington: Indiana, 2005).
30. Elaine Showalter, *The Female Malady: Women, Madness, and English Culture* (New York: Pantheon, 1985), 167–94.
31. Eric Leed, *No Man's Land: Combat and Identity in World War I* (Cambridge: Cambridge University Press, 1979), 164, 180.
32. Ibid., 186.
33. Virginia Woolf, *The Diary of Virginia Woolf: Volume 2, 1920–1924*, ed. Anne Olivier Bell (Orlando: Harcourt, 1980), 248. Virginia Woolf, *Mrs. Dalloway* (Orlando: Harcourt, 2005), 96.
34. Woolf, *Mrs. Dalloway*, 4–5, 112.
35. Controversial, that is, because many of Sebald's claims and conclusions about the paucity of German war representation, and specifically representations of Allied bombing and its effects, have been contested in recent years. See, for example: Volker Hage's two volumes, the anthology *Hamburg 1943: Literarische*

Zeugnisse zum Feuersturm (Frankfurt: S Fischer, 2003) and collection of companion essays and interviews, *Zeugen der Zerstörung: Die Literaten und der Luftkrieg* (Frankfurt: S Fischer, 2003); Lothar Kettenacker (ed.), *Ein Volk von Opfern? Die neue Debatte um den Bombenkrieg, 1940–45* (Berlin: Rowohlt, 2003); Susanne Vees-Gulani, *Trauma and Guilt: Literature of Wartime Bombing in Germany* (Berlin and New York: De Gruyter, 2003); and Wilfried Wilms and William Rasch (eds), *Bombs Away! Representing the Air War over Germany and Japan* (Amsterdam: Rodopi, 2006).

36. Rebecca L. Walkowitz, *Cosmopolitan Style: Modernism beyond the Nation* (New York: Columbia University Press, 2006), 153.
37. W.G. Sebald, 'Against the Irreversible: on Jean Améry', *On the Natural History of Destruction*, trans. Anthea Bell (New York: Modern Library, 2004), 150.
38. Ibid., 149.
39. Ibid., 154.
40. W.G. Sebald, *Austerlitz*, trans. Anthea Bell (New York: Modern Library, 2001), 153. All subsequent references are to this edition and are cited parenthetically in the text.
41. W.G. Sebald, *The Emigrants*, trans. Michael Hülse (New York: New Directions, 1997), 23.
42. Sebald, 'Against the Irreversible, 156.
43. Sianne Ngai, *Ugly Feelings* (Cambridge, MA: Harvard University Press, 2005), 2.

9
'The dangerous edge of things': Geopolitical Bodies and Cold War Fiction

Richard Robinson

The geopolitical fault line of the Cold War was more than a convenient backdrop to post-war espionage narratives. There developed in the imagination of British writers and film-makers a relish for the figurative potential – the sheer 'metaphoricity' – of newly-divided Central Europe. This setting became an increasingly fictionalized territory, a monochrome liminal zone which provided the thriller narrative with a new ambiguous space. The existential condition of the spy became archetypal, indeed formulaic, in the development of what might now be termed a Cold War aesthetic, whose appeal was dependent upon the obverse terrors of the nuclear age.

The Allied partitioning of Austria and Germany was initially exploited as a suggestive fictional setting by Graham Greene and film director Carol Reed. Their famous collaboration on *The Third Man* (1949) served as a template for further, minor work in occupied Central Europe: Greene's short story 'No Man's Land' (1950), set on either side of the newly-descended Iron Curtain in the Harz mountains, and Reed's *The Man Between* (1953), which takes place in a pre-Wall Berlin where the boundary between Allied and Soviet zones, though ostensibly porous, becomes dangerously contested.

John le Carré's *The Spy Who Came in from the Cold* (1963), credited with demythologizing espionage, is nonetheless as responsible for a stylized Cold War aesthetic as any British text. Although the novel stays on the surface of plot and largely avoids metaphor, its depiction of the Berlin Wall nevertheless assumes a full-blown symbolism as the disfigured frontier, a site of nullity and sacrifice. Ian McEwan's *The Innocent* (1990) is a late Cold War text which inherits and adapts a set of allegorized meanings from the pre-Wall period. The novel presents the Berlin of 1955 as a site of transgression, where states deposit their discontents below ground, and is notoriously unbalanced by a master-trope of geopolitical and corporeal dismemberment – a metaphor of the body politic, deriving from political science, which this chapter considers. The abject, parcelized German state is figured in *The Innocent* as a fallen Cold War underworld, where Allied 'innocence' may mask a will to retaliatory violence. Like Greene and Reed, McEwan inhabits the speleological spaces of the post-Nazi state (the 'bowels' of city and state), but also attempts to extrapolate the body politic metaphor by lingering on the sulphurous contents of an individual German corpse.

The early Cold War frontier

It was rather an accident that the Cold War aesthetic evolved as it did. The film producer Alexander Korda had stores of currency in various banks across the continent, but could not convert them back into sterling.[1] In the year of the Communist takeover of Czechoslovakia, the Marshall Plan and the blockade of Berlin, Korda decided to employ Graham Greene as a screenwriter for a film set in Europe, sending him off to Vienna and Venice.[2] But it was Vienna's bombed baroque landscape – together with the quiet desperation of citizens sequestered into occupied sectors – which proved irresistible to Greene, Korda and Carol Reed: *The Third Man* (1949) came into being. A proto-Cold War film which does not directly concern espionage, this work nevertheless is the *urtext* of the fully-fledged Cold War spy thriller.

Greene's fondness for Robert Browning's lines is well known:

> Our interest's on the dangerous edge of things.
> The honest thief, the tender murderer,
> The superstitious atheist, demirep
> That loves and saves her soul in new French books –
> We watch while these in equilibrium keep
> The giddy line midway.[3]

The green baize door that separated his headmaster father's study from the school was the first example of the threshold, a spatial figure which exerted a hold on Greene's imagination throughout his career. Vienna was part of an overarching authorial continuum: a 'dangerous edge' in formative Cold War geopolitics, it offered Greene a ready-made theatre for moral ambiguity and betrayal which he would continue to seek out in the 1950s. *The Quiet American* (1955) explores the contested ideological vacuum left by imminent imperial withdrawal in Vietnam;

Our Man in Havana (1958), set in Cuba, is a comic rendering of Cold War paranoia.

Although Greene had in mind the germ of a story about a man returning from the dead in London, it is still fair to say that the decision to set *The Third Man* in Vienna contributed decisively to its eventual impact. Greene commented that in Vienna '[r]eality, in fact, was only a background to a fairy tale'.[4] The documentary-style opening voiced by Reed establishes a geopolitical reality, but such *verité* is deliberately deceptive, merely providing the first defamiliarization of the city. Vienna's intrinsic fictive quality amplified the staple Greeneian symbology of thresholds.

Adam Piette's recent and brilliant reading of *The Third Man* details the psychopolitical topography of this archetypal Cold War setting. As the negotiations between Korda and David O. Selznick make clear, the film was a problematic UK–US collaboration: it duly explores the underside of the 'special relationship' through the interaction between Martins, Lime and Calloway. What Greene called 'the strange world' (127) of the famous Viennese sewer is figured by Piette as 'the secret state beneath the state', an illicit political unconscious where British and American allies shoot at one another.[5] Harry Lime takes refuge on horizontal and vertical axes: he is, to Piette, a titanic Cold War strategist on the Prater Wheel, a street-level ghost and a subterranean sewer rat, escaping to a political 'other-world' (the Russian zone) via a Dantean underworld (the sewers).

One facet of Piette's interpretation of *The Third Man* is that the subcutaneous spaces of Vienna suggest a new modelling of the body politic in the Cold War age. The sewers memorably represent 'a modern political Hades, a crypt of voices and secret identities that ramifies deep into the body of the emergent national security state'.[6] The Viennese labyrinth was sometimes compared to a digestive tract: Piette implicitly picks up on a Renaissance norm of the traditional body politic metaphor in writing that the sewer tunnels are 'facsimiles of the secret passageways of the body, its bloodstream and nerve fibres and intestinal tracts', and also updates politico-medical discourse: the sewer police in their protective suits pursue Lime like 'white antibodies zooming in on an antigen'.[7] Lime, the brother American in league with the Russians, the peddler of the false cure of watered-down penicillin, is the poison coursing through the system.

The success of *The Third Man* established the metaphorical dimensions of the early Cold War setting, which offered a classic set of tropes for thrillers. The formulaic 'love-across-the-divide' narrative (between German and British or American) was played out in a corrupt, politically ambiguous environment, still heavy with the sense of historical atrocity. Mario Puzo's first novel *The Dark Arena* (1955), for example, is a tale of an ex-GI returning to post-war Germany in search of his former lover, Hella. In a clear echo of the American *pharmakos* theme identified by Piette in *The Third Man*, Walter Mosca (*mosca* is Italian for fly: he is perhaps Beelzebub, an avenging angel) murders a black market drug supplier in revenge for Hella's fatal infection. In such narratives, the prostrate, occupied Germany increasingly became a moral exchange mart, in which the Manichaean distinctions between victor and vanquished started to disappear.[8]

Both Greene and Reed returned to divided Central Europe to create variations of *The Third Man* – work which inevitably felt a little *ersatz*, but also underlined the extent to which the coexistence of increasingly inimical states, contained within a defeated political body, dramatized an existential condition of 'between-ness' ideal for the modern spy thriller. Greene's 'No Man's Land', composed in 1950, was written with a view to a further collaboration with Reed, though the film was never made. This time, the Iron Curtain in the Harz mountains would provide the 'dangerous edge'.

The narrator of the story, a British boundary commissioner, speaks of 'an unfathomable emptiness that the propagandists of two worlds have imposed on our minds', and of the idea of the transcontinental 'over there', where a car may head towards the local village of Nordhausen, and then on to Asia.[9] Between these western and eastern zones lies a dead space: the story's title alludes to the murderous history of European no man's lands. The border trade in refugees, for which the narrator is responsible, throws up grisly murders in the forests, such as that of a Pole who is asphyxiated by having a handkerchief thrust down his throat with a walking stick. The boundary commissioner stresses what a dangerously permeable space he patrols, and takes issue with Churchill's famous metaphor of the iron curtain: 'It's a stupid phrase [...] even if the Great Man did invent it.'[10] In fact, Churchill did not invent it: a protective screen against fires in German theatres, 'iron curtain' was used metaphorically, in a similar sense to that of the *cordon sanitaire*, after the First World War. Goebbels had spoken of an iron curtain descending in front of Soviet territory two weeks after the Yalta conference – that is, well before Churchill's Fulton speech.[11]

Although the houses seem fancifully Swiss in style, suggesting a twee type of neutrality, this is *not* a hospitably liminal area: in the heart of the German body politic there is a stretch of land where, the narrator says, 'nobody can ever build or sleep'.[12] The association of *Walpurgisnacht* and the Harz mountains is briefly mentioned: the location thus combines a sense of ancient, pagan history (a mythic northern European immanence which provided Hitler and Goebbels with the date of their suicides) and the modern artifice of Cold War geography. In both senses there is a 'warding off' of unwanted others (spirits, inimical subjects). And we are aware, in reading this 1950 story, that the intra-German division would soon create a space, specifically built to be undwellable, which would include the *Todesstreifen* – a death-strip where licensed border guards would shoot to kill.

Greene's story anticipates the merging oppositions of later espionage fiction, in which protagonist and antagonist, agent and double-agent, become morally indistinguishable. It admits of no hermetic categories of 'Englishman', 'German' or 'Russian': the British spy, Brown, avenges the death of his half-brother, Paul, who is half-German; the Russian Starhov is more Anglophile than apparatchik. Both Brown and Starhov long for the pastoral, pre-modern sense of national belonging represented by their shared love of Turgenev. Between them is a type of femme fatale, whose betrayal of Paul and Starhov seems stereotypical in comparison with the compromised loyalty of Anna in *The Third Man*. The thriller's climax takes place at a Marian shrine within a grotto – a speleological space like *The Third Man*'s sewers – where pilgrims proceed through the predominantly Protestant Harz region. This religious divide has its counterpart in the geopolitical: the significance of a covertly contested uranium deposit on the Czech border confirms Piette's emphasis on 'the Plutonian realm' of nuclear secrets.[13]

Whereas Greene's original Cold War paradigm forces transgressors below ground, Carol Reed's later film *The Man Between* stays on the surface. Ivo Kern, once an idealistic lawyer who then 'obeyed orders' as a German soldier, now arranges abductions from West to East Berlin. His ex-wife, married to a British army doctor, is the spirit of the new West Germany trying to divest itself of the old. Susanne, the doctor's sister, is the English innocent who falls in love with Ivo, the smuggler of German bodies.

The Man Between reveals a model of Anglo-German relationships in which innocents become complicit and the guilty yearn attractively for redemption. There are thus continuities both with Greene's attack on deleterious (American) naivety in *The Quiet American* and with McEwan's later diagnosis of corrupted (English) innocence in mid-1950s Berlin. One scene rather flamboyantly illustrates how Reed casts a satirical eye on English innocence in *The Man Between*. Having cut his ties with the East, Ivo is the 'man between' sovereign and moral states: in his own fatalistic words, he is 'born to hang'. Susanne and Ivo take refuge in a prostitute's bedroom, close to the zonal border on the eastern side, where she impersonates a prostitute in order to hoodwink the *Volkspolizei*. Susanne loses her virginity to Ivo in the prostitute's bed. Whereas Ivo is markedly reticent, and amused by the inappropriateness of her disguise, Susanne declares 'I am not a child' with something approximating joy.

In this scene, Reed recognizes the plight of destitute German women like the prostitute, who were often the victims of sexual violence. This was a feature of other post-war narratives of German occupation, such as James McGovern's *Fräulein* (1957).[14] Reed inverts the sexualized encounter between the helpless *Fräulein* and the occupying Englishman/ American. The visiting English virgin innocent tries on, and thoroughly relishes, the role of her counterpart, the 'occupied' German prostitute, while the doomed ex-*Wehrmacht* man and dealer in bodies is the supine victim of his own worldliness.

The ending of *The Man Between* has Ivo, making a run for it at the checkpoint, shot down in no man's land – in order, it seems, that Susanne can get through to West Berlin. It has been characterized by film critics as an unsatisfactory and conventional act of stock heroism. As Robert F. Moss has written, 'where Lime sacrifices a woman to save himself, Ivo does just the reverse – thus substituting a hackneyed ending for the murky ambiguities of Greeneian betrayal'.[15] Dilys Powell, who had recently visited Berlin, felt that the ending was bizarre, in view of the fact that people were passing freely between the sectors – indeed, this is something the film itself shows us in its early stages, when Susanne goes on a tourist trip to an Eastern Zone festooned with posters of Lenin and Walter Ulbricht.[16]

Death at the Cold War border would become a historical common-place, but it is the internal law of the artwork which prevails here. Harry Lime is shot on a quasi-mythical, vertical axis, trying to escape from his Hadean underworld in the sewers, clasping the confessional-like grille, his face turned upwards as he falls back down the stairwell. Ivo is not quite one of Greene's damned, like Lime's 'tender murderer', but the strange formal and ethical logic of Reed's film suggests that Ivo *ought* to be sacrificed in the 'space between' the eastern and western checkpoints. Many noir fictions set in post-war Germany blurred the borders between the 'good' occupiers and the 'evil' defeated nation, and sometimes elided distinctions between the old Nazi Germany and the new democratic West Germany. For all the incestuous swapping of roles in the scene in the prostitute's room, however, the resolution of *The Man Between* has its own distinctive grammar. Allowing Ivo to cross the border may have implied a forgiveness of German past sins still too raw in 1953: though repentant, Ivo has talked of his involvement in razing

Czech towns, for example. However, the German bogey-man has been replaced by the Communist, and once Ivo has 'turned', he must not be subsumed in the 'East'. No man's land is the only space left him.

The 'tiny war'

John Lewis Gaddis has argued that, notwithstanding its localized wars by proxy, the Cold War should be counted something of a success precisely because it was not a war at all.[17] This sense of the Cold War as a non-war, or at least a different species of war, informs John le Carré's earlier fiction. *The Looking-Glass War* (1965), for example, tells of a ham-fisted operation over the East German border, and reveals how the obsolete Second World War mentality of 'the Department' (British military intelligence) has been superseded by the chicanery of 'the Circus' and its head, Control, who can pragmatically dispose of lingering post-war resentments in waging a new type of covert conflict.

This sense of continuity and discontinuity between the two wars is also evident in the novel which precedes *The Looking-Glass War*. *The Spy Who Came in from the Cold* is le Carré's most spare and resonant evocation of the Cold War. In what appears to be a justification of the spy's trade, Alec Leamas, who fought in the Second World War, says: 'This is a war [...]. It's graphic and unpleasant because it's fought on a tiny scale, at close quarters; fought with a wastage of innocent life sometimes, I admit. But it's nothing, nothing at all beside other wars – the last or the next.'[18] *The Spy*'s negotiation of Leamas's memories, of this 'wastage of innocent life', relates to the ways in which metaphors of corporeal violence are represented within the new international conflicts of the mid-Cold War period. During his discussion with Control about how Cold War operatives must live without sympathy, Leamas remembers witnessing a German aircraft bombing refugees as they fled to the coast from Rotterdam:

> Leamas saw. He saw the long road outside Rotterdam, the long straight road beside the dunes, and the streams of refugees moving slowly along it; saw the little aeroplane miles away, the procession stop and look towards it; and the plane coming in, nearly over the dunes; saw the chaos, the meaningless hell, as the bombs hit the road. (18)

Leamas's wartime memory is an unusual irruption into the typical le Carré narrative. Though it remains straightforwardly literal at this stage, it becomes one of the few overt metaphors of the whole novel. At narrative mid-point, it coalesces with another memory Leamas has, while driving in Germany: a small car, carrying four laughing children. He has a vision of the car being smashed into pieces by articulated lorries, and 'of the bodies of the children, torn, like the murdered refugees on the road across the dunes' (105). The figure of the torn body on the road yokes together the memory of the refugees and the image of the road accident. Leamas becomes the final victim of his vision: now one of the crushed innocents of the memory-turned-metaphor, he dies at the Wall. As Eric Homberger has written, 'the book ends with a symbol, not with a fact'.[19]

The double agent must lead a bodiless or disembodied existence, alienated from physical sensation and evacuated of personality and unitary meaning. At the same time, the idealized spirits or imagos of the state, like Control, are disengaged Cold Warriors, distant from physical conflict. They treat spies as expendable bodies on the road to a continually deferred outcome. Le Carré's organizing image of bodies on the road relates to Elaine Scarry's analysis of the 'road metaphor' in the traditional vocabulary of military histories. The road to a goal is figured as being unforeseeably blocked, and people are run over or cleared away in order that the destination (victory) may be reached. This masks the reality that '[i]njured bodies are the material out of which the road is built'.[20] More recently, Steven Poole's deciphering of 'unspeak' – spin and political propaganda – has inevitably included an inspection of the 'hideous' term 'collateral damage', which, as Poole says, denies human beings 'their personhood, their existence as individuals and their crucial difference from inanimate matter' and which also 'makes us think of something happening on the sidelines, in the wings: as it were, offstage'.[21] This last inference is relevant to how Leamas's memory first literalizes dead military metaphors and then transforms them into 'live' ones, focusing on the continuing victims of war, of whatever scale, 'onstage'.

Le Carré's early set-piece description of the Berlin border briefly moves into a figurative mode:

> There was only one light in the checkpoint, a reading lamp with a green shade, but the glow of the arclights, like artificial moonlight, filled the cabin. Darkness had fallen, and with it silence. They spoke as if they were afraid of being overheard. Leamas went to the window and waited, in front of him the road and to either side the Wall, a dirty, ugly thing of breeze blocks and strands of barbed wire, lit with cheap yellow light, like the backdrop for a concentration camp. East and west of the Wall lay the unrestored part of Berlin, a half-world of ruin, drawn in two dimensions, crags of war. (9–10)

Berlin is an illusion of the full-blooded, three-dimensional combat of the Second World War. The crags of the 'real' war now constitute a half-world in two dimensions; the arclights cast an 'artificial moonlight' on the unnatural, man-made border. The provocative simile with the concentration camp was one that had been drawn by Willy Brandt, who when he was governing mayor of Berlin wrote to Nehru (in August 1961) that the 'barred walls of a concentration camp have now been erected inside Berlin'.[22] Le Carré modifies the comparison: the cheap light reveals a 'backdrop' or backcloth – that is, a second-hand representation, a simulacrum, of a truly murderous place. The metaphorical disjunction self-consciously points up the 'tiny scale' of the Cold War while still laying claim to the existential plight of the spy's shadowy role in global politics.

The no man's land is presented as a *theatre* of war, revivifying a cliché of historiography which has its equivalent in the German *Kriegsschauplatz* (or 'war viewing place'). At the end of the novel Leamas is shot on 'an empty stage' (220), 'glaring around him like a blinded bull in the arena' (222). Martin Ritt's 1966 film of *The Spy* creates a plausible-looking Wall setting while retaining the stylized theatricality of the 'arena'. The film ends with the arclight (or spotlight) being switched off on a stage, empty but for two corpses. At this mocked-up Berlin site, we implicitly return to the theatrical origins of the iron curtain metaphor.

Leamas is a more hard-boiled sort of innocent than the idealists Liz and Fiedler, for whose deaths he is partly responsible. But he remains a victim, as all agents must be, of higher plots than those of his own making. Leamas voluntarily jumps to his death on the eastern side: the stark irony is that he has not been crushed by the pantechnicons of East and West, as the spatial metaphor would first suggest, but has been sacrificed by colluding 'opponents': the establishment mandarin (Control) and the *Abteilung*'s neo-Nazi (Mundt).

Despite this symbolic freighting of the border theatre, the plot of *The Spy* generally relies on an economical realism. Metaphor must be used sparingly because it will have a retarding effect on the syntagmatic mode of the spy thriller. This is why Graham Greene came to regret the 'poetic' nature of his earlier fiction, saying:

Excitement is simple: excitement is a situation, a single event. It mustn't be wrapped up in thoughts, similes, metaphors. A simile is a form of reflection, but excitement is of the moment when there is not time to reflect. Action can only be expressed by a subject, verb and an object, perhaps a rhythm – little else. Even an adjective slows the pace or tranquilizes the nerve.[23]

Thus, in the very middle of *The Spy*, the 'defecting' Leamas is hastily carried over the border without delay or elaboration. But the thrilling movement of events brings us back, in Cold War spy narratives, to the great geopolitical chasm. The border is the morphological frame where the novel begins and ends. As such a prominent narrative site, it becomes a stage, arena, threshold, point of physical collision, and tableau of violence – in Jakobson's and Barthes's semiological terms, a place which is metaphorically 'deep', inviting paradigmatic interpretation.[24]

   Franco Moretti has observed of nineteenth-century novels that 'figurality rises' when narratives reach borders: the interstate border 'is the site of adventure: one crosses the line, and is face to face with the unknown, often the enemy; the story enters a space of danger, surprises, suspense'.[25] In the unknown space, we need an immediate 'semantic sketch' of our surroundings – (Moretti quotes Ricoeur here), and '*only metaphors know how to do it*' – to express and contain this unknown.[26] However, as we have seen, too much metaphor *tranquillizes*. This may explain James Wood's criticism of what he calls le Carré's 'commercial realism'. The example he gives is of an 'old, thin terminus hotel' in Hamburg: though he praises the metaphor, it nonetheless speaks, through its very neatness and competence, of the way that metaphorical language must be used unthreateningly, fitting what Wood regards as the dead conventions of realism.[27] I would prefer to deflect this from a criticism of le Carré as a writer, and think of it more simply as a marker of how genre imposes limits on (any writer's) style. The filmic grammar of the espionage narrative demands that it largely remains within the discursive limits of the metonymic mode, avoiding the burden of fully embodied metaphors.

Impolitic body: Ian McEwan

Like le Carré, Ian McEwan visited the Berlin Wall in its early breeze-block form. McEwan's *The Innocent*, set in the pre-Wall Berlin of 1955, was in galley proofs when the Wall came down: indeed he was tempted to change its ending. It is thus a narrative that draws on the conventions of the Cold War spy thriller but comes after the apogee of that genre. In lingering upon sexual violence and corporeal violation, *The Innocent* self-consciously disturbs the surface of genre fiction, most notably in a bravura, gut-churning and well-researched sequence in which Leonard, the English innocent, and Maria, his German lover, kill her ex-husband Otto in self-defence – and then hack his body to pieces and store him away.

McEwan was explicit about the metaphor of body and state: 'I wanted to show the brutality man can aspire to by comparing the dismemberment of a corpse to the dismemberment of a city: the bomb-devastated Berlin of the post-war.'[28] But he regretted the way the dismemberment scene had dominated critical responses: these pages of forensic *grand guignol* sit – or as Kiernan Ryan said, squat – in the middle of the Cold War yarn.[29] It is the very conspicuousness of the corporeal trope which suggests *The Innocent*'s difference from le Carré's fiction, in which metaphor is circumscribed.

The figure of partition-as-dissection in *The Innocent* draws heavily on the traditional metaphor of the body politic, whose development in the discourse of political science is thus worth tracing in some detail. One of the first recorded elaborations of the body politic concerned the Athenian city-state: Aristotle wrote about it in the *Politics*, for example. In British culture, it is primarily associated with the Renaissance. The notion of the king's two bodies, as outlined by Ernst Kantorowicz, distinguished between the king's natural body (an incumbency possibly hapless or malign) and the untouchably divine body politic.[30] Such theories of kingship inculcated the sense of monarchic immutability and continuity. The body politic was essentially a conservative metaphor: every organ must keep its place to perform its function, just as every component of state must do its duty for the common good.

The most famous example of the body politic metaphor is to be found in Thomas Hobbes's *Leviathan* (1651). To Hobbes, the State is an 'artificial animal', an analogy founded on the notion that God is the artificer who has put the parts of Nature and Man together.[31] Hobbes's list of correspondences – sovereignty is the soul, wealth is strength, the magistrates are joints – also includes the equivalence of Civil War and death, reminding us that Hobbes articulates the body politic through the recent political history of a divided England. Hobbes's implication is that the decapitation of the king means the removal of the state's head – a mortal blow to the commonwealth.

After Hobbes, the body politic metaphor waned, to be superseded by an Enlightenment model of contractual citizenship and incipient modern democracy. But it reappeared in the mid-to-late nineteenth century, with Herbert Spencer's theories of the 'social organism'. Although Spencer coined the phrase 'survival of the fittest' after reading Darwin, he owed more to Lamarckian biology: his essay 'The Social Organism' was published in 1857, two years before *The Origin of Species*.[32]

Spencer takes issue with the correspondences drawn both in Plato's *Republic* and Hobbes's *Leviathan*, and thinks of the body politic as metaphorically useful when considered as a *living* rather than solely human body (271). He sees the opportunity for modern science to disclose further analogies: this is wedded to the idea of progress from the primitive to the civilized, or from the simple to the complex, and is clearly founded on a perceived hierarchy amongst 'races'. The essay is a veritable *bizarrerie* of equivalences: amoeba-like creatures are akin to two or three families of Bushmen (278), multi-cellular organisms are like aboriginal tribes, and finally large crustaceans have a centralized system which reminds Spencer of the fusion of England, Wales, Scotland and Ireland – the coalescence of provinces into a kingdom.

Spencer's application of the body politic metaphor had taken a wrong turn. If the body politic were organic, able to evolve, it could expand and supplant 'lower forms' of life. This sort of Social Darwinist theorization gave a specious, quasi-scientific justification to the 'mission' of the British Empire, and in turn validated the racialized German nationalism of the late nineteenth century. Although the term *Lebensraum* had had a specific botanical meaning ('habitat'), it was used metaphorically at the time of the 1871 German unification to refer to Germany's 'need' for colonies abroad, on the British and French model. As Mark Mazower has recently observed, in 1897 Friedrich Ratzel incorporated the term into the vocabulary of the new discipline of geopolitics, whose founder Rudolf Kjellén talked, for example, about 'the ambition of the state to become organically united with the soil'.[33]

The misuse of the biological metaphor in geopolitical discourse was thus established in parallel with late nineteenth-century imperialism, which the Greater Germany felt it had largely missed out on, before becoming central to Nazi ideology. Under the racist warrant of social organicism, it was easy for the European Leviathan to propagandize itself as in need of greater space. The *Reich* would grow – that is, grow into other territories – but at the same time saw itself, as Andreas Musolff has written, as 'a body that must be shielded from disease and parasites at any cost'.[34]

Although the whole discipline of geopolitics fell into disrepute after the Second World War, the idea of the body politic has remained popular in contemporary discourse, including the correspondence-seeking figures of literary criticism. Unmoored from its historical applications, it has become something of a dead metaphor, however. According to Lakoff and Turner, the body politic 'still exists as a folk-theoretical or 'contemporary unconscious cultural model'.[35] Steven Poole finds another example of 'unspeak' during the second Iraq war: continuing a historiographic tradition of anthropomorphizing 'sick' states, US 'Coalition' chiefs referred to the attack on Fallujah as a cleansing of the poison in the Iraqi body politic.[36] Such formulations, implying that a pre-existent 'natural' nationhood would be restored to Iraq, conveniently ignored the fact that the borders of the Iraqi state were artificially confected by the Allied Powers after the First World War.

Thus, when McEwan stated that he wanted in *The Innocent* to compare 'the dismemberment of a corpse to the dismemberment of a city', he was invoking a traditional metaphor with a chequered history. Although the cutting up of Otto has become something of a *locus classicus* of contemporary fiction criticism, the ramifications of the body politic analogy, though they have been alluded to in various ways, have not been fully explored.

Kiernan Ryan argues that McEwan's emphasis on the dismemberment metaphor is an authorial gloss which is no match for the 'untethered' imagining of brute physicality: 'the dead, dissected body is the point where signifying halts and hermeneutics ends, where the final ground of meaning is unmasked and metaphysical meanings implode'; 'the appalling spectacle of the demystified body [is] the black hole in the text through which meaning itself threatens to bleed away'.[37] Ryan is arguing against the metaphysical here, and against over-interpretation of the scene. The body is not a secret metaphor of something else, a representation of an as yet uncracked code (Platonic form, soul): rather, the body is the body. The reader experiences a suspension of signification. If we try to decode the metaphor of dismemberment, we realize that the quartering of Otto is an objective correlative overloaded by recent barbarism. History forces the metaphor into macabre excess.

But even here, knowing about the pre-history of the body politic metaphor deepens our understanding of this 'black hole in the text'. Ryan also comments that Leonard's view of our insides reveals that 'the accidents of evolution divide us from the most squalid life-forms'.[38] This reverses Spencer's evolutionary model, founded on the belief that a civilized state such as Victorian Britain was a higher – the highest – of life-forms. Distorted uses of Social Darwinism led to the feeling of apartness from the animal kingdom and difference from other 'races'; it encouraged a supremacist self-conception. That McEwan is concerned with 'de-anthropomorphizing' higher human forms into mere matter is congruent with his general co-opting of the body politic metaphor.

Mark Ledbetter's analysis of *The Innocent* is based on a conception of the body politic, but in mainly global terms: he alludes to the power games and secrecy of 'the world-body', and to the violence done between communities in general. Of Leonard's sawing off of the 'item' of Otto's lower leg, for example, he asks, 'Are we dismembering a body or isolating Poland? Bosnia? Iraq?'[39] This does not ask how far the dismemberment of Otto relates to that of post-war Germany in particular. Dominic Head has invoked Julia Kristeva's notion of the *abject*: 'the corpse, seen without God and outside of science, is the utmost of abjection'.[40] Head argues that Leonard and Maria's encounter with Otto enacts the collapse of the symbolic order of social identities, which had securely bounded them together against the Other. The discrimination between German woman and Englishman, selfhood and statehood, dissolves with Leonard's realization that 'all this stuff was also in himself'.[41] A corporeal limit, of individual and state, has been reached, reflecting earlier representations of post-war Anglo-German relations, which revealed the allegorical interpenetration of innocent or experienced bodies.

Once Leonard cuts Otto up, he has a problem: what to do with the corpse? Otto is parcelled into a pair of suitcases and placed under 'the Russian sector' (this last phrase itself encoding the metaphor of Allied privilege – the excision of German portions). The burying of Otto's body parts prompts the corresponding question: how does the new Europe dispose of the old Germany – how do Allies who are no longer Allies 'share it out'? Leonard has a nightmare in which, having put Otto back together like Frankenstein's monster, he offers his throat up to the remade German. Although the nightmare is read by Head as a guilty denial of the abject, it also remains interpretable within the frame of the body politic metaphor, standing rather instrumentally for the paranoiac British fear of revenant Nazism – for a new political subjection to the resurrected pan-German body politic. This sort of fear resurfaced at the fall of the Berlin Wall. Mrs Thatcher was so disturbed at the prospect of reunification that she called a meeting of British historians at Chequers: much of the discussion concentrated on alleged Teutonic character traits like 'angst, aggressiveness, assertiveness'.[42]

The historical narrative of *The Innocent* centres on the story of Operation Gold, the doomed Anglo-American plan to dig a tunnel under the Russian sector and tap the telephone lines to Moscow. The symbolism of the tunnel is established by the epigraph from Kafka's 'The Burrow', which implies a continuity between the labyrinths of Habsburg bureaucracy and the secret passageways of Cold War Europe. Christina Byrnes's Kleinian interpretation is that the tunnel, in 'treacherously robbing the adversaries of their secrets', is an 'envious spoiling'.[43] Cutting into septic tanks and graveyards, the tunnel is, to Byrnes, a desecration, a defiance of a taboo, like the invasion of Otto.

While travelling across Berlin from the tunnel, Leonard considers that he is either 'truly himself', in equilibrium between two secret worlds, or 'nothing at all, a void travelling between two points' (77). Although his lovemaking with Maria is presented as a form of burrowing ('these

Erkundungen, these excavations' (78)), the tunnel also remains, as it is for Kafka's rodent, an 'absolutely, pathetically private existential space', as Tamás Bényei has written.[44] The tunnel is an uninhabitable 'atopia', not a utopia: Leonard works in 'a world that is fallen (underground) from innocence'.[45] Eventually, at the end of their Cold War separation, Leonard reads Maria's letter by the mouth of the ruined tunnel shaft because, as Bényei says, it is the place which is between 'his time and her time, like so much unbuilt-on land'.[46] The tenor of this critical analysis reminds us of McEwan's inheritance of one component of the Cold War aesthetic. The metaphor of the tunnel revives Greene's Cold War topography: the 'Plutonian' sewers, or digestive tract, of *The Third Man*. The surface 'no man's land' of the border zones is *unheimisch* (unhomely), sending agents to *unheimliche* (uncanny) speleological spaces, such as the Marian shrine in the Harz grotto.

McEwan plays a variation on the Greeneian theme of harmful innocence: just as the American Pyle and the Englishman Fowler dispute the Vietnamese Phuong in *The Quiet American*, so Glass and Leonard are rivals for Maria. *The Innocent* inverts the compromised US–UK friendship: Glass is a worldly American, Leonard a naïve Englishman. Leonard's own betrayal of the special friendship (he leaks Operation Gold, unaware that double agent George Blake has already done so) may be more surprising, perhaps, than the world-weary Fowler's betrayal of Pyle to the Communists, but Fowler's cynicism is itself a mask for his idealized, old colonial love of Phuong.[47]

By undoing this opposition between innocence and experience, McEwan revisits the compromised moral territory of Greene and Reed. Thus, the virgin English gentleman has soon played out soldier fantasies on Maria, and shocked us (and Maria) by biting Otto's cheek during their tussle: his first subcutaneous incision, as it were. Leonard 'disarms' Otto and, having nearly carved right through the torso, looks down at his handiwork: 'What was on the table now was no one at all. It was the field of operations, it was a city far below that Leonard had been ordered to destroy [...] then the big one, the thighs, the big push, and that would be it, home, a hot bath, a debriefing' (178). Otto is an abject, militarily impotent state: the Allied firebombings of German cities are brought to mind. Just as Otto stands for Germany, Leonard, inured to the destruction he is causing below, represents the retaliatory Allied violence to 'no-one at all' – or rather, to a faceless civilian population.

Leonard has the RAF-language of Arthur 'Bomber' Harris ringing in his ears. British codenames for the bombing operations – Gomorrah (Hamburg), Thunderclap (Dresden) and Chastise (the Ruhr Valley) – were unambiguously vengeful. Disposing of the prone German corpse, Leonard speaks to himself in outdated anthropomorphizing discourse: compare, for example, B.H. Liddell Hart's description of Ludendorff's First World War offensive: 'He had driven in three great wedges, but none had penetrated far enough to sever an artery.'[48] By rehearsing this type of historiography, McEwan makes Leonard the object of his parody during this scene. This sits with the growing though still controversial recognition in Britain (for example, by A.C. Grayling in *Among the Dead Cities*) that Englishmen delivered the knock-out blow to the prone body of the enemy, and were thus rather unsporting. Leonard, the English 'innocent', inflicts retaliatory violence on the passively guilty body, now a Nazi corpse – and thereby becomes guilty himself.

Otto, reeking of beer and *Sauerkraut* and still in league with the presumably ex-Nazi Berlin police, is in one sense the Leviathan who, having devoured Europe, has over-extended his corporeal boundaries. We might even say that the death of the Nazi body politic – even the death of the discredited, deterministic metaphor itself – is suggested by his dismemberment. But Otto, perhaps surprisingly, is described as a small man: that is, he has already defeated himself. McEwan still clings on, I think, to an old analogy, Hobbes's equation of civil war with death, and implies that the parcelization of a country is a culpable act. Berlin, and by extension occupied Germany, is represented as a fractured political body whose nationally proportional sinews have been severed.

McEwan's next novel, *Black Dogs*, returns to Berlin in November 1989. Though a newly reconstituted whole, the city remains a topos of fallen innocence in this novel, too. At night the opened border has, for the narrator, 'the innocent brightness, the shameless indignity' of a place where states secrete their atrocities. The Berlin death-strip emblematizes, at least for former Communist Party-member Bernard, Sir Isaiah Berlin's comment about 'the fatal quality of utopias': it is a whited sepulchre.[49] Among the scenes of open-armed and pacific joy at the fall of the Wall, McEwan engineers a violent encounter between a Turkish Communist and a group of young neo-Nazi skinheads. This episode points uneasily forward, implying that the breaking of the ideological stalemate, even as it is being celebrated, is releasing a new set of ethnic tensions – as the Balkans Wars soon proved.

Spy fiction and postmodernist fiction

McEwan's *The Innocent* inherits and adapts a fully-fledged Cold War aesthetic, but by anatomizing the body politic in such detail it also seems to tell us that it is more than 'just' a spy novel. This reveals an instructive typological tension between metaphor and metonym which bears on the question of genre. The dominance of the master-trope of the body politic suggests the author's attempt to comment consciously and allegorically on post-war and Cold War history, and to transcend the 'commercial realism' of the spy thriller plot. Nevertheless, McEwan was aware of how genre fiction and 'high' modern literature were far from being mutually exclusive: 'I thought what a curious, useless thing spying is, what an oddly circular, self-contained, self-referential system it is [...] Spying is simply move and countermove within this closed system [and is] analogous to forms of literary modernism.'[50]

The idea was well-established that the espionage of the Cold War was like a 'god-game' with its own internal laws. In Len Deighton's *Funeral in Berlin*, for example, the chapter headings ('Exchange', 'Zugzwang') are taken from chess, though the geopolitical strategies to which these moves are analogous are not always clear. Like le Carré's 1960s fiction, Deighton's novel contributes to the Cold War aesthetic of the 'permafrost' years, though its brand-awareness and self-conscious anti-establishmentarianism now give it a hard and superficial glitter on the page: 'The night was young and it had nothing much to do.'[51] *The Innocent* has little of the disembodied quality of the 'high' Cold War era, reaching back to a more formative period, and to an earlier set of tropes – the speleological space of sewer, grotto and tunnel that we associate with Greene and Reed. McEwan's awareness of the imminent break-up of the USSR is finally narrated in an uneasy conditional mood: Leonard and Maria 'would take a good long look at the Wall together, before it was all torn down' (245). The teleological book-end to *The Innocent* precludes our sense of Cold War stasis.

Although McEwan spoke of the affinities between the closed system of espionage and the self-referential artwork, they are better illustrated, in the end, by le Carré. *The Spy Who Came in from the Cold* exemplifies the shared features of spy fiction and postmodernist fiction identified by Patricia Waugh: 'the fear of anomie, of disorder, of the insecurity of human life', the experience of 'existential boundary situations'.[52] Unlike Leonard and Maria, who we imagine coming together again in reunified Berlin, expendable spies like Leamas cannot cross the border and shape another post-Cold War telos. They are caught in another 'meaningless hell' – in Sartre's vision, a continuum without exits. We may even imagine that modernist 'arrangers' – Joyce and Eliot supposedly invisible within their artworks – have their counterparts in impersonal demiurges like 'Control', who is apparently indifferent to the spider's web at whose centre he sits.

Though limited in the language of metaphor and not formally meta-fictional, le Carré's novel relies on its own hermeneutic codes – what David Seed, invoking Cleanth Brooks and the literary artefact of New Criticism, calls its 'well-wrought' form – to fashion a mid-Cold War aesthetic.[53] Our perception of one plane of reality (Fiedler is trapping Mundt) is replaced by another (Mundt is trapping Fiedler): the bipolar world order, with its propaganda and counter-propaganda, excludes the philosophical middle. An image of the narrative whole, a recuperated fabula, is established – only to be replaced by its counter-narrative from the other side of the looking-glass. Like the postmodernist detective novel, le Carré's plot, for all its own morphological order, communicates 'not order but irrationality of both the surface of the world and of its deep structures'.[54] Those deep structures are not accessed by boring into the metaphorical body, the secret state, of Cold War Europe. Le Carré remains on a starkly two-dimensional horizontal plane – a paranoia-inducing surface under which the unknowable paradigms of mid-Cold War geopolitics are encrypted.

Notes

1. See Charles Drazin, *In Search of The Third Man* (London: Methuen, 2000), 4.
2. Drazin, *In Search*, 17.
3. Quoted in Bernard Bergonzi, *A Study in Greene* (Oxford: Oxford University Press, 2006), 5.
4. Graham Greene, *The Third Man and The Fallen Idol* (London: Heinemann, 1987), 4. All references are to this edition and are cited parenthetically in the text.
5. Adam Piette, *The Literary Cold War: 1945 to Vietnam* (Edinburgh: Edinburgh University Press, 2009), 35.
6. Ibid., 30.
7. Ibid., 31–2.
8. Robert Edric's *The Kingdom of Ashes* (New York: Doubleday, 2007), another love-across-the-divide narrative set in a British assessment and evaluation centre in a small town in Germany in 1946, has recently revisited this Cold War paradigm.
9. Graham Greene, 'No Man's Land', in *No Man's Land* (London: Hesperus, 2005), 7.
10. Greene, 'No Man's Land', 4.
11. Ignace Feuerlicht, 'A New Look at the Iron Curtain', *American Speech* 30/3 (1955): 186–89.
12. Greene, 'No Man's Land', 7.
13. Piette, *The Literary Cold War*, 30.
14. See Hsu-Ming Teo, 'Sexual Violence in Occupied Germany 1945–49', *Women's History Review* 5/2 (1996): 239–57. In McGovern's *Fräulein*, a Berlin woman, who has to work as a mud-wrestler and stripper in order to survive, is pulled between the love of a US soldier and a recidivist ex-Nazi.

15. Robert F. Moss, *The Films of Carol Reed* (New York: Columbia University Press, 1987), 207.
16. Cited in Tony Shaw, *British Cinema and the Cold War* (London: Tauris, 2001), 219, n.40.
17. John Lewis Gaddis, *The Cold War* (Harmondsworth: Penguin, 2005).
18. John Le Carré, *The Spy Who Came in from the Cold* (London: Victor Gollancz, 1964), 214. All subsequent references are to this edition and are cited parenthetically in the text.
19. Eric Homberger, *John Le Carré (Contemporary Writers)* (London: Methuen, 1986), 51.
20. Elaine Scarry, *The Body in Pain: the Making and Unmaking of the World* (New York and Oxford: Oxford University Press, 1985), 74.
21. Steven Poole, *Unspeak: Words are Weapons* (London: Little, Brown, 2007), 117.
22. Cited in Timothy Garton Ash, *In Europe's Name: Germany and the Divided Continent* (London: Jonathan Cape, 1993), 59.
23. Graham Greene, *A Sort of Life* (Harmondsworth: Penguin, 1971), 144–5.
24. See Roland Barthes's application of Saussure, and of Roman Jakobson's distinction between metaphor and metonym, in *Elements of Semiology*, trans. Annette Lavers and Colin Smith (London: Jonathan Cape, 1967), 121–2.
25. Franco Moretti, *Atlas of the European Novel 1800–1900* (London and New York: Verso, 1998), 43, 35.
26. Ibid., 47.
27. James Wood, *How Fiction Works* (London: Vintage, 2009), 174–5.
28. Quoted in Kiernan Ryan, *Ian McEwan* (Plymouth: Northcote House, 1994), 58.
29. Ibid., 60.
30. Ernst H. Kantorowicz, *The King's Two Bodies: a Study in Mediaeval Political Theology* (Princeton, NJ: Princeton University Press, 1997).
31. Thomas Hobbes, *Leviathan*, ed. Richard Tuck (Cambridge: Cambridge University Press, 1991), 9.
32. Herbert Spencer, 'The Social Organism', in *Essays: Scientific, Political and Speculative* (London: Williams and Norgate, 1891), 265–307. All subsequent references are to this edition and are cited parenthetically in the text.
33. Mark Mazower, *Hitler's Empire: Nazi Rule in Occupied Europe* (London: Penguin, 2008), 20.
34. Andreas Musolff, *Metaphor and Political Discourse: Analogical Reasoning in Debates about Europe* (Basingstoke: Palgrave Macmillan, 2004), 84.
35. Quoted in Musolff, *Metaphor*, 115–16.
36. Poole, *Unspeak*, 112.
37. Ryan, *Ian McEwan*, 59–60.
38. Ibid., 56.
39. Mark Ledbetter, *Victims and the Postmodern Narrative, or Doing Violence to the Body: an Ethic of Reading and Writing* (Basingstoke: Macmillan, 1996), 88–103; 91, 100.
40. Dominic Head, *Ian McEwan* (Manchester: Manchester University Press, 2007), 95.
41. Ian McEwan, *The Innocent* (London: Picador, 1990), 182. All subsequent references are to this edition and are cited parenthetically in the text.
42. Elizabeth Pond, *Beyond the Wall: Germany's Road to Unification* (Washington, DC: Brookings Institution, 1993), 157.

43. Christina D. Byrnes, *A Psychodynamic Approach to Ian McEwan* (Nottingham: Pauper's Press, 2002), 221.
44. Tamás Bényei, *Acts of Attention: Figure and Narrative in Postwar British Novels* (Frankfurt am Main: Peter Lang, 1999), 196.
45. Ledbetter, *Victims*, 97.
46. Bényei, *Acts of Attention*, 244.
47. See Piette, *The Literary Cold War*, for a Cold War reading of Anglo-American relations in *The Quiet American*, 152–67.
48. Scarry, *The Body in Pain*, 71.
49. Ian McEwan, *Black Dogs* (London and Basingstoke: Jonathan Cape, 1992), 92, 88.
50. Ian McEwan quoted in Peter Childs, *The Fiction of Ian McEwan* (Basingstoke: Palgrave, 2005), 84.
51. Len Deighton, *Funeral in Berlin* (London: Flamingo, 2001), 73.
52. Patricia Waugh, *Metafiction: the Theory and Practice of Self-Reflexive Fiction* (London and New York: Methuen, 1984), 84–5.
53. David Seed, 'The Well-Wrought Structures of John le Carré's Early Fiction', in Clive Bloom (ed.), *Spy Thrillers: from Buchan to le Carré* (Basingstoke: Macmillan, 1991), 140–59.
54. Waugh, *Metafiction*, 83.

Index

Allingham, Margery, 104
  Coroner's Pidgin, 104, 107–10,
    120–1
  Traitor's Purse, 110–11, 119, 121
Ambler, Eric
  Cause for Alarm, 83
Améry, Jean, 19–20, 164
  At the Mind's Limits, 164–81
Anglo–Irish War, 64
Auden, W.H., 83, 92
Austro–Prussian War, 12

Baring, Maurice, 49
Barrès, Maurice, 49
Barry, Sebastian, 20, 73
  A Long Long Way, 76–80
  The Steward of Christendom, 75
Benjamin, Walter, 16
Bion, Wilfred, 130
Blake, William, 26, 36–7
Blunden, Edmund
  Undertones of War, 30
body
  abject, 20, 47, 56–60, 148, 186,
    198–9
  as blood sacrifice, 7–8, 18, 66
  burial of, 20
  colonial, 64–80
  corporate, 6, 9, 117, 124, 130,
    132, 147
  as corpse, 2, 3, 5, 8, 10, 12, 16–21,
    42, 57–8, 73, 104–9, 116–22, 145,
    154, 167, 186, 193, 195, 197–8,
    200
  in disguise, 125–6, 129, 132, 138–9,
    190
  dismemberment of, 3, 21, 48, 58–9,
    83, 186, 195, 197, 200
  fascist, 20, 131, 143–63
  female, 110, 129, 136, 138, 146,
    148–9, 159, 190
  as geopolitical territory, 6, 33,
    185–202

grievable, 117, 123
  heroic, 6–8, 18, 41, 66–7, 108, 126,
    133, 146, 154
  Jewish, 20, 145–56, 164–81
  and machine, 11, 13, 96–7, 156
  as metaphor, 3, 11, 19, 172,
    185–202
  pacifist, 18, 46–60
  petrifaction of, 19
  tortured, 13, 19, 56, 148–9,
    154, 158, 161n14, 165, 171,
    173–4, 179
  and trauma, 13, 15, 19, 38, 68, 70,
    80, 85, 99, 108, 117, 164–80
  as uncanny, 65, 117
  in uniform, 2, 8, 21, 23n24, 32,
    68–9, 78–80, 92, 115, 125–41,
    145–50, 152, 154, 158, 167
Boer War, Second, 10
Bourke, Joanna, 2–3, 12, 20, 23n18
Bowen, Elizabeth, 3, 15, 109
  The Heat of the Day, 89–90
  The Last September, 69
Brittain, Vera, 3
  Testament of Youth, 128
Brooke, Rupert, 30, 35, 37
Brown, Gordon, 5
Browning, Robert, 60n1, 186

Chamberlain, Austen, 100
Chase, James Hadley
  No Orchids for Miss Blandish, 106
Christie, Agatha, 105, 107–8,
    117–18
  Curtain, 111
  The Moving Finger, 111–13, 118
  N or M?, 109
Churchill, Winston, 10, 12, 86, 94–5,
    101, 188
Clausewitz, Carl von, 13–14, 61n18
Cold War, 86, 101, 167, 185–202
Cornford, John, 99
corporeality, *see* body

Deighton, Len, 94, 201
Douglas, Keith, 92
Doyle, Roddy
  A Star Called Henry, 74–5

Eliot, T.S., 87–8, 93, 201
  Four Quartets, 87
  The Waste Land, 85, 87, 93, 98, 177

Farrell, J.G.
  Troubles, 72–3
Fenton, James, 87
First World War, 3–4, 7, 10–11, 15,
    17–18, 20, 26–80, 95, 108, 128,
    130, 136, 165, 177, 188, 197, 200
Franco–Prussian War, 12, 15
Freud, Sigmund
  Beyond the Pleasure Principle, 171–2
  'A Child Is Being Beaten', 159
  Studies on Hysteria, 172–3
  'Thoughts for the Times on War
    and Death', 124
  'The Uncanny', 150
Fussell, Paul, 4, 37, 39, 49, 128, 131

Globcnik, Odilo, 146, 148,
    151, 158
Graves, Robert, 42
The Great War, *see* First World War
Greene, Graham, 3, 107, 185, 193
  'No Man's Land', 185, 188–9
  The Quiet American, 186, 189
  The Third Man, 185–8, 199, 201
Gulf War, 12–13

Halifax, Lord, 86, 95
Hamilton, Patrick, 3
  The Gorse Trilogy, 139
Harris, Robert
  Fatherland, 20, 145–54
Heaney, Seamus, 92
Hillary, Richard, 101
  The Last Enemy, 96
Hitler, Adolf, 83, 86, 93, 96–7, 115,
    175, 189
Hobbes, Thomas
  Leviathan, 195
Holocaust, 15, 19, 117, 143, 146,
    164–82
  Auschwitz, 86, 149, 154, 164–6

commemoration of, 20, 143,
    149–58, 176
  Majdanek, 149–54, 159, 161n19
  Sobibor, 155
  Theresienstadt, 180
  Treblinka, 155
Homer
  The Iliad, 14, 17–19

Iraq War, 5–6, 13, 24n26, 196

Johnston, Jennifer, 72–3, 75–6
  How Many Miles to Babylon, 70
Joyce, James, 87, 178, 201
Jünger, Ernst, 3, 15

Keynes, John Maynard, 87–8, 91, 93
Klüger, Ruth, 20, 156, 164, 175–6
Kristeva, Julia, 58–9, 198

Le Carré, John, 87, 201
  The Looking–Glass War, 191
  The Spy Who Came in from the Cold,
    185, 191–4, 201–2
Ledig, Gert, 15, 17
Lee, Vernon, 17–18, 46–60
Levi, Primo, 152, 164–8

MacGill, Patrick, 68
Marinetti, Filippo Tommaso, 83, 100
Marsh, Edward, 30, 38
McEwan, Ian
  Black Dogs, 20, 145, 149–53,
    157–9, 200
  The Innocent, 21, 185–6, 189,
    194–201
McGuiness, Frank
  *Observe the Sons of Ulster Marching
    Towards the Somme*, 71–3
Miller, Betty
  On the Side of the Angels, 21,
    124–39
Miller, Emanuel, 130
Montgomery, Bernard Field Marshall,
    131–2

Napoleonic Wars, 9, 15–16
nation
  as anthropomorphic entity, 53
  as artificial construct, 52, 195

body politic, 20–1, 65–6, 80, 109–10, 120, 186–201
geopolitical territory, 10, 18, 26–43, 186–201
as 'imagined community', 27, 89–91
as machine, 13, 53, 75, 92, 109
and patriotism, 5–6, 10, 32–7, 51–60, 104–5, 125
sacrifical bodies of, 6–8, 18, 44n16, 47–60, 66–7, 71, 75, 95, 117, 144, 149, 185, 190, 193
social organism, 93, 195–6
see also body, corporate

O'Casey, Sean, 68, 74
Orwell, George, 106–7, 115–18, 168
Owen, Wilfred, 91, 127

Paulin, Tom, 18
 The Invasion Handbook, 83–101
Poole, Stephen, 3, 192, 196
Powell, Michael and Emeric Pressburger
 The Life and Death of Colonel Blimp, 116
 A Matter of Life and Death, 96
Priestley, J.B.
 Britain at Bay, 115
Puzo, Mario
 The Dark Arena, 3, 188

Reed, Carol, 188
 The Man Between, 185, 189–90
 The Third Man, 185–7
Remarque, Erich Maria
 All Quiet on the Western Front, 3, 17
Rhys, Ernest
 The Old Country, 33–7
Rivière, Joan, 129, 138

Sartre, Jean Paul, 100, 201
Sassoon, Siegfried, 18
 Memoirs of George Sherston, 26–31, 38–43
Scarry, Elaine, 2, 192
Schleger, Hans, 96, 99
Schwitters, Kurt, 87, 97
Scott, Sir Walter, 13, 33
Sebald, W.G.
 Austerlitz, 178–81

On the Natural History of Destruction, 178
 The Rings of Saturn, 16, 178
Second World War, 8, 10, 13, 17, 21, 83–185
Shoah, *see* Holocaust
Sontag, Susan, 4, 23n24, 143–4, 147, 151
Spencer, Herbert, 195–7
Stendhal, 15–17

Taylor, A.J.P., 86, 91
Thirty Years' War, 15
Thomas, Edward, 30, 38

Uklański, Piotr, 143, 159–60

Vietnam War, 12, 15, 186, 199

war
 and civilians, 4, 8–11, 13, 17, 21, 89, 104–43, 147, 167, 171, 199
 commemoration of, 2, 6–8, 16–17, 20, 73–4, 101, 155, 157
 and concepts of gender, 104–43, 154
 and detective fiction, 104–24
 euphemisms for, 8, 12–14
 and images, 1, 4, 8–10, 12, 17, 23n24, 27–37, 47, 57–8, 65–6, 71, 76, 78, 80, 83–104, 117, 119, 128, 143, 155, 192
 impersonalization of, 13, 109, 201
 and landscape, 26–46, 185–201
 and newspapers, 5, 8, 83–100
 propaganda, 10–11, 17–18, 26–42, 53–4, 89, 144, 154, 188, 192
 rhetoric, 4, 8–12, 19, 21, 52–3, 66, 196–7, 200
 technology of, 1, 4, 11–13, 53, 77, 94, 115
 as unrepresentable, 15
War in Afghanistan, 5–6, 13, 24n26
Weil, Simone, 19
West, Rebecca, 177, 182n10
Woolf, Virginia, 7n22, 178
 Between the Acts, 89
 Jacob's Room, 17
 Mrs Dalloway, 177–8
 Three Guineas, 54, 126–9

Yeats, William Butler, 67–8